W. E. Riddle   R. E. Fairley

Software Development Tools

With 26 Figures

Springer-Verlag
Berlin Heidelberg New York 1980

William E. Riddle
Cray Laboratories
5311 Western Avenue
Boulder, CO 80301/USA

Richard E. Fairley
Computer Science Department
Colorado State University
Fort Collins, CO 80325/USA

ISBN-13: 978-3-540-10326-4   e-ISBN-13: 978-3-642-46430-0
DOI: 10.1007/978-3-642-46430-0

Library of Congress Cataloging in Publication Data. Main entry under title:
Software development tools. "Proceedings of a workshop... held at Pingree Park,
Colorado in May 1979." Bibliography: p. Includes index. 1. Electronic digital
computers—Programming—Congresses. I. Riddle, William E., 1942- II. Fairley,
Richard E., 1937-
QA76.6.S617. 001.64'2. 80-20753

2145/3140-543210

Preface

This text contains the proceedings of a workshop on software development tools,
held at Pingree Park, Colorado in May, 1979. The workshop, for which we were co-chair-
men, was primarily, but not exclusively, concerned with a variety of tools supporting
pre-implementation phases of software development. The workshop brought together
researchers and practitioners from industrial, governmental, and academic sectors to
compare and assess current work and to set some directions for future work in this
emerging technical area. The fifty participants represented research and development
efforts in software tools within the United States, Canada, France, Great Britain,
and Japan. (A list of participants appears at the end of the text.)

Sponsorship was provided by the National Aeronautics and Space Administration,
the National Bureau of Standards, the National Science Foundation, and Digital
Equipment Corporation.

The conference consisted of seven formal sessions and numerous organized and
impromptu discussions. Each session (except the last) included invited papers,
prepared remarks by discussants, and an open discussion. The sessions focused on
the following issues:

Tool Needs: What tools are needed, how general or specific should they be,
and how are they affected by the type of user and the type of system under
development?

Tool Experiences: What has been learned about tools and their use, and how
can more be learned in the future?

Tool Integration: How should tools be delivered to software developers
in a unified, homogeneous fashion?

Procedural and Non-Procedural Description Techniques: What are the important
concepts for modelling of software during the pre-implementation phases,
and what are the trade-offs among formality, conciseness, ease-of-use, and
area of application?

Analysis Tools: Can existing analysis tools be "elevated" for use during
pre-implementation phases, and is it desirable and/or feasible to use
verification approaches during these phases?

Where to Next: What has retarded progress in the development and integration
of tools and description techniques, and where should the attention of researchers and developers be focused in both the short-term and long-term
future?

This text contains the invited papers as well as summaries of the discussants' comments and open discussions. We have chosen to summarize the discussions, rather than to present verbatim transcripts. An effort has been made to convey the major themes and issues, and to faithfully reproduce the intent of individual statements and comments. The comments by individual participants reflect their own, personal opinions and do not represent the opinions of the companies, agencies or institutions for which they work.

We would like to thank the sponsors, who made the workshop possible; the authors and discussants, who prepared the papers and made the presentations; the attendees, who provided timely and thoughtful comments; Tony Wasserman, who helped during the formative stage of the workshop; the staff of the Pingree Park Conference Facility of Colorado State University, who provided excellent facilities and services in a setting of spectacular natural beauty; and Irene Beckmann, who gave extensive and capable help with travel arrangements. We would like to especially thank the recorders (Bryan Edwards, Bill Ralph, John Sayler and Al Segal); they taped the presentations and discussions and prepared detailed reports on the discussions. And our special thanks also go to Dotty Foerst, Arlene Hunter, and Harriet Ortiz who typed the final copy of the text. The help of all these people is tremendously appreciated but we, of course, assume responsibility for the accuracy of this record and apologize, in advance, for undetected errors.

It has been said that the world of computer science technical conferences exists because of the services of a large number of first-time volunteers. Our experiences in organizing and running the Pingree Park Software Development Tools Workshop were entirely pleasant, however, and we found it a rewarding, albeit time-demanding, task. It was because of the capable help of all those involved that we experienced so few problems -- the most severe problem to our recollection was that squirrels found the telephone cable insulation rather tasty, making contact with the outside world erratic and difficult. We are indebted to many people for their pleasant, egoless participation and for their unselfish assistance.

Richard E. Fairley   William E. Riddle
Colorado State University   University of Colorado

March 1, 1980

Table of Contents

Chapter I. Introduction

Every profession has its tools of the trade, which are developed through the joint efforts of theoreticians and practitioners, and which generally evolve over many years of use and refinement. The tools which survive the natural selection process reflect the best ideas of theoreticians and inventors, the experiences of artisans and practitioners, and the contemporary technology of the field. Tools constantly undergo changes and refinements; but they provide, at any point in time, a collection of implements with which practitioners in the field may more effectively and efficiently perform their work.

Tools for software development can be categorized as cognitive tools, augmentive tools, and notational tools. Cognitive tools are the problem-solving techniques used to develop software systems; they include techniques such as hierarchical decomposition, information hiding, structured coding, and systematic testing. They are characterized by the fact that they enhance the intellectual capabilities of those who use them.

Augmentive tools are those which aid software development practitioners in much the same way that hammers, screwdrivers and saws aid carpenters — they increase the practitioners' "powers." They are typically software systems themselves and include implementation-oriented tools such as compilers and debugging packages, as well as tools for the pre-implementation (requirements definition and design) and post-implementation (verification, testing and maintenance) phases of software development.

Notational tools (i.e., languages) provide the media in which ideas may be expressed and communicated and they play an essential role in our ability to formulate concepts and solve problems. One of the best known examples of notational tools involves the controversy between Newton and Leibniz concerning the proper notation for expressing a derivative. The resulting vindication of Leibniz is a well-understood object lesson in the importance of notational tools.

The perceived advantages of modern software development tools include increased quality of the product, increased developer productivity, and enhanced job satisfaction for the tool user. The perceived disadvantages include the training/learning curve associated with new techniques, the constrained (and perhaps unsuitable) environment that may result from inflexible tools, and the cost overhead and lead time required to develop and integrate a tool as part of an ongoing software development project. These advantages and disadvantages are described as "perceived" due to the lack of quantitative data concerning cost overhead, cost effectiveness, and user acceptance of software development tools. The need for controlled experiments and better data is obvious.

The focus here is primarily, but not exclusively, upon environments that provide practitioners with a collection of augmentive and notational tools oriented toward the pre-implementation phases of software development. With regard to collections of tools, two extremes are *toolboxes* and *development systems*. A toolbox provides tools of general utility; it does not encourage or enforce any particular problem-solving technique, nor does it provide a uniform usage environment. Tools in a toolbox might include a line-oriented text editor, an assembler, and a breakpoint debugger, each with its own control language and input/output formats.

On the other hand, a development system enforces a particular development approach by requiring the user to interact with the system in rigid, fixed patterns of interaction. (A development system is akin to a "plant" in the manufacturing world.) Components of a development system might include a data base, a notation for project documentation, a preprocessor to ensure that certain coding practices are enforced, and a standardized configuration control system to "supervise" modification of the product.

There are inherent dangers in both extremes: a development system can be expensive to operate, inflexible, and stifling to creativity and innovation; while a toolbox provides no structure in the process of software development. Ideally, tool collections should be homogeneous, providing a uniform environment of usage with compatible interfaces between tools, and should be flexible enough to encourage good practices without enforcing rigid and arbitrary standards — we call such tool collections *development support systems*.

This text is the edited proceedings of a workshop on software development tools held at Pingree Park, Colorado, in May 1979. The major themes which emerged during the course of the workshop were:

- the critical need for high-quality data on the effect, both positive and negative, of collections of tools upon the development process,
- the degree to which development support systems should enforce methodological constraints, and
- the nature and variety of cognitive and notational tools upon which to base a development support system to aid pre-implementation development activities.

Comments concerning these themes pervade the text.

Other recurrent themes that are quite evident throught this record of the workshop are: the tradeoffs between formality, ease of use, and area of applicability for notational tools; the role of procedural and non-procedural notations in software development; the use of a single uniform notation throughout the pre-implementation phases of software development, as opposed to different notations to emphasize different aspects of the system; and the mutual influence that the development methodology, the structure of the development organization, the class of applications and users, and the software development tools exert on one another.

Finally, there were three major implicit themes which were seldom explicitly addressed during the workshop. They are, however, important "results"; we present a discussion of them here so that the reader may have the context which they provide for the text. These implicit themes concern the requirements for an "ideal" development environment, the reasons why the ideal has not been achieved, and the major problems to be solved on the way to achieving the ideal.

Requirements for an "Ideal" Development Environment

Various characteristics of an "ideal" collection of development tools were mentioned during the workshop and, taken together, they constitute a set of requirements for an ideal set of tools. Many of the requirements are obvious (at least with 20-20 hindsight) and some are well-known motherhoods. A few, however, are controversial in that they may not be universally accepted within the software engineering community at large.

The tools themselves should provide every audience (developers, managers, customers, etc.) with a high degree of visibility into the system under development, commensurate with their particular interest. Thus, tools should be able to provide descriptions of various system characteristics even though this information is not explicitly provided in the course of development. Tools should also provide visibility into the software development project itself and be able to present information useful in determining the extent of progress and the remaining tasks.

The tools should also provide a means for effective, unambiguous communication among and within the various audiences. They should encourage and facilitate the timely collection and dissemination of information concerning the system under development.

The effect of a tool's usage should be an increased leverage for the efforts of individual practitioners and teams of practitioners. Tools should serve to augment the abilities of the practitioners and allow them to do the same job in less time or a better job in the same period of time. They should primarily be oriented toward knowledgeable, relatively experienced practitioners because they will probably not be effective in making poor practitioners better.

The measurable benefit of tool usage should be an economic one. This could be

through a reduction in the cost of developing a software system using the tools, or
it could be through an increase in the quality of the developed system over that
which would be produced for the same cost without using the tools.

The language or languages upon which the tools are based should provide for a
multiplicity of views of a system under development. The different views could, for
example, arise because of a desire to see the data flow within the system after it
has been described from a process viewpoint, or vice versa. Also, the views may
differ because of the differing needs of the various audiences for the system description.

The language(s) used should directly support the modelling of a system's functions, performance and/or economic characteristics. Partially this is in order to
be able to prototype a system prior to a full implementation. Equally important,
it is to allow the abstract (non-detailed) and perhaps incomplete description of a
system as required during pre-implementation development activities.

The tools should be closely linked to a particular development methodology.
They should at least encourage the use of the associated methodology and could also
enforce its use. The tools and the methodology together should reflect some particular development metaphor.

The tool collection should facilitate the gradual, incremental development of
software systems. It should help practitioners make steady progress toward a fully
developed system. It should lead to a clear separation among the pre-implementation
phases but should make it easy to move forward and backward through the phases.

The tool collection should provide direct support for the management of multiple
versions of the system under development. These versions may be alternatives corresponding to differing development decisions, or they may differ for other reasons. In
any case, it should be easy to focus attention upon different versions and move
around in the space of versions.

The system which delivers the tool collection to practitioners should provide
facilities for monitoring tool usage and for collecting statistics useful in assessing the effectiveness of the tools. It should make tool use easy and allow development teams to work concurrently in a cooperative, non-conflicting way.

Why the "Ideal" Has Not Been Achieved

A number of pragmatic reasons underlie the failure to, as yet, achieve a tool
collection which satisfies even a majority of the requirements stated in the previous section. Adequate facilities for delivery of a tool collection to a team of
development practitioners are not generally available. Further, a small set of
demonstrably beneficial methodologies and, more importantly, metaphors has not

been identified and efforts are therefore diffuse and not easily transferred.

Other reasons are quality related. Tools are generally produced by a practitioner for individual use and little attention is therefore given to the tool's portability, its documentation, its robustness, or its user interface. In short, the tool falls prey to the single-user syndrome. Additional reasons include the "not invented here" syndrome (discussed by Ike Nassi) and the zealous oversell of inadequate tools by some researchers.

The most important reason that pre-implementation tools are not widely used is that they are viewed as high-risk ventures. They cost a good deal to adequately prepare and generally have an associated learning/training cost which is also high. Additionally, their production diverts, for too long a period of time, the attention of development practitioners from their more primary task. Finally, although there is a fair amount of experience in tool usage, data have not been collected which would allow either general or specific arguments to be developed concerning the value of tool usage or the benefit derived from the resources invested in developing tools.

Achieving the Ideal

During the conference, several topics emerged as requiring the attention of researchers and developers if there is to be significant progress in the area of software development tools. The issues identified at the conference undoubtedly reflect the interests of the attendees and probably constitute an incomplete list. Nonetheless, they provide some directions for future work in the area. They are presented below with no intent of implying their relative importance.

Since high-quality tools are generally very closely associated with a specific development method or metaphor, it is necessary to seek new methods and metaphors that utilize existing tools more effectively and lead to the identification of new, highly effective tools. Two approaches were suggested as deserving attention in the search for new development methods or metaphors. One can be called *constructive development* and involves the gradual preparation of system description text under the guidance of an intelligent text editor having knowledge about the syntax of the description language. The other can be called *gradual enhancement* and involves the preparation of a series of functioning systems, each more sophisticated than the previous. Methods and metaphors based on these approaches to development have been used in several instances, but the current thrust of tool preparation is more oriented toward traditional top-down elaboration approaches.

Another topic concerned the development of tools themselves. If they are to successfully satisfy the requirements indicated above, they must be demonstrably

cost-effective and must satisfy the criteria usually levied upon marketed
systems. At issue is how to gradually evolve tools in a cost-effective way. One
suggested attack is to use gradual enhancement in the development of tools themselves — minimally sufficient tools, particular to the specific task and easy to
modify, should be developed initially; usage should be monitored and, based on the
resulting data and the definition of new functions to be performed, these tools
should be gradually extended and enhanced. Another suggested route of attack is to
prepare tools in a "bottom-up" manner by taking tools proven to be useful during
one development phase (such as testing tools) and modify them so that they can be
effectively used during other phases.

The nature of the language or languages useful during pre-implementation development phases was also identified as a major topic. Particularly in question are
two aspects. First, is it sufficient to view the development process as a gradual
agglomeration of an eventually executable system description by the iterative addition of detail, or are different notations needed in different phases? Second, how
should the language, or set of languages, be developed so that multiple views of
the system (necessitated by the existence of multiple audiences) can be provided?

Another topic that was identified concerned the modelling of a system during
its pre-implementation development. Several approaches were discussed during the
conference, each providing the system developer with a different world-view, and
each therefore emphasizing a different set of system characteristics. The major
issues concerned when to use each of the various modelling approaches, and whether
or not one should be preferred over the others.

The final topic which emerged concerned the organization of the body of facts
collected together during system development so that it can easily and conveniently
be inspected, queried and modified. This issue extends past the questions of data
organization into the realm of representational issues associated with current artificial intelligence research activities.

OVERVIEW OF TEXT

The next six chapters present the prepared papers as well as summaries of the
comments prepared by the discussants and summaries of the informal discussions. The
final chapter presents three summaries of future needs and recommended research
directions.

Chapter II addresses the question: what support tools are needed? In the
first paper, Nico Habermann draws a distinction between tools for programming and
tools for system construction. He introduces the notion of a constructive programming methodology, and the use of a uniform notation for software development. The

paper by Vic Lesser and Jack Wileden discusses a number of issues which complicate
the problems of distributed system software design and proposes some requirements
for tools to handle the increased complexity of distributed systems. In the final
paper, Ike Nassi provides a critical look at tool needs from an industrial perspective. Reasons for the failure of tools are examined, and a model for tool development is proposed that accounts for the observed failures. The theme of experiences
with tools, opened by Ike Nassi, is continued in Chapter III by Bob Snowden. His
paper gives an experience-based assessment of software development systems. He
reports on experiences related to three software development systems. Following a
brief summary of each system, general comments and conclusions are presented.

Chapter IV covers toolboxes and development support systems. In his paper,
Lee Osterweil proposes a software lifecycle methodology and a development support
system tuned to this methodology. The development support system places major
emphasis on improved verification tools and techniques to be applied throughout the
entire software lifecycle, with the expected result being improved product quality
and enhanced product visibility. Tony Wasserman's paper discusses the User
Software Engineering (USE) project, which is an effort to develop a methodology and
a set of tools for the design and development of interactive information systems.

Chapters V and VI are concerned with procedural and non-procedural notational
tools for use during the design phase of software development. In Chapter V, Burt
Leavenworth discusses the use of data abstraction in program design. An extended
PL/1 notation incorporating abstract data types is illustrated by examples, and a
design methodology which uses this notation is discussed. In the second paper,
Bill Riddle discusses several approaches to software design modelling including
relational formalisms, functional formalisms, and procedural formalisms. It is
argued that procedural formalisms offer the most promising opportunity for developing a software design support system.

The papers in Chapter VI discuss notational tools based on regular expressions
and data base models of software. In his paper, Alan Shaw surveys and assesses the
use of event expressions, flow expressions, and several varieties of path expressions as non-procedural notational tools. John and Diane Smith describe the use of
data base models in the pre-implementation description of software systems, particularly those in which large quantities of intricately related data are manipulated
by multiple users.

The focus of Chapter VII is on the application of analysis tools and techniques
to the pre-implementation phases of software development. The papers describe the
use of formal verification ideas and tools and discuss software validation and pre-
implementation issues. The topics discussed by Ralph London and Larry Robinson include methodological concerns, applications to the language design, automated verification systems, new capabilities, and future directions. Dick Fairley surveys

several software validation techniques, discusses automated validation tools, describes current issues, and establishes several relationships between validation and pre-implementation considerations.

Finally, in Chapter VIII Nico Habermann, Alan Shaw, and Dick Fairley present summaries of discussions on "where to next?" with respect to support systems, specification languages, and analysis techniques. Each summary contains recommendations for short-term and long-term research directions.

CONCLUSION

This text offers evidence that future work in the area of pre-implementation tools can result in highly integrated collections of tools for software development. These support systems will provide notations that are convenient for the abstract, yet precise, description and modelling of software systems; reinforce particular development methodologies; be flexible enough to provide multiple views of the project, at varying levels of detail; and provide analysis tools so that practitioners can be assured that their development effort is proceeding in the proper direction. The deliberations reported here are an indication of the progress made to date, and how much remains to be done.

Chapter II. Needs

The workshop began with a concentrated assessment of tool needs from a number of perspectives: "traditional" software systems, distributed software, and industrial software development. This chapter presents the three papers addressing these topics and a summary of the discussion which followed their presentation.

In the first paper, Nico Habermann draws a distinction between isolated tools for the construction of individual programs and integrated tools for the construction of software systems. He introduces the notion of a constructive programming methodology, and the concept of a uniform environment for all phases of software development. All tools in the environment operate on objects built from basic constructs defined in a programming language. Some tools may generate alternate representations of the system, but the user works with a single representation. In this manner, uniformity of the environment for software development is achieved.

The second paper is by Vic Lesser and Jack Wileden. They discuss several issues that complicate the design of distributed software systems (e.g., concurrency, dynamic process structure, parallelism, redundancy, etc.). They present a set of requirements for tools to handle the increased complexity of distributed systems, and observe that distributed systems have many of the characteristics of complex organizational structures. An appendix illustrates the use of a process specification language to provide a high-level view of a large, complex process structure.

The third paper, by Ike Nassi, presents an industrial perspective of software tool development. Nassi observes that tools have a large potential payoff, but are expensive and risky to develop. Several necessary properties of successful tools are identified, and an evolutionary model for tool development is proposed.

Discussants Tom Love, Gary Nutt, and Terry Straeter provide numerous insights and comments concerning the three papers. The topics which emerged during the discussion include: the environment of the tool user, tool development issues, tool evaluation, models and formalisms, and miscellaneous smaller topics.

TOOLS FOR SOFTWARE SYSTEM CONSTRUCTION

A. N. Habermann

Computer Science Department
Carnegie-Mellon University

The environment in which programs and systems are developed provides
some isolated tools for constructing single programs, but support for
composing systems out of components is usually lacking. Each tool
uses its own vocabulary (e.g., characters and lines for text editors,
language syntax for compilers, machine code for debuggers). However,
uniformity can be achieved if the analytic approach to program development is replaced by a constructive approach. Taking this approach, all
program construction tools use a single set of programming language
constructs as their expression mechanism. This is exactly the set of
constructs that programs are written in. Building large software
systems is not merely a matter of programming, but also one of organization and management. A substantial amount of work goes into fitting
pieces together, trying different versions and checking interfaces. The
ability to separate module specification from implementation can be
utilized for defining precise logical interfaces and for version maintenance. System construction tools can be built that automate most of the
task of generating system versions.

INTRODUCTION

The need for partitioning a large software project into manageable subtasks has
been recognized from the early days of system building on, not only by system
designers, but also by language designers. Block structure in Algol 60, for instance, was included in that language with the idea that inner blocks might be
written by different programmers. Twenty years of experience have shown that block
structure is still useful, but more for localizing the existence of temporary variables than for partitioning the programming task.

A useful design concept for partitioning a programming task is the distinction
between *implementation* and *application*, between definition and call site. One writes
a program with the intent that someone else can use it in one of his own programs.
The user does not want to know about implementation details for two reasons. First,
the amount of implementation detail in a system would make it practically impossible
to build large software systems if every user must know every detail. Second,
system designers wish not to create strong connections between the implementation

---

This work is sponsored by the Software Engineering Division of CENTACS/CORADCOM,
Fort Monmouth, N.J.

and application of a function so that it is not impossible to change the implementation.

The procedure concept is more useful for partitioning a programming task than block structure, because it provides a clear distinction between *implementation*, described in a procedure declaration, and *application*, represented by a procedure call. The minimum amount of common knowledge shared by the implementor and the user of a procedure is what usually is called a *procedure specification*. This mechanism minimizes the common knowledge for both parties involved: a user can ignore implementation details and the implementor of a procedure needs to know neither the environment in which the procedure is called, nor the actual parameters to which it is applied.

The decision whether or not a design concept is adequate for partitioning a software product is primarily a matter of scale. The procedure concept is adequate for small programs (50 to 200 lines), but insufficient for larger programs. In order to divide the task of writing a large program into manageable subtasks, we need a concept which can be used to group procedures into meaningful program units. Data abstraction is the right concept. It allows a designer to group procedures by the class of objects to which they apply. This significant idea was first realized by the class concept of SIMULA67 [Dahl 72].

Systems are constructed out of units that usually are even larger than abstract data types. These units are commonly known as *software modules*. An example of a software module is a process management module for a multiprogramming operating system. This module defines several data types (e.g., *process* and *semaphore*) and operations on objects of those types (start, stop, P, V, etc.). In addition to these datatypes and operations, a process management module may contain shared objects (e.g., a ready list) and internal operations such as block and wakeup.

We wish to distinguish between the task of writing a single (large) *program* or single *module*, and the task of constructing a *system* out of a collection of modules. The tools needed for the first task are indicated by the term *program development* tools, and those for the latter by the term *system construction* tools. The term *construction tool* is used to indicate any one of these tools. Our discussion of programming tools centers around classical tools such as compilers and editors. We argue for a more constructive approach to writing programs and for more uniformity of the program development environment. Our discussion of system construction tools emphasizes the importance of specifications and system version maintenance.

The design principle for construction tools is based on two highlights in the development of software engineering methodology, one due to Parnas and the other due to DeRemer. The fundamental observation of Parnas [Parnas 72] is that a programming task is more manageable if it is partitioned by common decisions, rather than by specific characteristics such as control flow. Common decisions often center around classes of data objects. This is why a data abstraction mechanism is such a useful program concept. This is also why data types that share objects are placed in one software module.

The important observation of DeRemer [DeRemer 76] is that one should work with different representations of modules depending on what one is doing. DeRemer argues that one should use the *implementation* for what he calls "programming-in-the-small" and the *specification* for "programming-in-the-large". The former applies to writing single programs, the latter to composing systems. DeRemer's idea fits well with that of separating implementation from application. The knowledge shared by a system builder (who is the *user* of modules) and the implementor of a module is the module specification. Using specifications, one can build logically sound systems without knowing details of how modules are implemented.

The popularity of the Programmer's Workbench [Dolotta 76] should not make one believe that "building tools" is the entire answer to constructing large software systems. Tools are extremely useful, but are only means to an end. The real goal is to *control* and *manage* the development of a software product. This goal is achieved by providing a *software development environment*. Such an environment not only provides tools to its users, but also plays an active role in two other respects: 1) it maintains a representation of the *development state* and 2) it prevents user operations from leaving a project in an inconsistent state. These issues are discussed in [Habermann 79b] and in other papers at this workshop. The scope of this paper is restricted to the construction tools that exist in a software development environment.

PROGRAMMING TOOLS

The classical tools for constructing programs are: text editors, compilers, link-editors and interactive debuggers. These tools will also be needed in the future, but substantial improvements may be achieved in three ways, through:

- uniformity of the program development environment
- replacing the analytic compiling technique by a constructive technique,
- more efficient system construction.

Uniformity of Programming Environment

Currently, it is common practice that each programming tool defines its own vocabulary, independent of what other tools do. For example, programs are written using a text editor which defines a programming environment in terms of lines and characters. A text editor does not know that the character sequence *b e g i n* has a specific meaning. A compiler, however, defines another programming environment in which <u>begin</u> is recognized as a significant keyword. From the programmer's viewpoint it is silly to have such vastly different environments for typing in a program and for compiling it. A programmer should work in a single programming environment in which the constructs of his programming language are known.

It used to be the case that interactive debuggers defined a third programming environment in terms of assembly code, or, even worse, in terms of fast registers and memory addresses. Modern debugging systems allow a user to check the state of his program in terms of the symbolic names he gave to the variables and procedures of his program. We support the idea that debugging (if at all) should be done in terms of a source program (i.e., in terms of source language constructs). It should not be necessary for a user to understand the object code environment and its correspondence to the source.

From Analytic to Constructive Methodology

Uniformity of the programming environment is achieved by replacing the customary analytic compiling technique with a more constructive approach. The current practice is clearly expressed by the terms lexical *analyzer* and syntax *analyzer*. One of the main purposes of the lexical analyzer is to detect that the user meant the keyword <u>begin</u> when he typed the corresponding sequence of characters. The syntax analyzer, in turn, checks that the user also typed a matching keyword <u>end</u>. The lexical analyzer understands single keywords, but not the fact that some keywords must appear in matching pairs.

A more constructive approach is taken by replacing the triple (text editor, lexical analyzer, syntax analyzer) by a pair of tools (program constructor, unparser). A program constructor provides the editing environment which makes use of the programming language syntax. A program constructor is an editor in the sense that it is used for writing or modifying a program text. However, its instructions do not operate on lines and characters, but on program constructs. Instead of typing the character sequence for the keyword <u>begin</u>, a program constructor provides an instruction which has the effect of putting the pair of keywords <u>begin</u> <u>end</u> at the current position of the text cursor, provided that this is syntactically correct.

The main purpose of a program constructor is to build a syntax tree. This structure contains all the information necessary for generating intermediate code. Every instruction a program constructor receives is translated into a manipulation of the syntax tree. Problems of misspelled or non-matching keywords cannot occur, because language constructs are inserted by the constructor, not by the typist.

The major advantages of using a program constructor are that programs are

edited in terms of programming language syntax so that the user cannot write syntactically incorrect programs. One can expect greater efficiency in program translation, because the steps from character string to lexical units and from sequences of
lexical units to syntactic units are no longer necessary.

The *unparser* is internal to the program constructor. Its function is to map the
current syntax tree into user-readable program text. It should include pretty-
printing capabilities so that a program text appears well-structured and indented on
the programmer's terminal.

Two examples of program constructors are [Huet 77] and [Teitelbaum 79]. The
first is part of a verification system for Pascal programs. The second is part of
an interactive, interpretive PL/C system intended for students taking introductory
programming courses.

System Construction Efficiency

The path that leads from source program to system construction consists of
three phases:

    phase 1: from syntax tree to intermediate code
    phase 2: from intermediate code to optimized code
    phase 3: from single module code to link-edited code

Without a separate compilation facility, it is necessary to recompile the whole
program if some part of it is modified. This is not feasible for large software
systems. Compiling all the modules of a software system often takes an hour or more.
This situation is not likely to change in the near future. By the time that compiler
speed has increased considerably, our systems will be so much larger that total compile *time* is not drastically reduced.

System construction efficiency is achieved when the amount of recompilation and
relinking that is necessary because of modifications is reduced to a minimum. This
is achieved in two ways.

    • by postponing phases 2 and 3 until type checking and verification
      have been completed, and
    • by limiting the effect that modifying a module M has on modules
      that use M.

Provided that the logical interface with other modules is known (see the next
section), formal program verification and type checking can be completed without
applying phases 2 and 3. Not until a program passes these hurdles does it make

sense to apply the code generator and the optimizer. Phase 3, link-editing, should not be applied until a useful subsystem can be built out of several modules that went through phase 2.

The impact of a modification of a module M on modules that use M depends on the nature of the modification. Let Q be a module that uses facilities provided by module M. A modification of module M has one of the following three effects on module Q.

1. If we change the specification of the facilities provided by M and used by Q, it is necessary to rewrite, recompile and relink both M and Q. This type of change affects both the logical and the physical interface.

2. If the specifications remain the same, but we change some data representations of the facilities provided by M and used by Q, then it is necessary to recompile and relink M and Q. This type of change affects the physical interface.

3. If the specifications and data representations remain the same then it is not necessary to recompile Q, but it is necessary to relink M and Q. The modifications have a local effect on M.

It is likely that changes of the first category are fairly rare and changes of the third category most frequent. One does not change the specifcations that often, but changes in the source code or in the initial values of constants, ranges and variables are fairly common.

Recompilation and relinking are minimized by *incremental program construction*. If a subsystem is tested and a module M must be changed, the subsystem is halted and its current state is preserved. Module M is rewritten and recompiled. Assuming that specifications and representations provided by M and used by other modules are not changed, the old copy of module M is deleted and its new version is linked into the halted subsystem. Execution of the subsystem is then resumed. There is no need to start execution of a subsystem from scratch, nor is it necessary to reconstruct its state.

We achieve this flexibility by *invariant linking* of modules. The trick is to fix the *position* of facilities that module M provides to other modules. This is achieved by letting other modules access facilities provided by M through an *entry vector* which consists of pointers to these facilities. The position of a facility provided by M may change, but its position in the entry vector is invariant. Access to provided facilities goes through one more level of indirection. This is a small price to pay for the advantage of incremental program construction.

SYSTEM CONSTRUCTION

There are two aspects to system construction, a *logical* and a *physical* aspect.

The logical aspect has to do with composing systems out of modules. The physical aspect concerns the actual system generation by compiling source files and link-editing object files. We label these two aspects with the terms *system composition* and *system generation*.

System Composition

   The system designer who composes a system out of software modules wants to assure that the chosen modules are compatible and do provide the desired system facilities. While doing this, he acts as the *user* of these modules and is therefore primarily interested in the *application* of module facilities. System composition is primarily a matter of module *specifications*, because the information relevant to a user of an object is contained in its specification.

   Previously, we mentioned block structure as an example of a construct whose specification is implied by its implementation. It is generally thought to be better practice to represent the specification of an object explicitly as is done for procedures and abstract data types.

   Two modern programming languages, Mesa [Geschke 77] and Ada [Ichbiah 79] provide an explicit specification not only for procedures and data types, but also for software modules. Ada provides such a mechanism for processes as well. Another significant contribution of Ada to the state of the art is the physical separation of specifications from implementations for all four of these language constructs. This feature has the potential of making it much easier to read and understand programs. One of the most awkward problems with reading programs disappears: it will no longer be necessary to scan a program in order to find out which parts one should skip if one wants to understand the structure of a program.

   The programming environment in which systems are constructed needs to provide ways for such tools to describe a system in terms of the specifications of its component modules and subsystems (what DeRemer calls "programming in the large"). A system description shows not only which building blocks were used for its construction, but also how these building blocks depend on one another. Modules are specified in Mesa and in Ada by listing all the facilities that are exported, including their names, types, and parameters and their types. This information is sufficient to achieve *independent* type checking. Various languages provide *incremental* type checking, which requires that all modules that provide some facility used by a module M are compiled prior to M. This assures that all type information is available when M is compiled. Independent type checking means that modules can be compiled in any order. It is obvious that Mesa and Ada permit independent type checking because the necessary type information is in the explicit module specifications.

   One can make a case for including more information in a system description than

the full specification of the facilities provided by its components. It is useful
to include not only the facilities *provided*, but also the ones *required*. One may
argue that it is not necessary to list the required facilities because this information can be derived at compile time. Also, independent compilation is not jeopar-
dized because full specification of the provided facilities is sufficient to achieve
this.

The reason for including a require clause in a module specification is that one
can more precisely express the *intended* use of the required facilities. For example,
a module M provides a data structure s{f,g}, where f and g are fields of some type.
It may be that some module A should have read/write access to the fields of s, while
a module B should have read access only. There may be a third module, module C,
which requires access to s.f, but not to s.g. Another example is a module that provides a data type and its operations (e.g., mailbox, send and receive). Other
modules need to use different subsets of these operations. A require clause makes
these restrictions explicit and checkable.

Since a user module determines how it will use a facility provided by another
module, the specification list of that user module is the natural place for describing the facilities it requires. This leads to a module specification consisting of
two parts, a *provide* and a *require* list. What one gains by having a require list is:

- the intended use of required facilities is explicitly stated,
- a compiler can check more accurately for correct usage (e.g., for
  read-only access),
- module specifications are self-sufficient for checking the logic of
  a module; it is not even necessary to know the specifications of
  other modules.

The purpose of a system composition description is to show the structure and
specification of a system in terms of provide and require lists of its components.
The structure is determined by some simple nesting rules. The validity of a system
is determined by composition rules such as:

"Each facility provided by a system must be provided by one of its
components"

or

"Each facility required by a component must either be provided by one
of the other components or it must be required by the system"

A system composition tool enforces such rules and checks for system consistency.
Another task performed by the system composition tool is to translate the provide
and require lists into compiler usable form. If the tools are well-integrated, the
system composition tool generates a pre-filled symbol table which is expanded by the

first compiler phase. Otherwise, it generates a definition part which is added as a
prefix to the module body. A system that works this way is presented in [Tichy 79].

System Generation

Specifications define the logical module interfaces. There is sufficient information in a specification to apply the first compiler phase which checks types and
generates intermediate code. But there is insufficient information for the second
compiler phase, because real code can be generated only if physical properties such
as sizes of objects are known.

In analogy to type checking one can think of *incremental* or *independent* code
generation. The former requires that the code generation phase is applied to
modules in some order so that physical interfaces are known when needed. It is not
difficult to make a system construction tool that derives the necessary order from
a system specification. However, the incremental method is somewhat restrictive
because it cannot handle circular dependencies.

Independent code generation is possible only if the physical properties of
required facilities are known. This is achieved in Mesa by restricting the kind of
facilities that can be required to those whose physical properties can be derived
from the specifications. In Intercol, described in [Tichy 79], physical properties
are added to the specifications.

A more important issue than that of incremental versus independent code generation is that of generating different *versions* of systems. A given system specification may be realized by different compositions of modules. It is conceivable that
two different collections of modules each provide the same set of facilities. It is
also conceivable that one writes different implementations of a module, each providing the same set of facilities. Alternatively, different versions of modules may be
created by slight modifications of the kind that turn range checking on or off.

Management of module and system versions requires an adequate *representation* of
version definitions and version instantiations, and a construction tool for *generating* a particular version from a representation. We discuss first module versions,
because these are the building blocks of system versions. For the sake of simplicity we consider a scheme in which only *source versions* are explicitly described.
In fact, one may take a broader view and describe not only source versions of a
module, but represent its specification, its object code, its documentation and all
other representations also as versions of a module.

If one takes the broader view, a more general description is needed than a
specification of provided and required facilities expressed in the syntax of a
particular programming language. This view is taken by Cooprider [Cooprider 79].

He describes a module by a *diagram* which lists provided and required resources and also the module's various versions. The essence of a version description is a *construction rule* which can be executed to generate that version.

A drawback of this general approach is that the system construction environment has no knowledge of the nature of the versions being described. Version management becomes much simpler if the environment knows about various types of versions and relationships between versions. Simplification is achieved in two ways. First construction rules are not needed, because the various types of objects each have their construction rule. For example, an object of type *source program* is compiled into an *object program* and an object of type *text* is formatted into a *document*. Second, it is not necessary to list all kinds of versions. Objects such as object code or documents are derivable from source objects and can be generated when needed. If one adopts the rule that all derived objects are deleted when a source object is deleted, then derived objects can be left out of the version description.

For compilable systems, module specifications can easily be extended to describe versions. With this extension, a module specification now consists of three lists, a *provide* list, a *require* list and a *version* list. An element of a version list identifies an implementation which designers wish to consider as different from other implementations. There are as many different implementations of a module as there are elements in its version list.

Designers may often revise an existing implementation and not want to consider the resulting version as a totally different implementation. Revisions of this kind are handled without extending the version list. Conceptually, the latest revision of a particular implementation is put on top of a pile of revised implementations and each element of a version list points to the top element of such a pile. This is more economical than representing each revised implementation separately in the version list. Piles of revised implementations are typically managed by a backup facility which orders them by creation date, most recent on top.

We now turn to system versions. An element of a system version list describes a system *composition* (instead of an implementation). A composition defines in fact not just one, but a whole family of system versions. A particular family member is selected by specifying for each component of a family composition which revised version should be used. The resulting version scheme has three dimensions: *composition, implementation* and *revision*.

> *Example:* Let EM and IM be modules; let B = EM.bss, C = EM.c, D = IM.bss and G = IM.c be implementations of these modules. If A = (EM,IM) is a composition of a module S, then three examples of version instantiations are:
> S.A(B.780626,D.790410), S.A(C,G), S.A.
>
> All these versions are instances of the composition S.A. The first two select the ".bss" implementation of both components EM and IM.

The first version specifies exactly which revised implementation of these components it wants to use. The second version does not specify so much detail; we assume it will be composed of the most recent revised implementations of the ".c" implementations. The third version of S is a composition of the most recent revisions of the standard implementations of EM and IM.

We mentioned above that, for compilable systems, versions can be generated without describing a specific construction rule. All a system version generation *tool* needs is a version instantiation parameter. The tool applies to that parameter a standard compile, link-edit sequence. This scheme is simple enough for a user to write his own version generation rules which perform additional tasks such as code optimization.

The proposed scheme allows for either *incremental* compilation or *independent* compilation. If one chooses incremental compilation, the order in which modules and systems must be compiled can be expressed in the composition rules of systems. If one chooses independent compilation, physical interfaces can be specified either as an extension of the provide and require lists or as part of composition rules.

CONCLUSION

A major improvement of system construction methodology is achievable by creating a uniform environment for program development and composition of systems. All tools operate on objects built out of a single set of basic constructs defined by a programming language. These constructs are represented in several ways (e.g., as character strings on a terminal, as a syntax tree, as object code), but a user works only with a single representation. Other representations are generated by the construction tools, some automatically, others by explicit user commands. A significant contribution toward achieving uniformity of the program development environment is the constructive compile-edit approach.

Explicit representation of system and module specifications is crucial for both system composition and single program construction. Program development tools use the logical interface defined by specifications for *independent* type checking and verification of the logic of single modules. System specifications are used for checking that all necessary facilities are provided correctly and that the components are consistent.

Final code generation and linking of modules cannot take place until the physical interfaces are known. If this information is included in module specifications, it is possible to generate code and link-edit modules in any order (*independent* construction). Without this information, code generation and link-editing require a definite order (*incremental* construction). This order can be expressed in the representation of a system composition.

Changes in the interface of modules usually require recompilation of both providing and using modules. However, these changes are rare compared to local changes in the code or changes of constant or initial values. For these simple but frequent changes, it should not be necessary to recompile modules that use a revised module. Program development tools can be constructed so that in most cases only modified programs must be recompiled and relinked. The effort of recompilation can be reduced significantly.

Some modern languages provide useful language constructs for representing module specifications. This language tool can be extended to apply to systems as well, and also indicate the various module implementations or system compositions. The software development environment should know how versions are represented and automatically generate them from the specifications.

The most important issues not discussed in this paper are those related to system state description and project management. The tools discussed in this paper are part of a software development environment which also maintains various forms of system documentation and checks that users do not leave their project in an inconsistent state.

ISSUES IN THE DESIGN OF TOOLS
FOR
DISTRIBUTED SOFTWARE SYSTEMS DEVELOPMENT

Victor R. Lesser and Jack C. Wileden

Computer and Information Science Department
University of Massachusetts

A number of issues which complicate the problem of distributed software
system design are discussed. These issues occur because distributed computing entails substantially more complex computational structures than
arise from traditional approaches to structuring process-based problem
solving. We discuss the requirements for tools which can handle this additional complexity.

INTRODUCTION

Distributed computation is becoming an increasingly popular and prevalent approach to problem solving. Indeed, distributed computation has been embraced so
rapidly and widely that the term itself is threatened with meaninglessness through
overuse [Enslow 78]. For purposes of discussion, we define distributed processing
as computation involving the decomposition of the problem solving task into subtasks
that are executed on relatively independent processing elements. We differentiate
distributed processing from multiprocessing by defining distributed processing systems as those systems where the cost of maintaining a centralized global view of the
problem solving database and control structure is prohibitive.

The dramatic growth of distributed computation is due in part to the emergence
of hardware technologies (e.g., VLSI) and communication structures (e.g., packet
switching) which have made it possible to construct networks of tens to hundreds of
processors. These range from loosely-coupled geographically distributed networks,
like the ARPA-Network [Kahn 71], to closely-coupled networks, such as the UC Irvine
Loop system [Farber 75] or the Carnegie-Mellon CM* system [Swan 77]. Equally important, however, has been the recognition that solutions to many complex problem-
solving tasks may be more easily conceptualized in terms of cooperating, semi-inde-
pendent agents working collectively toward an overall goal. This has been especially
true for large, knowledge-based, artificial intelligence systems (e.g., Hearsay-II
for speech understanding [Erman 79], VISIONS for natural scene recognition [Hanson 78])

This work was supported under National Science Foundation grant MCS78-04212 to the
University of Massachusetts.

in which different areas of knowledge (e.g., syntax, semantics, phonology, etc.) are decomposed into independent, self-directed modules which interact anonymously and are limited in the scope of the data which they need and produce.

The distinguishing properties of distributed computation systems require that support tools useful in the development of distributed software systems must possess capabilities beyond those sufficient for aiding designers of more traditional software systems. In the remainder of this paper, we discuss the special problems of distributed software design and consider the features which tools and support systems should possess if they are to facilitate the development of distributed software systems. In the next section, we first enumerate the characteristics of distributed computation which aggravate the problem of software design. Then, in the following section, we describe some of the capabilities which we feel must be provided to designers of distributed software. In the final section, we address the issues of tool integration and utilities desirable in a distributed software development environment.

SOFTWARE FOR DISTRIBUTED COMPUTATION

The primary complication in designing distributed software systems which is not found in more traditional software design arises from the possibility of concurrent activity in a distributed computational system. Indeed, managing the complexity introduced by concurrent activity is the central challenge to the designer of distributed software and hence to the tools intended to aid that designer. Concurrency gives rise to subtle interactions among various components of the software system. It leads to the possibility of conflicting usage of shared resources. It demands that every possible sequencing of interleaved or overlapping actions by the system's components be considered and deemed acceptable as a potential behavior of the overall system. Providing the distributed software system designer with capabilities for coping with concurrency must be the overriding objective in the development of tools for distributed software design.

However, distributed computation possesses properties in addition to concurrency which complicate the problem of distributed software design. As stated in the introduction, we distinguish a distributed system from other computational systems which admit parallel or concurrent activity by observing that components of general parallel systems may communicate and coordinate their actions through access to shared variables in a shared memory while in distributed systems intercomponent communication is restricted to the transmission of messages among the components. This distinction, based upon the bandwidth of the communication channel available between system components, is generally recognized, but its implications for software system designers have received less attention. Designing software for a

distributed system requires consideration of some issues unique to distributed computation and also of some issues, relevant to other types of software as well,
which acquire added significance in the distributed setting. Among the issues of
particular concern to designers of distributed software are fault tolerance and dynamic process structure, communication cost, allocation and synchronized usage of
shared and/or duplicated resources, the binding of conceptual to physical processing
entities and appropriate decomposition of a computational task for distributed
processing.

Since the paradigmatic example of distributed computation is the computer network,
it is perhaps not surprising that issues of fault tolerance arise more commonly in
the design of distributed systems than in other circumstances. Questions can mean-
ingfully be asked about the viability of a distributed system in which some components
or communication linkages either have completely ceased to function or are functioning only intermittently or erroneously; the answers can have important consequences
for system design. Neither the domain of sequential systems nor the domain of centralized, parallel systems is particularly conducive to a similar level of concern
about the impact of changes in configuration. Thus, on the one hand, a designer of
distributed software needs to worry about low-level issues of message transmission
protocols, timeouts, and noisy transmission. However, these concerns also manifest
themselves at a higher level as a need to describe dynamic aspects of the process
structure of a distributed system.

The distributed system designer must, therefore, be provided with facilities
(e.g., [Wileden 78]) for describing the creation and deletion of system components,
and the appearance and disappearance of intercomponent communication linkages during
system operation. Such facilities will be required if designers are to attempt to
build fault tolerance into their distributed systems. Moreover, these capabilities
are necessary simply to permit designers to explore the full range of potential
distributed computation solutions to problem-solving tasks. Thus, the ability to
handle dynamic process structure ranks a very close second behind the management of
complexity due to concurrency as a requisite feature of any tools which are intended
to aid designers of distributed software.

Communication cost is another issue of concern to the designer of distributed
systems which does not arise in more traditional sequential or centralized parallel
situations. Communication among components of a distributed system may be costly in
the literal, financial sense of requiring expensive telecommunications equipment, or
in the more figurative sense of consuming a disproportionate amount of component
activity and possibly substantially slowing the individual components as they await
messages from one another. In either case, it is important that the designer of a
distributed system be provided with tools which permit the early and accurate assessment of the communication costs implied by a proposed design. Lacking such aid,

designers can all too easily produce designs whose impractically high communication overheads will not be discovered until the system is implemented and found unusable.

Synchronization of concurrent, conflicting activities of processes in a centralized parallel system is a major consideration for designers of such systems. However, numerous techniques have been developed for dealing with the synchronization problem in this setting, so that designers at least have reasonable alternatives to consider in deciding how to handle potential conflicts among process activities. Unfortunately these techniques generally depend upon common access to some entity in shared memory and are thus inappropriate for use in solving distributed system synchronization problems. For this reason, a distributed system design tool should offer capabilities which allow the designer to explore various approaches to synchronizing activity within a distributed system ([Bernstein 78], [Lampson 77b], [LeLann 77], [Thomas 76]).

A closely related problem concerns the replication of shared resources in a distributed system. The possibility that, for example, multiple copies of a file may exist at various locations within a distributed system raises questions regarding where those copies should reside and how to maintain the consistency of the information they contain. Addressing these questions should be within the capabilities provided by a distributed software design tool.

More generally, a distributed software design tool should permit the description and investigation of various possible bindings between the conceptual process structure and the physical processing elements on which it will eventually be running. In a more traditional setting, although the software system might be conceived of as a collection of processes, the binding of those processes to physical processors is either trivial (e.g., all processes bound to the single processor of a uniprocessor system) or essentially irrelevant (e.g., all processes interchangeably bound to any available processor in a centralized multiprocessor system with identical processors). In a distributed system, however, the binding of processes to processors may have a significant impact on the system's behavior; particularly in terms of its performance characteristics. For instance, it would be useful to be able to specify that certain processes should be allocated on nearby processors because they communicate often.

In the previous paragraphs, we have raised a number of software issues with respect to distributed processing system design which in some sense are already found, although perhaps less important, in process-based computational models implemented on either a single processor or a closely-coupled processor network. We believe, however, that there are new issues involved in the design of distributed processing systems which may necessitate a radical shift in our perspective on how to organize computational algorithms for such systems.

In order to fully exploit the parallelism and redundancy of these potential processor networks of hundreds of processors, large and complex process structures

will be required. For the most part, current tools have been designed with small
and simple process structures in mind. In order to manage the complexity of large
and complex process structures, a shift in viewpoint is needed. Rather than viewing
a system as a simple network of producer and consumer processes, it is more appropriate to view it as a society of interacting processes whose structure is similar to
that of a complex organization. For instance, such organizational structuring ideas
as Simon's "nearly decomposable hierarchical system" [Simon 62] should be reflected
in tools used to develop such process structures.

Another, possibly more fundamental, shift comes from the inadequacies of conventional approaches to distributed system design. Conventional approaches can be
characterized by their emphasis on the maintenance of information correctness in all
aspects of the distributed computation. Using this approach, the distributed processing system is organized so that a processing node's local data bases contain exact
copies of appropriate portions of the overall problem solving data base necessary for
the node's algorithms ([Peebles 78], [Bernstein 78]). In these systems, a processor
rarely needs the assistance of another processor in carrying out its problem solving
function.

We call this type of distributed process decomposition *completely-accurate*,
nearly-autonomous (CA/NA), because the processors' algorithms operate on complete and
correct information ("completely-accurate") and because each processor usually has,
in its local data base, the information it requires to complete processing ("nearly-
autonomous"). When this information is not locally available, a processor must request another processor to calculate the information, which is returned as a complete
and correct result. This form of processor interaction can be characterized as
asynchronous subroutine calls, and is fairly easily modelled in existing parallel
process specification tools ([Bell 77], [Campbell 79a], [Estrin 78], [Feldman 79],
[Riddle 78a]).

The CA/NA approach, however, is not suitable for applications in which algorithms
and control structures cannot be replicated or partitioned based on the distribution
of data in the network. In this situation, a CA/NA would be very expensive to implement due to the high communication and synchronization costs required to guarantee
completeness and consistency of local data bases. We feel that the almost exclusive
use of this approach has severely limited the application areas to which distributed
processing has been effectively applied. This is especially true for distributed
interpretation and monitoring applications which seem suited to distributed processing implementations because of the natural spatial distribution of their sensors and
effectors.

An alternative and new approach to structuring distributed problem solving systems is to allow incorrect and inconsistent intermediate results and a range of
acceptable answers ([Lesser 79a], [Lesser 79b]). In this approach, internode

communication can be reduced at the risk of inconsistency and incompleteness of local views, and at the risk of unnecessary, redundant, or incorrect processing. We call a system with this problem solving structure *functionally-accurate* (FA) because it exhibits correct (within tolerance) input/output behavior but is distinct from *completely-accurate* problem solving structures, in which all intermediate aspects of the computation are required to be correct and consistent.

FA distributed systems are more complex than CA/NA distributed systems because the algorithms and control structures operate on local data bases which are incomplete, inconsistent, and possibly erroneous. In order to resolve the uncertainties in these local data bases and still keep communication bandwidth low, nodes must exchange partial results (at various levels of abstraction) and share common goals. Since new information may be based on processing which used incomplete or incorrect data, *an iterative, coroutine type of node interaction is required* to resolve uncertainty. This type of interaction leads us to view such a distributed system as a "cooperative network of interrelated tasks." Therefore, we call such FA systems *functionally-accurate, cooperative* (FA/C).

In FA/C systems, it is often appropriate to have the control of cooperation among the nodes decentralized and implicit. Each node uses its local estimate of the state of network problem solving to control its processing (i.e., what new information to generate) and its transmissions to other nodes [Lesser 79b]. This allows node activity to be *self-directed*. For instance, if a node does not receive an appropriate partial result in a given amount of time, it is able to continue processing, utilizing whatever data are available at that time.

When organizing a FA/C distributed system, it is appropriate to think of the system as being *synthesized* from local systems operating at each node. This perspective shifts the view from that of a system distributed over a network to that of a functionally-accurate network of cooperating systems, each performing significant local processing on incomplete and potentially inconsistent information. This new perspective is not easily represented using existing tools for parallel process specification.

Consideration by designers of issues regarding the appropriate decomposition of the computational task, such as the choice between CA/NA and FA/C organizations, will demand a tool equipped to facilitate the description and investigation of various alternatives. This will probably involve tools that integrate deterministic and probabilistic modelling and specification of distributed system designs.

In this section, we have highlighted a number of issues which complicate the problem of distributed software system design and pointed to the need for tools to assist in the design effort. In essence, we have enumerated various facets of the fundamental fact that distributed computing entails substantially more complex computational structures than do the more traditional approaches to process based problem solving structures. This complexity calls for design tools which support a global, high-level view (both deterministic and probabilistic) of a system's design, and also the ability to focus in on specific local aspects of the design. In fact, the need for both local and global viewpoints is not restricted to the design stage of distributed software development but pervades the entire development process. For instance, both specification of requirements and debugging can benefit from the maintenance of local and global viewpoints on a distributed computing system.

One final consideration which must be kept in mind by those building tools for distributed software system development is the relative infancy of distributed computation. It is almost certain that completely unanticipated issues, such as dynamic interaction phenomena among interacting processes, well outside the scope of our discussion in this section, will turn out to be of great importance to the designers of distributed systems. This likelihood underscores the need for tools which support analysis of evolving designs and which support both local and global views of a system. It also calls for design tools which are non-prescriptive, that is, do not enforce nor even strongly suggest a particular approach to system implementation. Tools which bias designers toward some particular computational organization for distributed systems will inhibit the exploration of alternatives which is necessary to the successful exploitation of a technology as new as distributed computation. Non-procedural description techniques, which indicate the intended behavior of a system or component without specifying precisely how that behavior should be realized, represent one approach to non-prescriptive design and therefore seem particularly appropriate for use in distributed software system design tools.

A HIGH-LEVEL VIEW OF THE PROCESS STRUCTURE

In the preceding sections, we discussed a broad range of issues which contribute to the difficulty of designing distributed software systems, and we suggested some of the capabilities needed in design tools for such systems. Perhaps the central and most compelling among these issues complicating the design problem for distributed systems is that of managing the complexity inherent in sophisticated process interaction protocols and dynamic process structures. These issues will naturally arise when the designer tries to maximally exploit the capabilities of a distributed computing facility.

In this section, we consider some approaches to this particular problem in order to illustrate techniques which may be useful in tools for distributed software system development. We will concentrate on the particular problem of how to integrate an appropriate high-level viewpoint of a large and complex process structure into a process-specification tool.

An appropriate high-level viewpoint of the process structure should integrate

both the structure's static and dynamic characteristics. For example, it should include the data requirements of individual processes and the frequency of access to
these data. It should also make clear how processes are connected, both in terms of
direct communication through messages and indirect communication through shared data.
Those processes which run in parallel, as coroutines or sequentially, should be
discernable. Finally, this view should include the characteristics of the process
structure's dynamic responses to new data.

One of the main ideas that can be used to accomplish this integration is to structure the specification on two levels. The first level corresponds to a static description of the process structures. This static description specifies the potential
components in the process structure, and the nature and the structure of possible
communication paths among the components. Given this static description, the more
dynamic characteristics of the process structures can be described on a separate
level in terms of this static structure. As will be discussed, this two-level specification framework allows non-procedural specification of many of the dynamic characteristics of the process structure.

The static structure of complex process structures can often be decomposed in
terms of subtasks or process clusters. This decomposition is somewhat arbitrary and
may be based on shared data within a subtask, functionality of a subtask, interaction
intensity, or component life histories. Clusters are themselves made up of sub-
clusters, in terms of both information and control flow. This permits a hierarchical
description of a process structure. The use of hierarchy in specifying a process
structure is very useful but should be formulated so that non-hierarchical communication still can be represented conveniently. This method of describing a process
structure is very compatible with Simon's view of an organization as a "nearly decomposable hierarchical system."

Within this hierarchical framework, there are a number of other important structuring principles. Parallelism in a decomposition is often obtained by replicating
the structure of a subtask and partitioning the data among the instances. A wide
variety of different process structures can be constructed by specifying the replication attributes of the components of the subtask. For example, within a substruc-
ture, a component may be replicated or may be shared by other components which are
replicated themselves.

Replication implies the need for synchronization and communication paradigms in
order to coordinate and communicate with the multiple component copies. These paradigms include lock-step control and broadcasting of data. Many control paradigms
can be implemented directly by communication protocols that deal with groups of
processes. For example, the lock-step control paradigm can be defined by combining
two group communication protocols. One protocol broadcasts the same message to a
group of processes, the other protocol waits until all processes in a group have

replied before sending a composite message.

The communication paradigms linking components of a process structure can be made independent of the number of replications and the manner of component sharing. A given link is statically specified to connect certain components with a specified communication protocol. When this link is instantiated, it should connect all copies of the components in its static specification with the specified communication protocol. For example, a simple link should be replicated for each instantiated process so that messages can be directed to specific instantiations. A broadcast link should send a copy of each received message to each receiver, independent of the number of receivers.

Decomposition of a process structure must also address the structure's dynamic behavior. When the process structure associated with a subtask is constructed it can be used repeatedly to perform the same function. Each use might require only minor modifications or re-initialization of the process structure. Thus, in order for the process structure to be effectively implemented on a processor network, it is important to be able to specify that particular processes and their communication links do not have to be completely disassembled every time they complete a task.

By describing and manipulating a structure's evolution state, its dynamic behavior can be controlled. An evolution state describes the extent of instantiation of a component. A wide range of dynamic behaviors can be described by pre-specifying how the evolution state of a component is related to the evolution state of its enclosing structure. The description and parameterization of the subcomponent structure simplifies these minor modifications for each repetition and permits the system to automatically modify appropriate parts of the process structure upon certain predefined events.

Using these mechanisms, a process-oriented job control language (PCL) has been developed [Lesser 79c]. The PCL provides a high-level view of the process structure and allows the modular and non-procedural specification of both the static and dynamic characteristics of a process structure. The PCL thus offers a number of the essential capabilities which will be needed in software development tools for distributed computing systems (see the Appendix of this paper for an example of a PCL specification).

THE DEVELOPMENT ENVIRONMENT

A hospitable environment for development of distributed software systems should include both utilities to ease the eventual implementation and usage of distributed software, and a collection of design support tools to aid the designers of such software.

Among the utilities useful to distributed software development is a process-oriented job control language (such as the PCL discussed in the previous section). Such a control language would support the global and local viewpoints at the level of the operating system under which the development effort is carried out. Not only would this present distributed system developers with a more homogeneous environment, unifying the descriptions used during the design and implementation phases of the development, but it could also facilitate the assessment of their designs for distributed software systems. Even in the absence of a truly distributed computing system, a process-oriented job control language could support the execution or simulation of software designed for a distributed system. Thus, in this environment developers would not need an actual distributed hardware system in order to begin testing out a distributed software system.

The PCL could also be augmented to support the simulation of process structures on networks with different topologies and communication structures. This would permit accurate measurement and comparison of process communication events across simulated nodes in the network. This type of approach has been recently used to evaluate the performance of a distributed interpretation system [Lesser 79b]. A multi-job coordination facility for the Decsystem TOPS-10 operating system was developed. This facility coordinates communication and concurrency among a collection of independent processes. The network communication structure is simulated by a shared file that holds a record of each transmission in the network and additional information, such as when and by which node it was generated and which nodes have read it. All processes can access this file through an inter-node communication handler. The simulation of concurrency among the processes is accomplished by keeping the processes' clock-times in step; each time a job makes a request to transmit or receive inter-node communication, it is suspended if its local processor time is no longer the smallest. In this way, the simulation of concurrency is event-driven rather than sampled, allowing accurate analysis of process interaction.

For certain distributed computing applications, a useful utility would be an interface to the distributed network which normally made the network's topology transparent, but still permitted this topology to be visible if the user so desired. Such an interface would allow most users to ignore the details of the underlying distributed structure, providing them with a virtual view of the system as if it were a monolithic facility. At the same time, sophisticated users would be permitted to influence system activities based upon their understanding of the underlying distributed system. Among the capabilities available would be direct control of how various functions are distributed across processors (i.e., what is done where) and indirect control of distribution by providing information (hints) which would permit more intelligent and efficient scheduling by the operating system. Thus, either directly or indirectly the user could assist the system toward optimum utilization of its processing facilities.

Many of the features desirable in design support tools for distributed software system development have been suggested in previous sections of this paper. Under-lying all those features, and fundamental to their fruitful usage, is the appropriate type of bookkeeping aid or data base. Bookkeeping aid helps in the orderly develop-ment of a design by providing a repository for fragments of the evolving design de-scription, permitting elaboration, modification, or replacement of design fragments, and making up-to-date versions of the design available to members of the development project. Ideally, the data base used to provide bookkeeping aid in a distributed software design support system will be structured so that access and modification of its contents can be done in terms of units natural to the description of distributed software.

The flexibility required for developing good designs in an area as new as dis-tributed computing will likely, at least for the foreseeable future, call for a set of tools rather than one single design support tool. In particular, various levels of tools may be needed corresponding to the various viewpoints which a designer should have of the system being developed. Thus, low-level tools may be needed for develop-ing such low-level details as message transfer protocols, while higher level tools may be required for obtaining a global perspective (e.g., statistical properties) on the behavior of the evolving distributed system. Tools supporting specification from the viewpoint of an individual process will be needed, in addition to tools support-ing specification from the viewpoint of an outside observer. However, a unified framework within which these various tools (with their various viewpoints) can be used is most desirable. At the very least, a common command language interface between the developer and the assorted tools can significantly increase the useful-ness of the collection and contribute to making the developmental environment hospit-able to a distributed software system designer.

CONCLUSIONS

We believe that the computational structures required to maximally expolit the capabilities of distributed computing are significantly different in character from existing structures used for conventional problem solving. These differences arise because of the need for fault-tolerance to improve reliability, the need for large, complex and dynamic process structures to exploit parallelism, and the need for functionally-accurate problem solving structures in order to minimize inter-node synchronization and communication. These requirements will lead to computational structures which have many of the characteristics of complex organizational struc-tures. This new view of computational structures calls for design tools which support a global, high-level view (both deterministic and probabilistic) of a sys-tem's design, and also the ability to focus in on specific local aspects of the design.

APPENDIX: An Example of a Process Structure in PCL

Consider a network system for automated air traffic control (ATC). At any given time many planes are in the air. Each plane sends information about itself (position, speed, amount of fuel, etc.) in a burst of data. These bursts of information are sent periodically or on demand from the system. The controller process receives each burst of information, updates its global information, and based on that information decides which planes to contact next and what messages to send to those planes.

We will describe the system with the process structure in Figure 1. CONTROLLER, the master process, takes all bursts received but not processed. With these it updates a global data base, IN_AIR, and after initiating two processes for each plane in the air, goes to sleep. These processes are DISTILL(i) and NEXT_ACTION(i). DISTILL(i) preprocesses information in IN_AIR for the use of NEXT_ACTION(i). NEXT_ACTION(i) determines the message to be sent to plane i and the priority of that message. DISTILL(i) and NEXT_ACTION(i) are coroutines with NEXT_ACTION(i) initially in control. They share PLANE_LOCAL(i), a working memory segment. When NEXT_ACTION(i) is completed it places its results in POSSIBLE_ACTIONS and signals its completion to CONTROLLER. When all NEXT_ACTION(i) are completed, CONTROLLER is awakened, selects which messages in POSSIBLE_ACTIONS are to be sent to the planes, sends them, and reinitiates the cycle. The number of NEXT_ACTION and DISTILL processes varies from cycle to cycle based on how many planes are in the air.*

First, let us consider the static characteristics of the ATC process structure. We must specify the type, number, and interconnections of structure components. In some cases this information is parameterized. For example, there are n copies of DISTILL, NEXT_ACTION, and PLANE_LOCAL, where n (the number of planes in the air) is determined by CONTROLLER and communicated at run-time.

We must describe the nature and the structure of the communications among the components. For example, the data link between CONTROLLER and the memory segment IN_AIR specifies the read-write access capability of CONTROLLER to IN_AIR. The communication link between CONTROLLER and NEXT_ACTION components has a broadcast structure; the same message is sent to the n NEXT_ACTION processes in order to wake them up to work on new data. The structure of this link is different from the one going back from NEXT_ACTION(i) to CONTROLLER. This return link acts as a "concentration semaphore," a single message is received only when all n are sent. Finally, component *sharing* is to be described. For example, multiple links connected to the memory segment IN_AIR indicate that it is shared.

Figure 2 summarizes these static characteristics. The diagram lacks information

---

*In order to keep the example simple, we have not specified a process structure that reuses structure based on expectation of a plane remaining in the air from cycle to cycle.

34

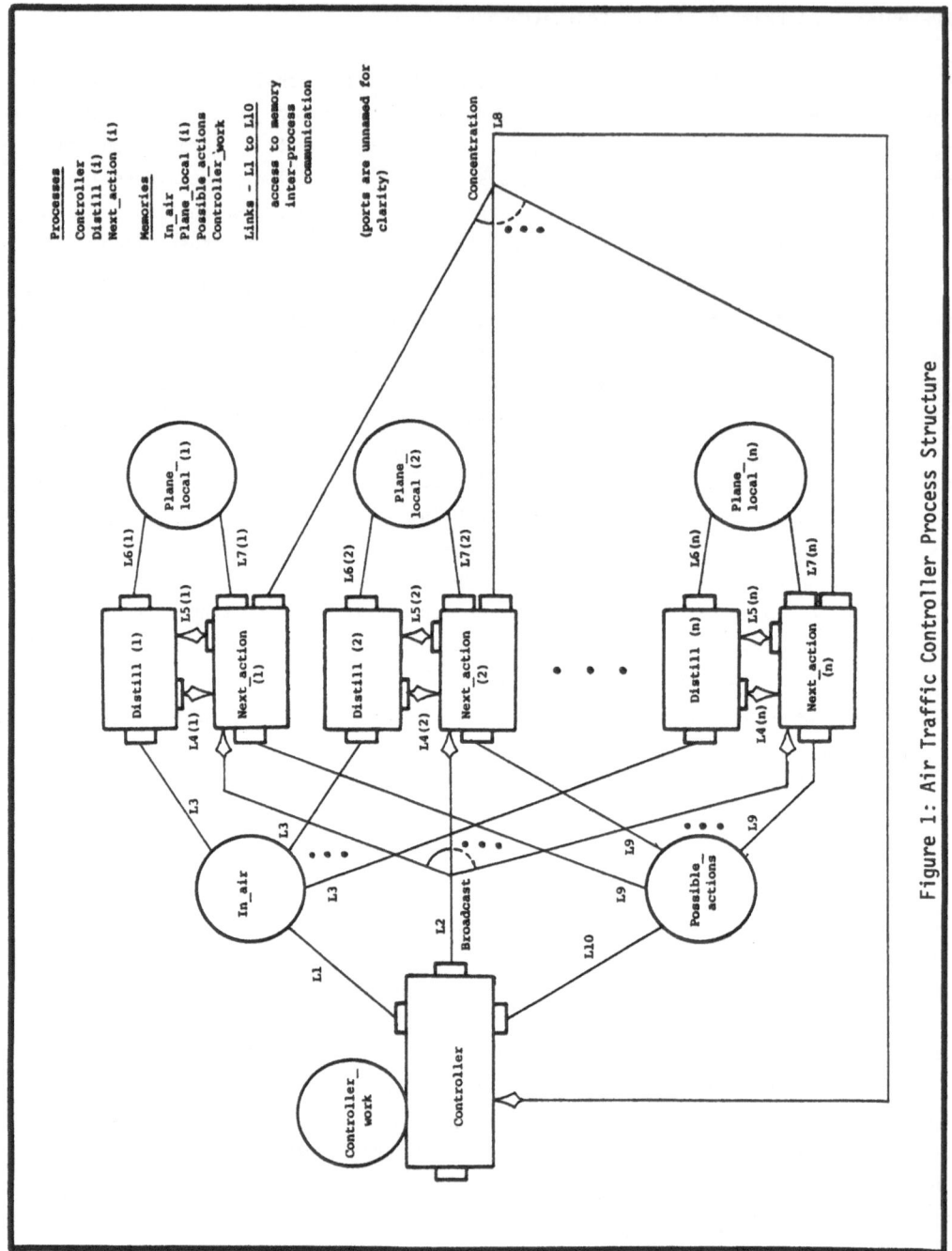

Figure 1: Air Traffic Controller Process Structure

Processes
Controller
Distill (i)
Next_action (i)

Memories
In_air
Plane_local (i)
Possible_actions
Controller_work

Links - L1 to L10
access to memory
inter-process
communication

(ports are unnamed for
clarity)

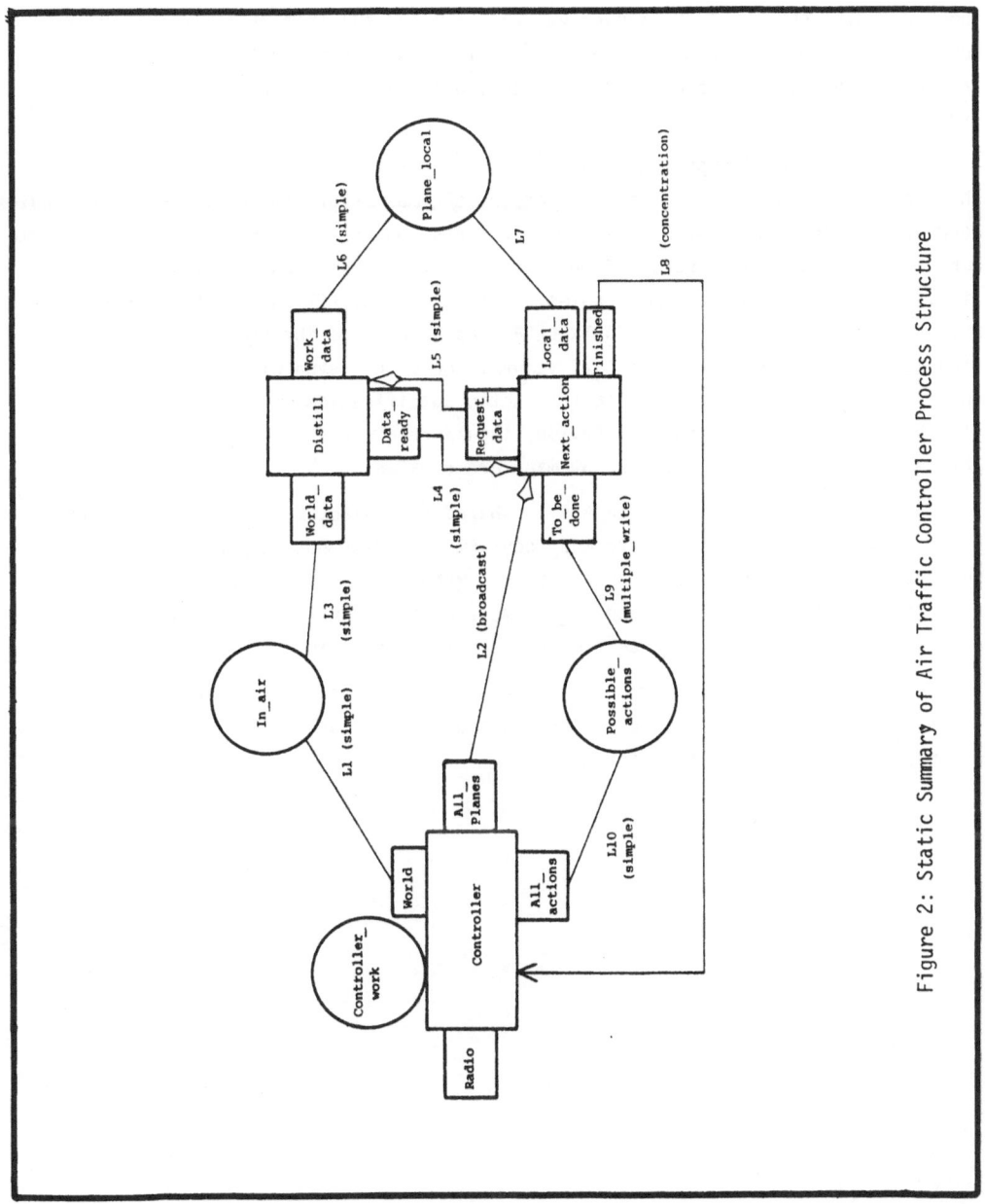

Figure 2: Static Summary of Air Traffic Controller Process Structure

about dynamic aspects of the structure, but contains all information necessary to build an arbitrary dynamic structure out of the static components described. One task of the PCL is to capture and localize the static characteristics of a process structure.

There are several important dynamic characteristics of the ATC process structure. There are *master* processes. In the example, the master process CONTROLLER distributes work in parallel with many NEXT_ACTION processes, which themselves locally distribute work to the DISTILL processes. Components or groups of components can be *copied* at will. For example, there are n copies of DISTILL, NEXT_ACTION, and PLANE_LOCAL where n is determined dynamically by CONTROLLER. Each copy has the same internal process structure but with different initial values. Note that even with potential sharing, the link structure must conform to the static specification. For example, L2, the link between CONTROLLER and NEXT_ACTION, should remain a single broadcast link to all NEXT_ACTION processes, no matter how many are created.

Components can be *shared*. IN_AIR is shared by CONTROLLER and all DISTILL processes. Again, the link structure must conform no matter how components are shared. Components can be *instantiated* dynamically. When the process structure is initialized, for example, CONTROLLER and IN_AIR must be fully instantiated. The rest of the structure, however, can exist as simply a static description.

PCL must allow a user to represent these dynamic aspects of a process structure, as well as the static aspects previously discussed. Figures 3 and 4 show the PCL description and skeleton code for the ATC.

```
Cluster  Air_traffic
    Internal_port Radio
    Master Process Controller (copies = 1,
                               phase = execute
                               creation = local )
            external port Radio
            internal port World, All_planes, All_actions
            memory Controller_work (size = 1000,
                                    mode = readwrite,
                                    creation = local,
                                    phase = execute )
            end/* Controller */
    Memory  Possible_actions      (size = maxplane,
                                    mode = read,
                                    creation = local,
                                    phase = execute )
    Cluster Plane  (phase = bind, expand with (N),
                    creation = local, copies = N )
            internal port  Finished, To_be_done
            master process  Next_action  (copies = 1,
                                          phase = initialized
                                          creation = local )
                external port  Finished, To_be_done
                internal port  Request_data, Local_data
                end  /* Next_action */
            process  Distill  (copies = 1,
                               phase = initialized
                               creation = local )
            internal port  World_data, Work_data, Data_ready
            end  /* Distill */
    Memory  Plane_local   (copies = 1,
                           phase = bind,
                           creation = local,
                           size = 100,
                           mode = readwrite )
    Memory  In_air  (copies = 1,
                     phase = execute,
                     evolves with Controller,
                     creation = own,
                     size = (N*40),
                     mode = readwrite )
    link  (connections = Next_action. Request_data: Distill,
           type = simple,
           carry = control,
           traffic = high )
    link  (connections = Next_action. Local_data: Plane_local,
           type = simple,
           carry = data )
```

Figure 3: Air Traffic Controller PCL

continued on next page

38

```
Figure 3 continued


        link   (connections = Distill. Data_ready: Next_action,
                type = simple,
                carry = control,
                traffic = high )
        link   (connections = Distill. Work_data: Plane_local,
                type = simple,
                carry = data )
        link   (connections = Distill. World_data: In_air,
                type = simple,
                carry = data,
                traffic = high )
                end  /* Plane */
        link   (connections = Controller. World: In_air,
                type = simple,
                carry = data,
                traffic = medium )
        link   (connections = Controller. All_planes: Plane,
                type = broadcast,
                carry = control )
        link   (connections = Controller. All_actions: Possible_actions,
                type = simple,
                carry = data )
        link   (connections = Next_action. Finished: Controller,
                type = concentration,
                carry = control )
        link   (connections = Next_action. To_be_done: Possible_actions,
                type = multiple_write,
                carry = data )
        end  /* Air_traffic */
```

```
Controller:
  while true do
    begin
      while not IS_EMPTY (Radio)
      do begin
             RECEIVE (Radio, Controller_work (1) , Length_radio_message);
             Update_all_planes
           end;
        EXECUTE (All_planes, N = Numplanes_in_air);
        SLEEP
      end

Next_action:
  begin
    Compute own_situation;
    /* Examine all near-by planes */
    for i := 1 to n
    do begin
           Plane_local (COPY NUMBER)   := i;
           EXECUTE (Request_data);
           SLEEP;
           if Plane_local (Plane_near)
                then Update_situation

         end;
    Compose message;
    SEND (To_be_done, Local_data (Final_situation), Situation_description_length);
    WAKEUP (Finished);
    BIND
  end

Distill:
  begin
    Get_raw data (In_air (Plane_local  (COPY NUMBER)));
    Massage_data;
    Construct_situation;
    WAKEUP (Data_ready);
    INITIALIZE
  end
```

Figure 4: Skeleton Code for the Air Traffic Controller

A CRITICAL LOOK AT
THE PROCESS OF TOOL DEVELOPMENT:
AN INDUSTRIAL PERSPECTIVE

I. R. Nassi

Digital Equipment Corporation

Tools, while having a large potential benefit, are expensive and risky
to develop. In this paper, some factors are identified that are necessary properties of successful tools. Tools must be supported, easy to
use, easy to learn, reliable, modifiable, and culturally compatible
with the development environment. An evolutionary model of development
is presented which places strong emphasis on interactive design and
design iteration. The need for early consideration of success criteria
is discussed along with some points for management consideration.

INTRODUCTION

As hardware costs continue to decline, the cost of software is becoming the domi-
nant factor affecting the cost of computer systems. Industry is more aware of the
important role of software in the years ahead because it is becoming an important
contributor to total revenue. Software will become more important in the marketplace,
as customers expect more sophisticated and easier-to-use application programs. Since
there will have to be a significant amount of software written to exercise the increased capacity of current and future technology, and since that software becomes
necessarily more complex, we can expect to continue to seek ways to reduce both the
complexity and the cost of software development.

In the next few years, integrated sets of tools will continue to be developed to
decrease the cost associated with software production. The pressure for this will
come from both industry and government. The Programmers Work Bench [Dolotta 76] is
an example of industry attempting to provide tools in an integrated package. The
PEBBLEMAN [DoD 79] effort is an example of the government providing an impetus for
researchers to look at ways of reducing development cost.

Producing software development tools is expensive. The reasons are fairly obvious.
Software is expensive, and tools are software. Additionally, as in other professions,
there is a significant cost of learning how to use tools. Finally, heavy investment
in tool development is risky. Many tools are built to be used for either a short
time, or on a particular project, and thus are not easily generalizable. Many tools
are "throw-away."

Because of the pressure to build new tools, the high risk involved, and the expectation of increasing emphasis in this area, some analysis of the process of tool development is justified. In this paper, we look at the process of tool development from a broad, industrial perspective and try to arrive at some requisite fundamental principles for successful tool development.

PRELIMINARIES

A software development *tool* is any software application program that a user invokes to perform a task associated with a software development project. This includes compilers, editors, table generators, debuggers, document preparation aids, etc.

An *environment*, as used here, refers to the interface the user interacts with while working on a development project. This includes the development operating system, the target test system (usually but not always the same) and any clerical or administrative procedures the user is required to conform to while working on a task.

WHY TOOLS FAIL

While no tool can be expected to be perfect, it is very clear that some tools are more successful than others. In this section, we examine some reasons why a particular tool may not meet with widespread acceptance in its intended user community.

Learnability

First, it may be difficult to learn how to use the tool. The interface may be difficult to learn because it may be culturally very different from other tools in use in the same environment.

The documentation may be nonexistent, not easily available, obsolete, or sketchy. Alternatively, it may be large and not organized for quick reference, or for the novice. There may be no one to ask questions of when the answer cannot be found in the documentation. It may have a steep learning curve, even to do something relatively simple. It is wise to remember that while a well-run software project may have a detailed schedule, learning a new tool is often likely not to be included in that schedule.

Usability

Once it is known how to use the tool, a user may still find it difficult to use the tool in practice.

For example, the tool may require the presence of an environment that is not created or generated by the tool itself. If the tool operates on files, it may require that they be of a certain format, but the user may discover that no ancillary file conversion or initialization utility exists.

It may require a long, involved dialogue with the user without providing an interactive help facility or meaningful prompting (in which case it is no dialogue at all). There may be many positional parameters for instance, or there may not be enough defaults, or the defaults may be set incorrectly or counter-intuitively.

The tool may be part of an existing environment that is difficult to learn to use. It may make many assumptions about the development process (or the developer!) that are not satisfied when a developer tries to use the tool for the first time.

Functionality, Reliability and Performance

The tool simply may not be suitable for the intended job, but may appear close enough to be used in the absence of a more appropriate one.

Little, if any, attention may have been paid to performance issues. Tools are strictly an overhead item and are useful as labor saving devices. If it requires more time to run than it saves, then it should not, and probably will not, be used. If it is too costly to run in terms of system resources, and is the kind of tool that must be run frequently, alternatives will be sought. For example, a language's pretty printer that runs almost as slowly as the corresponding compiler is not likely to be used after each edit.

The reliability of the tool is extremely important, since often the tool is operating directly on user source files. For example, an editor that manages to delete random characters in a source file after an editing session is not likely to see much use. The tool must do no harm.

In a more general sense, tools must be of a very high quality because it is easy for a software developer to think he knows how to do it better. It follows that there will be many low quality tools "born at midnight." These can serve as good points of departure, especially for the functionality they define, but are unlikely to be a good basis for further implementation.

Degree of Integration

The tool may be a compromise, i.e., a selective fusion of features from some existing tools. To integrate such features is likely to be difficult, and it will be difficult to convince proficient users of the older tools that the new tool is better. The new tool is expected to have what each user thinks are the best features of the existing tools, but it may not be possible to get agreement from those users on what those features are or should be. The resultant tool is likely to be broadly perceived as being cluttered with unnecessary functions at the expense of other more important functions.

The tool may be solidly integrated into an environment that the user does not want or cannot use. There are several very useful tools, for example, that run under UNIX. These tools are useless to the user who needs to do development under a system devoid of a C compiler, pipes, or other UNIX specific features.

The tool may not be well-integrated with the remainder of the user's environment. This is especially true of transportable tools, that is, tools which run on a number of different operating systems or architectures. As each operating system has a certain kind of culture, the tool may be seen to be a singularity, and hence avoided. There is a relationship here to learnability, since if the tool were well-integrated, it would be easier to learn as it is likely to be similar to the other tools or commands a user already knows.

Not Invented Here (NIH)

The fact that a tool was simply "not invented here" often contributes to a tool's non-acceptance. While it is easy to attribute this attitude to the immaturity of the profession, its widespread occurrence calls for a more detailed analysis.

Integration of the use of a tool into the development process can be an expensive operation. Often, the development process is different from one environment to another, and one project to another. The fact that a tool was produced to work in some environment strongly contributes to its likelihood of being used on another, similar project with the same environment. There are several reasons for this. First, it is likely that prior experience in the use of the tool will be available to the new user. Second, any operational "bugs" in using the tool are more likely to have been worked out, or at least the information generated on how to circumvent them. Third, the fact that a tool was constructed and used successfully in an environment increases programmer confidence in using it again in the same environment. The comparative success in using "invented here" tools versus those "not invented here" produces a conditioned reflex in software engineers. The avoidance of tools "not invented here" is a manifestation of this reflex.

One way to avoid the NIH syndrome is to produce tools that are easily modifiable and thus can be tailored to specific environments. Often, a small modification can convert an unacceptable tool suffering from the NIH syndrome into an acceptable tool. The ability to easily modify a tool also can provide an opportunity for the local toolsmith to "bless" the tool.

Other Reasons

Another reason for a tool's failure is the lack of sophistication of the user population, or a general negative attitude toward change, and specifically, the use of tools as a way of partially automating the development process. This is similar to the anti-automation reflex that exists in many industries. In order for tool usage to become widespread, there must be a general attitude that selective tool usage is the "nifty" and professional thing to do, but only if the use of the tool is justified in a particular situation.

Another factor is the reputation of the tool developer. If the tool developer has produced even a single tool that proved to have a negative effect in the development process, there will be a fair amount of skepticism about any new tools from the same source the next time around.

Inertia is a strong factor in a tool's non-acceptability. Users who are quite adept at using very primitive tools may tend to resist change. The tool developer must be prepared to deal with this and to make the transition to the newly introduced tool as painless as possible.

As developers move among differing environments, they begin to appreciate the transportability of key tools. Tools that are inherently non-transportable will tend to be less enthusiastically received than those that can be moved between environments frequently.

A PROCESS MODEL

Experience and common sense show that the most successful tools are the ones that evolve over time and through actual use. This evolutionary approach to tool development is in contrast to one consisting of one-time requirements analysis, design, construction, and delivery.

The mechanistic approach can be summarized by the following steps:

1. Understand the environment
2. Obtain a first approximation to the requirements
3. Iterate until convergence is reached

3.1. design it

3.2. build it

3.3. package it for delivery and installation

3.4. gain experience using the tool

3.5. update requirements

In general, there will be many iterations of small steps, that is, they will be evolutionary rather than revolutionary steps.

The following examines each step in turn.

The Environment

The very first step is to understand who is going to use the tool, i.e., the customers. These are the people who must be satisfied. Then, one has to develop an accurate model of the operating environment. The best way to obtain an understanding of the environment is to work within it. There is no substitute for experience. One of the reasons for the observed success of tools born "in the heat of the battle" is that they were constructed with a very clear understanding of the environment.

Many times it is far easier to work within the constraints imposed by an existing environment than to create a new one, as the tool developer might be tempted to do. There are likely to be very good (but perhaps non-obvious) reasons why the environment has evolved the way it has. The tool developer who attempts fundamental environmental changes not only runs the risk of rediscovering those reasons now lost in antiquity, but also must overcome a fair amount of inertia.

Requirements

There are several classes of requirements. First, there are *general requirements* that every tool must satisfy, like correctness, reasonable performance, usability, etc.

Specific requirements are those that are particular to a tool. Four kinds of specific requirements are identified: perceived, projected, requested and accepted. Hopefully, requirements are generated by the intended users who first recognize the need for a tool meeting these requirements. These are the *perceived* requirements. *Projected* requirements are generated by the tool developer; however, these tend to reflect the tool developer's perception of the user's requirements, a potential source of error if the user and the developer are not the same. There are also the requirements that are *requested* by the user, and these may or may not be precisely the same as the requirements perceived by the user. Finally there are the requirements actually *accepted* by the developer, which may be different again.

Assuming that the tool is being designed in more than one iteration, these distinctions may not be all that important. But in the case that iterations are few, or far between, either because of contractual, geographical, or other external reasons, they should be understood.

The goal, of course, is ultimately to converge on the actual requirements, but these change over time also.

Design

Early design interaction between users and developers enables users to spot limitations in the design caused by an implicit, incorrect understanding of one or more requirements. It also enables users to understand limitations in the design and encourages them to think about these limiting assumptions as early as possible. An important reason for having an interactive design is to give users the opportunity to participate in the design in such a way as to make the user feel part of the process. This also proves to be helpful in trying to "sell" the tool later on, if the tool's use is optional.

Build it

There is not too much to be said about building the tool. Simply be prepared to change every line of code.

Package it for delivery

At every release, care should be taken to ensure that the tool is packaged properly. This means making sure there is adequate, accurate user documentation, that sufficient testing has been done, and that there is a helpful and friendly user interface. It is hard to imagine a case where too much effort can be expended in this area, for this provides the basis for the first user contact.

Use it

The tool developer should find good initial users, and cultivate them. These users should be willing to experiment and innovate. The most effective ones are respected by their peers, and they will help sell the tool. They should be willing to spend the time to tell the developer what is good and bad about the tool. As the tool improves the developer should attempt to get a larger set of users.

When the use of a tool is optional, it must be sold: that is, it must be pre-sented to users for their examination on a trial basis. Ideally, the well-engineered tool should sell itself. One philosophy is the *potato chip principle*, which says that what is initially presented is the skeleton of a tool with only a few features that caters to a direct need. Initial customers are chosen carefully. As they use the tool, and come to rely on it, they ask for more and more features, because they cannot stop with just the skeleton. In this way, the users are happy, the tool development project is started at low cost, and only when it is demonstrably success-ful, is a further investment made.

The potato chip principle works well only for tools that make relatively small improvements (at the 10% level) in the development process. More innovative or sophisticated tools are much more difficult to sell. In general, more effort is required to develop them, and there is a correspondingly higher risk in return for much higher potential benefit. It is probably the case that these more ambitious tools should be avoided unless there is significant support for them from the start, so that there is enough time, money, and moral support to lay the necessary ground-work for both the development of the tool and its acceptance.

IDENTIFYING SUCCESS

In this section we identify some success criteria for tools and relate them to two examples: a parser generator and an (emerging) text editor.

Example: Parser Generator

PAT is a LALR parser generator which was developed some years ago in Digital's Research and Development group. The development of PAT was internally funded, and was intended only for use in the company to aid the development of software products. PAT was originally written in Pascal and ran under TOPS-10. It was used to develop software for various PDP-11 and VAX based products, and thus users required access to at least two different machines, with differing hardware and software architectures.

PAT ran satisfactorily on TOPS-10, and there were few complaints. It was easily modified to run on TOPS-20 when a Pascal compiler became available for the DEC-20.

Because users of PAT made much higher use of PDP-11's and VAX's than DEC-10's or DEC-20's, a group of people rewrote PAT in assembly language for the PDP-11. It performed poorly on the large grammars given to it, but in spite of its poor perfor-mance, it was used.

The original author has long since stopped maintaining the program as he has become interested in other projects, moved up the management ladder, and never planned on maintaining it in the first place.

There are now several versions of the program, and there is no central control or source of information.

It has been a successful tool as determined by its use on multiple projects. But today's project leader undertaking a new project may not use it because:

- it is rumored to run slowly,
- it is rumored to have bugs,
- it is rumored not to run on anything but a giant DEC-10,
- it is rumored that there are better generators that run faster, accept a wider class of languages than LALR(1), or operate on a small PDP-11 configuration,
- the latest version of the program or documentation is unavailable,
- no one is supporting it, so that there is no one to ask questions of should problems occur.

Example: Emerging Editor

Software engineers at Digital have their choice of a number of different inter-active editors. Some of the widely available ones are:

TECO-10	TV	EDT
TECO-11	EMACS	
TECA	SOS	

None of these editors is a widely accepted standard. TECO is too primitive; EMACS is too slow. SOS is the one that can be considered closest to fully trans-portable (in terms of functionality) since it runs on DEC-10's, DEC-20's, PDP-11's and VAX's, but is line-oriented whereas most terminals in heavy use are CRT's, for which screen-oriented editors are more appropriate.

In addition, there is currently emerging a new generation of screen-oriented editors which have been influenced by word processing systems. These editors are themselves an interesting case study in tool evolution. They are written in TECO-11. Because they are interpretive (each one is just a very large TECO macro), they can easily be modified to adapt to new requirements very quickly.

These new editors are satisfying a number of requirements as these requirements emerge.

- Transportable - at least between PDP-11's and VAX's
- Programming Language Oriented - some have knowledge of programming languages, e.g., BASIC-PLUS and BLISS
- All are culturally compatible with word processing systems which know something about language (words, paragraphs, sentences, etc.)

This suggests that what is needed is a transportable, multi-language, screen-oriented, interactive text editor. A number of people have built prototypes and want to build a production version.

Analysis

The previous discussion suggested criteria for evaluating these examples. The PAT example provides an opportunity for systematically analyzing a project in its historical perspective according to these success criteria. The editor example provides an opportunity for using the success criteria to help establish some guidelines for a tool project just starting out.

Consider the following set of requisite characteristics for a software tool:

- easy to learn
- easy to use
- well integrated
- easily modifiable
- transportable
- high reliability and good performance
- easy to migrate to
- supported
- meets a clear need

The two examples described above will now be examined with respect to these characteristics.

PAT

PAT was easy enough to learn how to use in theory, since it required that an implementation grammar be written and fed through the analyzer. In practice, however, there were some difficulties in using it. There was an auxiliary postprocessor that would convert the PAT output (tables of integers) into a set of Pascal declarations. Developers using anything but Pascal were expected to write their own postprocessor, or edit the output directly. The machine readable documentation for this process, along with the table driver, was separated from the program itself, so that users running PAT were presented with tables of integers. The only way to make sense out of it was to find someone who had successfully been through the process before for the subtools necessary to produce the working parser.

PAT was written using non-standard Pascal, so migration proved to be difficult.

Performance was acceptable on the DEC-10, but unacceptable on the PDP-11.

Modifiability was not much of a problem. Modification of the user interface was straightforward. Few attempted modification of the internals since to do so requires highly specialized knowledge of LALR parser construction. Many, if not most, developers would rather write or modify the code of a parser than modify the parser generator.

In summary, PAT was deficient in some of the characteristics outlined above.

Language-oriented Editor

The tool requirements proposed above should provide guidelines for new tool development.

Of course, the editor should be easy to learn to use. The editor should be usable on the range of (text) file organizations supported by the underlying system. Invocation of the editor should look no different than invocation of any other tool in the environment.

Provisions should be made to allow new commands to be added to the editor. There is a variety of ways to do this ranging from modifiable source code (of the editor) to an extensible editor that interprets personalized operator or command definition files.

The editor should be transportable so that users need not learn a new editor when they move between systems. (Learning to use an editor is particularly sensitive to being able to integrate typing ability with touch coordination to invoke keys whose function is specific to a particular editor. Thus, learning to use an editor is more expensive than learning to use many other tools.)

MANAGEMENT CONSIDERATIONS

As more effort is invested in tool development, and as tool development is being funded at the corporate level, the method of choosing where to expend the effort becomes increasingly important. (One method of doing this is to have a board of senior software developers and line managers, or their representatives, give guidance in this area to both tool developers and to corporate funding organizations.)

There seem to be two approaches to building tool systems: the integrated tool system approach which is inherently top-down, and the bottom-up approach which tries to satisfy a set of key needs in an existing environment.

In the bottom-up approach, the selection of the first tools will be relatively easy. The tools will likely be fun to build, but as a general awareness of the tool development process emerges, some form of economic feedback will be required, and this should be anticipated by the tool developer at the outset.

This feedback will ultimately relate usage characteristics and productivity, but initially the tool developer should provide mechanisms to collect usage information, to observe and document users interacting with the tool, and assess the costs costs associated with running it. This information is also extremely useful in successive refinements of the tool.

There are still many questions in this area, including:

- What are the characteristics of an integrated tool set?
- Bottom-up or top-down? When should one be preferred over the other?
- Should internal tools be made available to customers? What are the risks? What are the benefits? How should a price be determined?
- What percentage of resources should be put into tools? Certainly one percent is too low and sixty percent is too high. How much do other industries spend on tool development?
- Should tool development be in a separate central group or distributed throughout an organization?

SUMMARY

Tool development is becoming increasingly important for economic reasons, but it is both expensive and risky. Tools that are difficult to learn, or are not easily modified, or do not have a high degree of reliability and support are not likely to be successful. It is important that a user perceive the tool as well-integrated with the development environment.

An iterative, evolutionary, and interactive approach toward tool development is necessary for a tool to become widely used. Success measures for tools are difficult to establish, but important to consider. Early thought should be given to determining success.

ACKNOWLEDGEMENT

I want to thank Peter Lipman, Maurice Marks and Bill Segal for their help in preparing this, and to Bob Gorman for suggesting the name of the *potato chip principle*.

The issues raised during the presentations by the authors, the prepared remarks by the discussants, and the open discussions are arranged by topic, without regard to the actual order in which the remarks occurred.

THE ENVIRONMENT OF THE TOOL USER

A recurring theme throughout the session was whether, and to what extent, the user environment should be an integrated one. "Integration" turned out to have two distinct meanings during the discussions: the first was the issue of a common inter- face amongst all the tools that the programmer uses, so that the user need not, for example, be forced to memorize numerous command structures and protocols; and second, the issue of a single command environment for the user - a program development system - which would allow the user to enter and edit designs, write code at the terminal, run and debug programs, and re-edit designs and programs within the same facility.

Tom Love presented the following remarks concerning tool integration:

> MVS, UNIX, and Interlisp are three systems which are in some sense integrated. The integration methods differ substantially. When toolsmiths call for an "integrated" system, what do they really mean?

> Must the collection of tools simply reside on the same system (a toolbox), or must the output of one tool be valid input for another (a workbench), or must each tool have knowledge of what other tools have done (a capable assistant!)? I suspect that we should at least be thinking of integration of the second type where the results of any tool on the workbench can be made directly available to any other tool. This is the fundamental philosophy of the UNIX system which is probably the most widely used collection of tools in the industry today.

Love also pointed out three topics that had not been addressed: graphics, tools for designing user interfaces, and tools for teams of programmers:

> The importance of graphics in specifying, designing, and documenting software systems should not be overlooked. A brief glance at the

blackboards in any software house will demonstrate that these problems
are dealt with using graphic media, yet rarely do we provide machine
assistance of this type. In particular, distributed system specification and design could really benefit by appropriate interactive graphics
facilities. One could imagine some benefits from animated representations of the dynamic behavior of a distributed system.

A second tendency is a bias toward tools that support code development,
rather than total system development. In particular, we should not
assume that when the system produces the "correct output" for the first
time that the job is finished. In parallel with algorithm design and
development there should be an effort to design the user interface to
the system. Many systems which could perform useful work are not used
because they are so unnecessarily difficult to use. If a tool performs
some tremendous service which cannot be performed otherwise, users are
willing to tolerate substantial abuse -- TSO and the calculus would
seem to fit this category! If the tool is only of marginal utility,
it had better be easy to learn and easy to use.

Another unnecessary bias is the idea that tools are built for single
users. Most sizeable commercial organizations have, at one time or
another, amassed 10 or more programmers and chartered them with building some new and important system to support the business. Organizations like the U. S. government and IBM have often amassed many more
than 10 people on a single project! For many reasons these projects
are difficult to manage and often consume more time and dollars than
originally estimated. Why can't we build some tools to help these
projects in the same way we build tools for university research projects?

One simple tool which is being used more commonly is an electronic
message and mail system as a part of the development machine. Any such
tool which facilitates communication among developers is likely to be
worthwhile. Other tools of this variety, while not intellectually
challenging to design and build, might prove to be more beneficial than
expected.

To stimulate budding toolsmiths, a couple of "team tools" will be
suggested.

- on-line war-room: most large development efforts attempt to
  "display" the project status in some central location; due to
  antiquated tools this display is difficult to maintain and rarely
  up-to-date; large screen projectors could provide up-to-the-
  minute data directly from an automatically updated database.

- meeting scheduler: considerable time is consumed in a large
  development effort searching for a time and place for a group
  of people to meet; if all personnel schedules were maintained

online along with those for conference rooms, an easy mechanism
could be provided to not only schedule but track meetings.

While these tools are comparatively easy to construct from a technical
viewpoint, they in fact rarely exist in today's software projects.

Today there are literally thousands of useful software tools available
to most software developers. How does the individual developer or even
a manager select among these tools? Typically the tools that get
selected are those tools that were used in the last development effort
that the key individuals were involved in.

Toolsmiths should undertake an obligation to the future editors of
"Consumers Guide to Software Tools" to quantitatively evaluate the
actual benefits resulting from the use of their tools.

Love concluded his remarks with the following thoughts concerning future directions:

At General Electric Information Systems we are currently in the process
of building a set of tools which is integrated to the extent that different tools will be able to access common information stored in a database and all the tools work together on top of PWB/UNIX. Like the CADES
effort this work is preceding a particular development effort and it
will produce a single set of integrated tools which span the software
life cycle beginning at the system design stage.

Some distinguishing characteristics of the system include:

- extensive use of graphics to allow the designer to interactively
  generate software designs,
- strong emphasis upon human engineering throughout,
- a laissez-faire philosophy which measures success based upon the
  number of developers who choose to use the tools because they
  believe the tools simplify their job.

Our approach is pragmatic; our criterion easy to measure.

One very fundamental question has been raised which is not possible to
answer -- is the laissez-faire approach more desirable than a strong
methodology driven approach? I believe that no set of tools can be
built which does not exhibit some particular preference regarding software development methodologies. So undoubtedly there is not a simple
dichotomy and the question is really "how strongly should the methodology shine through the toolbox?" I believe it to be the case that
opaque toolboxes have been preferred in the past -- UNIX being a good
example.

Gary Nutt's comments also focused on the environment of tool usage:

It is a naive cliche that better tools are needed in order to cope with
the increasing complexity of software. Even before we have been able
to develop superior tools for software development in a single-user,
batch environment, the technology is offering us interactive, distributed systems. A significant transition in this spectrum is that from
the single-user to the multiple-user environment, i.e., the problems
seem to be inordinately magnified when more than one user is involved
in the development of software. Even though there is much to be gained
by concentrating on tool building for single-user systems, I believe
that the multiple-user needs will influence the direction of much future
research in software tools development. (Note that this distinction is
not one of program building versus system construction; small systems
can be built by one person and large programs may require several
people.) Further, I believe that modern software tools should exist in
a highly interactive environment, relying on (color) CRT displays with
local intelligence.

As Habermann and Nassi have pointed out, it is important that the
environment be constructed from a set of tools having a uniform, integrated interface. Most of us have experienced the frustration attendant to the traditional edit-compile-load-execute-debug cycle of software development. As the software construction schema becomes more
complex, the interfaces among the development steps can become more
ragged. For example, it can be particularly awkward to change from the
editor environment to the compiler or runtime environment. The debugger
ought to be able to access symbols and source code. Smalltalk [Ingalls
78] is an example of a high level of integration of the parts of this
cycle: the programming environment includes the editor, operating
system, compiler, and debugger: one programs a Smalltalk machine,
rather than machine X in language Y under operating system Z. A wide
variety of interactions with the system occur in the same manner;
messages directed to the user (i.e., output) appear in a window on a
CRT screen, while input messages can be passed to the parts of Smalltalk with an especially uniform set of conventions.

The user interface to software development tools is sometimes as important as their integrated functionality. Even the most uniform set of
facilities will not be used if they are difficult to manipulate. A
large part of the choice of the tool interface is dictated by the physical environment. Low speed alphanumeric terminals do not offer the
same flexibility as refresh CRT terminals (with local computing power).

The Smalltalk interface makes heavy use of the graphics devices of the computer systems on which it is implemented.

A short remark is in order about the trend toward the use of modules and implementation/specification distinctions -- programming-in-the-large. My personal experience with the Mesa environment shows that there are many positive aspects to this approach, similar to those pointed out by Habermann. However, the requirement for early interface specification is disruptive to anything other than pure top-down development. The usual iterations require interface redesign, with the attendant extra work (some might say that this is proper).

A large part of the future software tool needs will revolve around the notions of computer networks and personal computers. Cost-effective computing can often by accomplished by interconnecting small, independent computers which retain most of their autonomy. For example, we speculate that the "office of the future" will be implemented in an environment of personal computers with sophisticated graphics, file servers and hardcopy servers. This environment will encourage "communal computing" in which there are shared facilities such as compilers which check for consistency among the constituents (e.g., consistent use of facilities, consistent message protocols, absence of deadlock, etc.), and in which the computing is implemented on loosely-interconnected nodes. This environment will tax our understanding of integration and encourage the demise of the "not invented here" syndrome. Developers of tools for composing systems must not rely on the presence of a single computer; many future research problems in computer science in general, and software engineering in particular, are inherently tied with the network approach to computing. I also believe that this network environment especially emphasizes the need for orderly development of systems from specifications, through models of varying detail, to the implementation. It is through the use of such refinement techniques that one can evaluate the design at the various stages both for specification analysis and performance.

Terry Straeter presented the following comments:

It is clear with the rapid increase in hardware technology that computing systems, both large and small, will grow at an ever-increasing rate over the next several years. The effective use of such systems will depend, of course, on the ability of people to develop effective software. This software development must be of the highest quality, while the cost of developing this software must be kept as low as possible. In order to keep the cost low, or at least manageable, automation will play a large role. The key element is that automation will be the development of software tools. The major issues associated with the development of these software tools will be:

- the tools must form an integrated system which support software throughout its life cycle;
- the role of breadboard models in the requirements analysis and design phases of software development must be supported more fully;
- these tools must be developed in a manner which assures their successful use.

While a good deal of progress has been made and will continue to be made in program development tools, it appears that the greatest progress and improvement can be made in the area of system construction tools. We must be able to support incremental program construction through separate compilation facilities and through tools which support the independent specification and implementation of software modules.

The introduction of distributed systems on a large scale will bring a number of new challenges to the development of software. The design, development, testing and use of these systems will demand an increased role for simulation testing and analysis tools in software development. In many hardware development activities, this phase of product design requires the development of breadboard versions of the system which investigate various difficult issues of system construction. It is apparent that there is a great need for the ability to very quickly put together breadboard versions of a system in order to analyze and solidify the design of the software before the implementation phase begins.

The use of tools which are available today is spotty at best. It seems that even when quality tools are available, it requires an extensive training program, management edicts, or a dedicated set of evangelistic users to swing the large body of programmers to the use of these tools. We have all seen examples of situations where the use of some tool, be it a dynamic test analyzer, a documentation aid, or a debug feature of a compiler, is demonstrated to exert a substantial time or cost reduction in the software development cycle. And yet the use of this tool does not become the standard operating practice, but rather is only utilized in the rarest of circumstances. Therefore, the issues identified in the Nassi paper of tools being learnable, usable, functionally reliable, and supporting some integration are clearly important issues. The model for tool development proposed by Nassi is indeed sound. It is most important that tool developers get solid and immediate feedback on the utility of the tool being developed. The area of tool develop-

ment for particular projects should be carried out by personnel closely
related to the project for which the tools are to be built. While it is
important that tool builders be able to look across the broad horizon
and develop high-quality systems, it is also more important that the
systems which they develop be useful to the intended users.

During the discussion, it was observed that the system described by Nico Habermann
is knowledge-based; the program entry system has extensive knowledge of the language
being used, and so can guide the programmer through program construction. It was
suggested that some of the advances being made by the Artificial Intelligence community could be of help in developing program construction systems that have knowledge
of the specific language being used, and also of the problem domain.

Habermann's talk also drew attention to the fact that his system relies on the
use of a CRT terminal. Thus, the physical aspects of the programming environment
were deemed very important, in particular it was noted that more attention should be
paid to software tools which take advantage of the new physical environments available.
This in turn raised the question of the role of microcomputers in program development
tools.

TOOL DEVELOPMENT ISSUES

The major point in this area was whether tools should be developed by evolution
or by revolution. The different approaches were characterized by the "potato chip"
principle (due to Ike Nassi) and by the "sunbelt" principle (due to Carl Hewitt).
The potato chip principle decrees that the toolsmith build a lovely, desirable, small
tool to begin with. The user will respond appropriately (with gusto) and ask for
features to be added. Pleased with the nice additional capabilities, the user will
ask for more --- and more. Ideally, the edifice construction will be stopped before
it exhibits the "rococo" phenomenon. When/if the environment becomes rococo, or
when/if the environment is simply not up to doing the job that needs to be done, it
is time to embrace the sunbelt principle, to wit, when there is nothing more to be
done in the current environment then it is time to move to a new environment.
Numerous questions and points of view emerged concerning evolution versus revolution:

- How does one know when revolution is necessary?
- A good example of successful revolution was the adoption of time-
  sharing over batch processing.
- Industry can ill-afford unsuccessful revolutions. ("Cost accoun-
  tants run businesses.")
- Industry can well-afford successful revolutions. (much laughter)
- Only those toolsmiths with credibility will have the chance to lead
  revolutions.

- A small group will be much more successful at a revolution than a large one.

Importance was attached to the idea of bread-boarding. Rather than devoting an undue amount of time and energy to the specification phase of development it appears to be sometimes wiser to mock up a prototype of the system to be developed. This approach has the advantages of getting user response (acceptance or rejection) quickly as well as identifying the problem areas that must be dealt with in the full blown implementation effort.

Another question which arose was who should be responsible for changes to the tool -- the users or the developers. The consensus was that people will more readily accept a tool if they can play with it. Further it was noted that toolsmiths have a dual role -- they are both developers and users of tools. On the other hand Terry Straeter emphasized that we should try to abolish the "patch technology" so obvious today. Further, good tools will be exported, and will thus be altered by people not within the original target group. Several examples were given of tools that appear to owe their success to the fact that documentation regarding them was widely disseminated; hence the tools could be tailored to new users' requirements or desires. An associated question was whether toolsmithing should be the province of a single group, or should it be distributed. Ike Nassi pointed out that even within a single group it is impossible to keep a current database of information about tools.

Finally there is the question of what role tools play. Some felt that tools have the status of laws in that they enforce a specific methodology while others suggested that tools may function as educational devices.

TOOL EVALUATION

A major consideration during the discussions was the need to measure, somehow, the effectiveness of the tools that we develop and use. Further, some suggested that tools should not be released until they are accompanied by some means of measuring their utility. This raised the spectre of "productivity": management wants tools which increase productivity, but nobody really knows how to measure it. It was suggested that even if one could measure productivity that might be too narrow a criterion to use. Other considerations are 1) learnability of tools, 2) programmer contentment with tools, 3) portability of tools, 4) cost of developing the tools, and 5) cost of maintaining the tools. There was some agreement to the point that some tools which are hard to learn are still valuable, e.g., (for some) calculus and (for others) Basic.

J. C. Rault commented that productivity can be measured, or at least quantitatively assessed for several instances of tools; this is particularly true for testing and quality control tools. He also commented that a carry-over from conventional

CAD/CAM is feasible, and that study of CAD/CAM literature should be beneficial to software toolsmiths.

MODELS AND FORMALISMS

Consideration of pre-implementation issues gave rise to a discussion of methodology. It was noted that management is quite wary of funding research on "methodology" but that industry does look at what the universities are doing and has no reluctance to use whatever advancements are made there.

It was pointed out that among the things we need are better analytic models, and that this need may take precedence over the need for more software tools. Along with the need for better analytic models is the need for more formal specifications for software. Tom Love mentioned a project with a 350-page requirements document, and the difficulties of using it to produce a set of coherent functional specifications. Along these lines people asked: What should be included in a high-level description language? How should one describe the static and the dynamic structure of a system? It was observed that the job of the conference was to pose a solid set of questions to be answered rather than to try and arrive at solutions to the (software) world's problems.

MISCELLANEOUS (SMALLER) TOPICS

Consideration of distributed systems led to some lively discussion about the carry-over of knowledge from other disciplines to our problems, and the nature of scientific exploration. Taylor Booth pointed out that many of the problems being faced with respect to distributed systems were problems that hardware control engineers have been wrestling with for years. This led to the point being made, by Vic Lesser, that the difference between the two fields is that distributed software systems are very concerned with the semantics of the messages being communicated, in addition to the problems associated with the existence of the communication pathways.

The topic of distributed systems also led to some remarks about verification; in particular, how does one specify/know what's correct with respect to a message received from some remote sensor or computer?

Many participants brought up the requirement to consider the user's needs and knowledge. In particular, sophisticated toolsmiths should avoid the tendency to tailor tools to their own knowledge and proclivities.

Transportability of tools would seem to be a desirable goal. However, the more that tools are integrated, the less likely it is that the system as a whole will be transportable, since several tools are welded together. The issue of transportability is thus of importance with respect to the environment of tools, as well as to the area of tool development itself.

Chapter III. Experiences

Several development support systems have been prepared and future advancement will best be done by "standing on the shoulders" of these previous efforts. The second session of the workshop was oriented toward gaining some knowledge of what as been learned from previous efforts so that this information could be factored in during the discussions in the rest of the workshop.

A number of insights into development support system organization and componentry are provided by Bob Snowdon in his paper. Basing his assessments on experiences with three systems (PEARL, TOPD and CADES), Snowdon provides observations concerning: 1) the ways in which a development support system allows a developing system to be viewed, 2) the development methodologies supported by a development support system, 3) the lifecycle phases supported by the different development support systems he reports on, 4) the need to clearly distinguish separate development concerns, 5) the data base forming the core of a development support system, 6) the tools to be included in a development support system, and 7) the development support system's interface to the user.

Discussant Sabina Saib initially directs the discussion toward a number of questions which address the extent of Snowdon's experience base and his overall impressions of the value of the development support systems he reports on. The lack of concentrated collection of evaluative data is the focus of the remarks by discussant Carl Davis who proposes well-defined efforts in this direction as the only way we can successfully learn from the past. The remarks by the discussants form the basis for a discussion that centers more on what data should be collected and how to do the collection than on what data have already been collected. There seemed to be unanimous agreement that this important aspect of tool development has been neglected and done only relatively haphazardly when done at all.

R. A. Snowdon

International Computers Ltd.

INTRODUCTION

"Systems" which aid the development of other software systems have existed for several years. They have evolved and broadened in scope considerably. We can class-ify such systems as *toolboxes* or as *development support systems*. The former are loosely-connected systems composed of individual development aids (e.g. editors, compilers, languages) which are relatively easy to use together. Development support systems, on the other hand, attempt to provide an integrated approach to the whole task of system development. They normally encourage a particular development metho-dology, the individual facilities of the system being designed for this purpose.

Particular development support systems offer different capabilities dependent upon various factors. No such system is "perfect" in that its use guarantees the orderly design and development of the highest quality software. The reasons for this include the most basic reason -- we do not know how to do it. Additionally, these systems tend to have deficiencies derived from the environment of their own develop-ment. It is instructive to note some of these deficiencies, and also some of the strengths, as they are observable from some development support systems which have been built and used.

The author has been closely involved with three such systems: PEARL ([Snowdon 73], [Snowdon 74]), TOPD ([Henderson 74], [Henderson 75b], [Snowdon 78]), and CADES ([Pearson 73], [Pratten 78]); the purpose of this paper is to give some observations based on experiences with these systems. First, in the next three sections, a short introduction and history is given for each, noting particular attributes. The fifth section draws together comments about these systems and gives several conclusions about development support systems in general.

PEARL

PEARL was an early development support system, essentially experimental in nature. It was basically a program development aid designed to be used interactively. PEARL viewed programs as being developed in a top-down manner using a language allowing abstract data types and operations. The language was similar to the sort of language in which one performs "step-wise refinement" of a program and its vintage was that of Dijkstra's report *Notes on Structured Programming* [Dijkstra 72]. An explicit language construct relating data and operations together was not provided although the PEARL system itself understood these relationships.

A deterministic finite state machine model was utilized in order to allow "execution" of abstract programs. Such executions were intended to run interactively with the programmer providing assistance when an undefined operation was encountered.

Information representing the evolving program was stored in a structured file but little use was made of this file as a true data base. The mechanisms provided for updating the structured file were those which encourage the discipline of top-down development.

PEARL was a primitive development support system in that it addressed only a small part of the software development problem. It could only be considered as a software design aid, rather than a programming aid, if one viewed the language as providing a procedural description. There was, however, no mechanism by which the design could be translated into code.

PEARL was a uni-programmer tool. No facilities were provided for multiple access, although the information in the structured file could be shared among a number of different programs or designs.

TOPD

TOPD was developed as a successor to PEARL. It took the development support system idea a little further and its viewpoint was somewhat different from its predecessor.

The TOPD notation allowed programs to be developed in terms of classes (abstract data types) whose representation was given in terms of instances of other classes and invocations of operations on these instances.

A non-deterministic finite state model was used to allow description of the effect of unelaborated procedures (operations). This description capability was included to allow designs to be evaluated without the requirement that operational detail be specified.

Program development, though expressed in terms of hierarchies of classes, was not constrained to be either top-down or bottom-up. However, the various tools tended to favor a top-down style of development.

The trend in TOPD was away from interactive program development. The more powerful analysis tools of TOPD were concerned with design evaluation and involved "execution" of a particular level of the design in terms of the underlying finite state machine models. Display of the resulting effect was via annotated program text listings showing possible state sets. Facilities for checking an implementation against the finite state model were also provided.

The underlying information storage system of TOPD was a relational data base in which the objects were individual pieces of program text having certain properties of semantic integrity. Data base retrieval capabilities were provided to allow the user to inspect his design, although the retrieval forms were limited. A primitive version handling capability was provided by "stamping" each stored object with the time and date of insertion into the data base. This made it possible for the user to view the system's design as it stood at any particular point in time during the design process.

TOPD was more of a software design system than a programming system. TOPD embodied the idea of mapping the design as represented in the TOPD design notation into statements of a "real" programming language wherein program details were encoded The design notation, while providing a fixed set of data and operation combinators, made no commitment to a base programming language in terms of primitive types or operations.

TOPD was also primarily a uni-programmer system, although the data base was more amenable to sharing than that of PEARL. Again, as in PEARL, several designs could co-exist within the same data base sharing common parts as appropriate.

CADES

CADES is a different, and potentially more embracing, development support system than either PEARL or TOPD. Its nature is different in that CADES has evolved over a period of years (since 1971) while all of the time being used within a computer manu-facturer's environment supporting the development of a large operating system (i.e., VME/B for the ICL 2900 series).

CADES is a development support system addressing most activities involved in producing and maintaining a large software system. The development methodology supported by CADES is called *structural modelling*.

Structural modelling encompasses the ideas of multi-level, top-down system design Software is designed in terms of levels. At each level, a complete description of the system is given in terms of the abstract concepts (functions, data) characterizin that level. The relationship between descriptions at neighboring abstract levels is one which expresses component hierarchy and is not directly related to call or struc-tural hierarchy as in TOPD or PEARL. This means that a system description at each level is complete in its own right without recourse to higher-level structures. The other major emphasis of structural modelling is that design is driven by considerations of data rather than by considerations of algorithm. The designer is encouraged to determine the data transformations that take place within and by the system and to design suitable structures before he considers algorithm design in detail.

The relative independence of the individual levels of system representation is reflected in that only semiformal descriptions are encoded. The design notation associated with CADES (System Description Language or SDL) provides little more than a framework for describing relationships at the more abstract levels. As the design becomes more detailed, programming language features are introduced to the descriptions until the designer achieves a description entirely in source code statements.

In addition to the source code description of a system and its development in terms of higher level abstractions, CADES supports other descriptions of the software under development in order to cover the total software development and support activity. These descriptions are in terms of such concepts as compiled units called *modules* (allowing support for the system building function) and representations of the binary image and its relationship to hardware (or more accurately the architecture of the underlying computer system). SDL formalism is extended "downwards" to cover all of these views and thus to integrate standard software development tools such as compilers, link editors, system loaders and generation tools.

CADES has evolved in an environment of large development teams and thus has had to recognize various managerial aspects of software development. The stance has been taken that these aspects are equally important and CADES thus supports aspects of software development concerned with planning, progress reporting and project organization.

As well as supporting software production, CADES provides support for the documentation of the emerging system. As an adjunct to the semiformal system descriptions expressed in SDL there is an integrated documentation system known as the project log. This is, in effect, a scheme wherein narrative descriptions of the system are recorded as additional commentary on the more formal encoding.

The data base component is extremely visible in the CADES scheme. The heart of the scheme is a regionalized data base in which is recorded all of the information describing the system under development. This information includes the abstract descriptions, the source description, the lower level construction and architectural descriptions, as well as organizational structures such as plans and unscheduled work. The project log (system documentation) is also conceptually part of the data base structure although physically separate. Normal data base tools are available (query facility, report generators, etc.) to enable easy access to system information. Production tools (compilers for example) are integrated with the data base software in order to achieve control over their use and to insure that their outputs are also returned to the controlled environment of the data base.

The data base system, itself, provides protection mechanisms in order to allow concurrent activity by many system developers. Integration facilities are also provided to support the fusing of separate developments into a larger unit within the developing product. These facilities reflect the planning and authorization schemes by which development is controlled and are one aspect of the larger problem of version control [Henderson 79]. This version problem is very important in a "real" software development situation.

EXPERIENCES AND REFLECTIONS

The sections above provide a brief introduction to three development support systems. Of these, PEARL and TOPD were essentially academic in that they were developed in a university research environment and have been used only for illustrative software development. CADES has been developed by a major computer manufacturer for its own use and has evolved with that use over a period of years. These two different backgrounds are complementary. PEARL and TOPD offer some insights into development support systems which are some distance from contemporary programming approaches, while CADES offers more realistic, real-world observations of what can and should be provided.

The Nature of Software

Development support systems encourage the software system designer to consider the system under development from one or more viewpoints, each encouraging insights and decisions to be made in particular directions. The encouragement is derived from the design notation "recognized" by the support system and from any tools which reflect characteristics of that notation.

Thus, in TOPD the designer developed his system in terms of classes grouping states and actions, whose meaning was expressed in terms of a non-deterministic finite state machine. With CADES, the designer expresses his design essentially as programs (divided into modules) for different abstract machines with operations having an effect known to the designer. TOPD and CADES are thus dissimilar in their attitudes to the nature of software. TOPD attempted, through its design notation and its testing ideas, to encourage the view of classes and finite state machines, whereas CADES provides less direction to the designer beyond the separation of data and function modules. TOPD's view was not correct as can be seen by the difficulties that could occur in expressing certain constructs in the required manner (see comments in [Snowdon 78] and [Stavely 77]). It is more difficult to question whether CADES correctly views the nature of a software system or not, precisely because it says so little about it. If we measure proximity to nature as some measure of software system quality, then CADES has not got it right either. Design and implementation bugs also appear in CADES developed systems, although their effect tends to be more contained than in systems which are simply "designed and coded."

It is not obvious that we yet appreciate what is the nature of software systems, or, perhaps more importantly, even how bad is our current understanding. What is obvious is that it is not very good. This is important if we want to comment on the value of a development support system, or to compare such systems. Presently our comparisons tend to be by feature (as here!), rather than by measurement of the quality of the product that is so developed. Experience with a system such as CADES in its support of VME/B development leads one to believe that CADES and the encouragement it gives to system developers (e.g., its emphasis on data rather than function) is a step in the right direction. VME/B development is a well-understood task and the VME/B product which results has certain nice properties in terms of software system quality (e.g., measurements indicate a long lifetime). However, it is easy to criticize it as well if one is a purist. It is also easy to say that it was no fault of CADES that VME/B turned out like it did, because CADES is not absolute in its methodological demands nor in the type of software system it encourages. Of course, this latter view is very similar to criticisms of the use of high-level programming languages.

It is likely that, in experimental support systems, particular views on the nature of software can be supported, even when these views can be undermined. This was the case with TOPD, for example. For "real" development systems less rigid views must be taken to enable problematical situations to be encompassed without too much heartache.

Methodology

The issue of development methodology obviously cannot be clearly separated from the issue of the nature of software (or from that of design notations). Design methodology encompasses the way in which the software system is designed and in which its development proceeds. If we have a particular view of what software is, then a design methodology, and hence the support system, should encourage the designer to understand and design a particular system within the bounds of that view. However, the methodology should not discourage or dissuade the designer from viewing a system from a number of points of view at its more abstract levels before choosing a particular structure in order to achieve an executing system on whatever hardware is available. This flexibility tends to be missing in current design methodologies and support systems, even to the extent that designers are unable (and therefore do not try) to appreciate aspects of a system except those which the particular methodology dictates. Design notations are probably very much to blame for this situation. One suspects, however, that as a result of the deficiencies noted in the discussion of the nature of software, we do not really know how to provide the flexibility usefully.

There are numerous illustrations of the problem. For example, in designing at abstract levels there is a tendency to describe systems in terms of certain concepts, colored by our particular view of the nature of the system under design. This is equally true of hardware designers as it is of software designers. Hardware designers tend to talk in terms of processing components (logic circuits) on the one hand and wires carrying signals between processing components on the other. An abstract representation of hardware will be expressed in this way as will be the detailed diagrams from which hardware is built. Software designers tend to describe systems using the analogous concepts of procedure (or module) and procedure call. Such concepts will appear in high-level descriptions as well as in the source code. In a design methodology in which multiple representations of a system are produced and related to one another, one might expect that the relationships between abstract processing units and wires and "real" processing units and wires (or procedures and procedure calls in software) would be complex. However, the tendency is that, while abstract processing units tend to be related to both real processing units and real wires, an abstract wire tends to be related quite directly to a real wire. In software, an abstract procedure call will be rather directly related to a real procedure call. These effects (which we have called the *wire syndrome* and the *procedure call syndrome*, respectively) are powerfully encouraged by existing design methodologies. CADES allows a little flexibility in that calls between processing units (called *holons*) are abstractly considered as a "message in, message out" sequence. In many cases, the mechanism which implements the communication may be either a procedure call (in a number of variations) or a macro expansion. The designer has to choose from a fixed set, however, and has no means of supplying his own communication mechanism.

Other deficiencies in methodological considerations are all concerned with particular, but different, views of a system that are important. These include areas such as name scopes, protection, sharing, synchronization, event scheduling, mapping of concepts, binding of parts at different times, etc. Development support systems tend to be weak in most of these areas.

The Software System Development Cycle

The development of a software system is a complicated process, involving a number of interrelated subprocesses. This is emphasized in an environment such as that in which CADES is used for operating system development. Development is a long-term

and continuing activity involving many people. At the outset of a system's development there are various requirements to be met. Plans must be drawn up to control
progress towards achievement of a system satisfying these requirements. Design
work must proceed to determine the "shape" of the system. This is followed by
detailed design, coding, compilation, unit testing, system integration, system testing and system release, with accompanying documentation being produced at each stage.
While work is in progress, new requirements appear and plans are made for second and
third releases of the system to satisfy these new requirements. Once a system is
released, bugs will be found and provision must be made for their correction.

Early versions of CADES were, like TOPD and PEARL, concerned primarily with the
"glamorous" end of development support. Structural modelling concentrated on the
design of a system and tools were produced aiding the software designer and coder.
Little was done for the remaining aspects of the development cycle. However, gradually, CADES facilities have been extended to cover more of the whole cycle, thus
integrating all aspects of software development and support into a single scheme.
This has benefits in that much redundancy is removed and standard tools are available
for information display where they did not exist before. System developers are thus
made more aware of exactly what the system looks like. Feedback from different stages
of the cycle is facilitated, thus reducing unnecessary compartmentalization of effects
with benefit to the whole system development process.

Separation of Concerns

In designing software systems there are many things that the designer has to
take into account. We have already mentioned several during our comments on the
nature of software. One very important feature of a good design methodology seems
to be that the designer be able to concentrate on as few aspects of design at any
one time as possible. If the designer wishes to concentrate on algorithm design,
then he should be spared any worries about packaging of his algorithm into program
modules, blocks or whatever. If he wishes to concentrate on understanding and concep-
tualizing the system he is designing, he should be free to ignore details which
reflect particular machine structures.

Software development systems must encourage such approaches to design through
the facilities they provide. Evolution of such systems demonstrates recognition of
this. PEARL failed to encourage the distinction between programming and system
design. TOPD recognized the distinction in that systems represented in TOPD design
notation were expected to be coded subsequently in a programming language such as
COBOL. DREAM [Riddle 78a] goes further in emphasizing the role of system design.

The evolution of CADES provides good evidence of increased understanding of the
importance of separate development views. Early versions of CADES placed major

emphasis on system design. Structural modelling encouraged the system designer to produce "data trees" and "holon (or function) trees" and to give abstract descriptions of how the system worked at each level of the trees. Little emphasis was placed on packaging the design into features of a particular programming language. But, at the lower level of the "design trees," it becomes essential to cope with such aspects as software modularity. Detailed questions concerning use of procedures, macros or subroutines need to be answered. Support for interfaces needs to be defined. Data storage questions become appropriate (e.g. should certain data objects be represented as arrays, or record structures, should they be held in files or distributed within a data base). It is possible to represent these issues by further interpretation of the holon and data trees, adding "annotations" and "codes" as necessary. However, and this is the view supported by CADES today, it is better to separate the issues of "high-level design" from those of a low-level nature. Thus, CADES provides different levels of system representation with explicit relationships (mappings) between them.

Data Bases

A feature of the support systems considered has been the use of a structured information system as a central component. The software system being developed is described in some notation and this information is submitted to the information system for storage to augment the design already recorded.

In PEARL, the information system was little more than a structured file effectively hidden from the user. Thus the PEARL system itself dictated how this file could be used, in particular its structure and the manner in which information could be retrieved. TOPD recognized that a data base was required and provided one in the form of a single relational data base for storing fragments of program text. A reasonably general retrieval mechanism was available, although no general relational operations were supported. The structure of the TOPD data base was relatively trivial.

The entities stored in a TOPD data base were relatively large program fragments with relationships sufficient to give a proper lexical structure to the design composed from sets of such fragments. No attempt was made to decompose the information further (e.g., to store call or use structures). Work extending the TOPD data base capabilities did in fact include these structures [Gimson 78].

The CADES data base utilizes IDMS, although a gloss has been applied to provide certain necessary capabilities such as many-many relations, version handling, protection and a textual interface. Advantage has been taken of the necessity of producing a schema for such a data base. The CADES schema reflects a simple view of the information structures necessary to support software development [Pratten 78]. The data base stores information in a more structured form than pure text, the entities of the data base including most items which may have an independent interest at any stage in the development cycle (e.g., individual literal values are regarded as separate entities rather than being embedded in source code statements). Generalized retrieval capabilities based on a navigational descriptive language are provided, together with report generation to enable display of information in the appropriate forms.

The data base aspects of development support systems are important for a number of reasons. First, from a theoretical point of view, the need to provide a schema accommodating software design information forces some decisions as to what software is, or what a system is. The CADES schema has proved reasonably resilient to extended interpretation perhaps as a result of its simplicity. On occasion, we have been confronted with different options for its use which merely emphasizes that we have not really grasped what software and systems are.

Second, the actual existence of a data base having a homogeneous structure has a number of important practical results. In a many-person development environment there are problems of authority and responsibility. The centralized data base means that these problems can be overcome in a completely general manner. The data base is "regionalized" according to the gross structure of the system under development. Local versions of regions can be developed in isolation and thus responsibility for the logical content of that region can be delegated. Integration facilities, coupled with planning and progress reporting tools, allow local developments to become public and hence part of the whole system.

Data base regions, localized developments, integration and the like are all part of a significant problem -- the problem of versions [Henderson 79]. A complete system is made up of many components. There will be several complete systems co-existing and, generally, a number of versions of individual components. It is necessary to keep control over which version of which component goes into which version of the whole. A solution needs to allow frequent change without excessive overheads in processing or in wasted storage (multiple copies).

Tools

Development support systems provide tools to aid the system developer. Some of these tools are those in normal use for software development. Compilers are needed to transform source code (or its equivalent) into object code. Link editors are necessary to compound object code into larger units. System loaders are necessary to load the system into actual machines. In a development support environment, these tools are more closely integrated with the support information structures thereby saving the user from information management concerns.

74

Development support systems will also tend to provide additional tools. For example, in PEARL and TOPD tools were available for design analysis in the form of finite state testing [Henderson 75a]. In CADES, there was an experiment with an "animation" tool whereby the higher levels of system description could be exercised to provide summaries of system characteristics. A test-bed generator tool was also proposed making use of the information within the data base to establish appropriate test-bed skeleton software. An observation on all of these tools is that they each stand or fall by how much useful return the user gets for the extra effort involved in submitting the necessary additional information. Finite state testing can work only if the designer describes the finite state model. If this is awkward or unnatural to produce, or the inadequacies of the finite state model place unnecessary demands on the designer to understand what has happened, then the value of the tool is the less. Problems such as these are compounded when the person who wants the analysis is not the person who has to supply the additional information.

Development support systems provide an opportunity for a review of traditional development tools as well as being the basis for experimentation with new ideas. The data base of a development support system has much more information readily available concerning the system under development. The additional information makes it possible to conceive of more "intelligent" transformation tools or tools which will report on the implication of proposed changes (e.g., "If I change the value of this literal, then how many recompilations will I need to perform?").

User Interface

The appeal of many systems is that they are well-engineered for easy use. More interesting is the nature of user/system interaction. PEARL was designed to be essentially interactive in use. The designer was guided by the system as to what he should do next; the analysis tools interacted with the designer at a terminal when they were uncertain as to how to continue.

That this was a good idea was unproven. Indeed it appeared to be counterproductive in some ways. In TOPD, therefore, the system was weighted away from interactive use except for text preparation, submission and retrieval. The system did not guide the designer as to how to progress. The analysis tools were designed to produce hard copy listings which the designer could study away from a terminal. This approach was predicated on the availability of appropriate hard copy facilities and satisfactory machine scheduling so that the designer did not sit around awaiting output. However, given such conditions it appeared better than the PEARL approach. In the CADES environment this is also what happens. It may be, of course, that what is lacking in all of these systems are facilities by which the designer can "see" his design at a terminal. However, with low-cost character display terminals it is not obvious how to provide such a picture. Even with more powerful terminals, it is likely that there is no substitute for quiet study away from the demands of the system.

CONCLUSIONS

Development support systems have been built and used in several different environments. There is still much to be learned about the process of software system development and this is reflected in the immaturity and incompleteness of present development support systems. However, such systems are useful both as vehicles by which our understanding of software systems and the development process may be increased, and in real-world development efforts as is demonstrated by the VME/B operating system for ICL 2900 Series computers designed and developed by using CADES. (For an appraisal of CADES and the nature of the VME/B product produced by using CADES see [Pearson 78], written by one of those responsible for early versions of CADES).

ACKNOWLEDGEMENTS

Acknowledgements are due to P. Henderson, of the University of Newcastle upon Tyne, with whom the author worked on the TOPD system and to B.C. Warboys and G.D. Pratten of ICL who have both been closely associated with CADES, its design and its use for VME/B development.

The discussion was first directed, by several questions posed by Sabina Saib, toward understanding the extent and nature of the experiences reported by Bob Snowdon. In addressing these questions, Snowdon indicated that Pearl had received little usage because it was a doctoral project aimed at exploring requirements and feasability, that TOPD was used by a large number of students, and that CADES had been used by about 200 professional developers working on an operating systems project. It was also reported that only CADES had been used in the design of (a subsequent version of) itself and that this use had been fairly successful.

With respect to a question concerning the suitability of commercial data base systems to support development systems such as CADES, Dave Pearson indicated that the general, broad-scale data base system (which had been adopted because of the inadequacy of the pre-existing, in-house system) used for CADES delivered essentially all the necessary facilities but was lacking in two respects. First, the facilities for sharing of information were "not quite right." Second, the data base system lacked version control facilities requisite to coping with the complexity inherent in large-scale systems. This generally positive assessment was not supported by two other reports on the use of commercial data base systems. Steve Zilles reported that experiences in implementing the TELL system [Hebalkar 79] indicated that: 1) a good, general-purpose query system was absolutely mandatory, and 2) the space requirements are generally larger than necessary when the data base system has been engineered for general data handling rather than for the specific problem of handling system descriptions during development. Sabina Saib reported that her experiences also indicated that space requirements were prohibitively large for production implementations, although the requirements may be acceptable for exploratory implementations. Bob Snowdon indicated that experiences with CADES did not reflect a prohibitively large space requirement.

With respect to an overall assessment of CADES, addressed first with respect to a metric of "benefit derived per resources required," Bob Snowdon indicated he felt developers got farther faster than they would have without CADES. Dave Pearson argued that one was really comparing "apples and elephants" and the availability of new capabilities made assessments according to such a metric difficult. He did, however, indicate that he felt the cumulative machine time used over the entire development period was less.

Assessing CADES from the alternative viewpoint of its most important contribution to the development process, Bob Snowdon said that its real value was in facilitating the control of the evolution of a system's structure so that the system had a longer lifetime. Dave Pearson added that the visibility into the detailed design process offered by using CADES was also extremely important.

In the remainder of the discussion, a number of observations were reported concerning the assessment of tools through exploratory, experimental usage. A number of these observations pertained to the usability of tools. It appears that the usage of tools by others in addition to the tool developers reveals that a good deal of flexibility must be permitted since it is difficult to pre-guess the purposes giving rise to the use of a tool even though the tool itself may have a relatively narrowly defined "mission". Further, the tool must be robust and able to function under a broader range of uses than generally anticipated, some of them seemingly quite bizarre — failure in this regard can negatively affect the tool's acceptance. Further still, the ever-present command language design problem is exacerbated by having to try to minimize the amount of superfluous output produced by the tool (in order to enhance its acceptability) without extensive knowledge of what output is needed or useful.

Another theme threading through the observations was that testing and coding tools, the most prevalent types of tools produced so far, do not adequately provide support for some very difficult development activities. Several people indicated that maintenance tools would perhaps be more cost effective and give rise to more benefit than testing and coding tools. The infeasibility of using some potentially beneficial tools during maintenance was also noted — testing tools, for example, cannot generally be effectively used because a one-line change generally requires a complete re-test of the entire system. The view was also expressed that programming-language-based tools provide help too late.

A final theme evident in the observations was the difficulty of gathering meaningful data and drawing inferences from it. One problem is that of drawing inferences from usage by users who do not satisfy some of the assumptions under which the tool is developed — the fact that these assumptions are frequently not explicitly stated makes this problem all the more severe. Another problem is that support is frequently not available to perform modification, enhancement and experimentation, all of which are critical to any meaningful assessment. Finally, the absence of meaningful metrics was uncovered by the fact that none could be proposed without serious argument questioning their validity. (One metric of overall quality did, however, survive being cast in doubt. This was the "door knocks" metric which measures a tool's overall quality as inversely proportional to the number of questions posed to the developer by the users.)

One question that arose was: which version of a system should be stored in the project data base, the source text or an abstract version of the source text? There was (short-lived) agreement that in any event only one of the versions should be

stored. This notion was dubbed the "Pingree Park Principle." Since the format of
the text is important to many people, it was agreed that there is some legitimate
reason to store <u>both</u> versions of a system, as CADES does, so the Pingree Park
Principle was abandoned.

Sabina Saib gave a short report on an experimental evaluation of the effectiveness of path analysis tools for testing. A large, (supposedly) bug-free Fortran
program was seeded with a number of errors. It was then debugged using three
approaches: 1) inspection of code and program output, 2) inspection of code, program output, and output produced by a debugging aid which performed tracing, dump-
ing, etc., and 3) inspection of code and program output with the help of a path
analysis testing tool. The major conclusion drawn from the experiment was that the
testing tool greatly hastened the discovery of some errors, but it was pointed out
that this was perhaps due to the help afforded in "understanding" the program.
Saib's assessment of the experiment was that it indicated "a tool can save you some
time in finding some types of errors, but then you're still going to have to use
everything you've got."

The discussion during the report on this experiment indicated that even well-
planned, well-executed experiments raise more questions than they answer, many of
them concerning methodological issues. This was also the focus of Carl Davis'
comments in which he suggested that an evaluation technology is needed. Davis
stated the case for such a technology with the following argument:

> Learning by experience has been the cornerstone of many techno-
> logical advances. However, when we ask what we are obtaining from
> experiences in software development we must face up to the fact that
> we are not benefiting as much as we should. The problem is making our
> experiences useful to others, so that when a software development
> technique is selected for a project we can have the appropriate data
> to make a correct decision. In order to make these kinds of deci-
> sions we need to know what environment the technique is appropriate
> for, what can be expected in terms of payoff from its use, what
> character an organization should have to support the tool, etc.
> These questions must be answered and verified by our experiences, it
> is the only way. However, we must couch our experiences in a broader
> framework of a measurement technology in order to make them more bene-
> ficial to the software development community.
>
> If we ask why we are not obtaining the information we need, we
> see several things that could be improved. First of all, we are
> not collecting the specifics which are most useful. This is mainly
> due to a lack of understanding as to what they are, as well as an
> unwillingness to pay the costs of collection and analysis. Most of

our analysis of experience is after the fact, "monday morning quarter-backing," when much of the detail may have been forgotten or lost. Granularity and accuracy of the data greatly affects its usefulness. Secondly, we don't have a good set of evaluation criteria. We constantly try to compare apples and oranges. Data collection that is not uniform makes correlation nearly impossible.

In short, while experimentation is the only way to collect what we need we are going to have to be much more specific about what we need for the process to give the payoff we need. We need a technology for evaluating methodologies.

In the discussion following this proposal, a number of potential problems were raised. It was pointed out that the negative impact of a technique and/or tool supporting it is generally more obvious than the positive impact. The practice of collecting (and disseminating) data only after the technique and/or tool are deemed successful, and the resultant skewing of the data, was mentioned. The lack of accurate characterizations of development techniques, system development problems, development practitioner styles, and project management approaches was indicated as a major problem which severely impacts the transferability of evaluative data. (A particular problem of this latter type is the variability of practitioner experience and ability, making it especially hard to conduct controlled experiments.) The difficulties of measurement without perturbation were mentioned. Finally, the lack of time and money was indicated as a severely limiting factor, exacerbated by the absence of scaling laws which allow conclusions regarding large development efforts to be drawn from experiments involving somewhat less complicated development efforts.

Despite the skeptical tone introduced by noting these difficulties, there was general agreement that well-conceived, controlled experimentation was crucial to both the improvement and increased acceptance of tools. Until this is possible, however, it is the case that improvement is dependent on exploratory usage and that acceptance (and development support) is dependent on good reports from credible people which, as Steve Zilles pointed out, usually means from other project managers.

Chapter IV. Development Support Systems

To be of real value, tools must be delivered to development practitioners as a well-integrated, homogeneous collection. It is desirable for the tools to support each other's use and present the tool user with a supportive environment in which to carry out development. The two papers in this segment of the workshop both address several questions concerning tool collections, particularly what capabilities belong in a collection and how should these capabilities be provided as a collection of complementary tools?

In his paper, Lee Osterweil proposes a software lifecycle model and a development support system attuned to the model. Major emphasis is placed on improved verification tools and techniques that can be applied throughout the entire software life-cycle. The expected results are improved product quality and enhanced product visibility.

Tony Wasserman's paper presents a discussion of the User Software Engineering (USE) project, which is an effort to develop a methodology and a set of tools for the design and development of interactive information systems. Components of the system that are discussed in the paper include the PLAIN programming language, the USE specification aid, and the Module Control System. The current status and intended use of the system are presented, along with some general observations on software tools.

Discussant Paul Zeiger raises several questions suggested by the papers, and discussant Ray Houghton comments on reasons for resistance to change in organizations, and issues of particular concern to the government. The general discussion focuses on the desirability of prototyping, the nature of formal description media, and the problems of extending development tools and techniques into the maintenance phase.

A SOFTWARE LIFECYCLE
METHODOLOGY AND TOOL SUPPORT

Leon J. Osterweil

Department of Computer Science
University of Colorado at Boulder

This paper describes a system of techniques and tools for aiding in
the development and maintenance of software. Improved verification
techniques are applied throughout the entire process and management
visibility is greatly enhanced. The paper discusses the critical
need for improving upon past and present methodology. It presents a
proposal for a new production methodology, a verification methodology,
and the system architecture for a family of support tools.

INTRODUCTION

There has been growing interest recently in the problem of producing high-
quality software at reasonable cost ([Brown 73], [Brown 75b], [IEEE 75a], [IEEE 76],
[IEEE 78], [IEEE TSE]). The cost of producing programs has been observed to range
up to and sometimes beyond $200 per line [Boehm 75]. In spite of these costs, em-
barrassing and occasionally disastrous errors and shortcomings have been found in
such code. People actively involved in software development have become all too
accustomed to a variety of problems, including:

> cost/schedule overruns,
> poor visibility into development status,
> unreliability,
> maintenance difficulties,
> inconclusive verification,
> inadequate or nonexistent documentation.

These problems have received much attention during the last few years, and the
quest for improved, modern software practices has generally been a search for ways
to eliminate or at least alleviate these problems wherever possible.

As a consequence of intense multidisciplinary investigation of these and related
problems, some basic findings have emerged ([Black 77], [Brown 74], [Brown 78],

———————————
This work was supported by NSF Grant MCS77-02194 and U.S. Army Research Office
Grant DAAG29-78-G-0046.

[Williams 75]). The key findings are that software is an intangible product; and
that it is critically important that its production be carefully managed. Unfortunately, software management is currently more of an art than an exact science.
This is because software is not tangible (hence much management science does not
apply directly), and because there are few if any basic software development principles and disciplines.

In view of the growing magnitude of U.S. software activities (currently estimated at $10-20 billion per year [Boehm 73], [Carlson 76]), it is not surprising
that considerable effort is being spent on discovering workable software development and management principles. An important step in this direction is the realization that software production is an activity that properly takes place in phases,
and that it should be managed as such. The phased approach to software development
is now widely accepted as a basis for improving project cost effectiveness through
improved visibility and control.

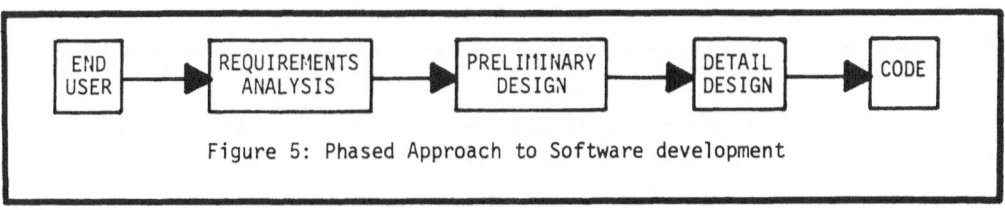

Figure 5: Phased Approach to Software development

Figure 5 illustrates typical names and the usual ordering of some of these
phases. Generally, the first phase, requirements analysis, should result in the
production of a requirements document specifying the end user's need and wishes for
the software. The next phase, preliminary design, should be the identification and
analysis of the functional capabilities needed to achieve the requirements. The
next phase, detail design, should be the derivation and definition of specific data
aggregates and algorithmic modules capable of effecting these functional capabilities. The final step, coding, is then the process of implementing these specifications as computer source code.

Many discussions of the phased approach also include documentation, testing and
maintenance as sequential phases of software production. It is our opinion that
documentation and testing should not be considered phases, but rather pervasive
activities throughout the development process. The next section explores this idea
more fully. Maintenance also should not be considered a sequential phase, but
rather an activity continuing throughout the useful life of the software.

Maintenance has become a catchall term for all activities occurring after the
code is declared operational. In practice these activities are quite diverse, encompassing such things as: 1) correcting coding errors, 2) repairing design flaws

(and impacted code), and 3) upgrading of basic capabilities (resulting in redesign and recoding). It now becomes clear why 50-60% of total software lifecycle costs are ascribed to maintenance ([Alberts 76], [Gansler 77]). Figure 6 illustrates this notion of maintenance as the iterative alteration and correction of requirements, design, and code.

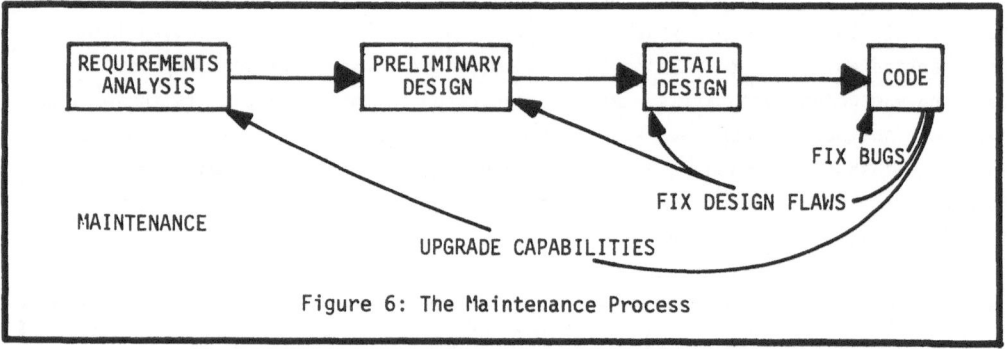

Figure 6: The Maintenance Process

We believe that the greatest benefits of this phased conceptualization of software development and maintenance will not be obtained until the conceptualization is supported by adequate tools and automation ([Brown 72], [Osterweil 76a], [Reifer 75]). Specifically, what appear to be needed are tools and techniques to: 1) facilitate the transition from one development phase to the next, and 2) determine that the transitions have been made correctly. This paper proposes an integrated, tool-supported methodology to effectively address both of these objectives.

LIFE CYCLE VERIFICATION

Careful management throughout the life cycle is critical to the success of any software project. This careful management must be based upon adequate visibility into the development (and hence maintenance) process. The phased approach dictates that milestones be inserted into the process as monitoring points. By itself, however, it does not specify how this monitoring is to be done. Clearly the intangible nature of the evolving software product is the problem.

Thus the driving philosophy behind our approach is that project-related products and information be made as visible and tangible as possible. It is important to observe that such things as reports, summaries, and analyses must be considered key project information. Indeed, such information may be more useful in improving project visibility and manageability than more obvious and mundane items, such as listings and design diagrams. For this reason, much emphasis is placed upon techniques for producing useful reports, summaries, and analyses at all phases of the development (and hence, maintenance) cycle. Ideally, these reports, summaries, and analyses will be automatically drawn from rigorous representations of requirements, design, and code. Thus, important emphasis is also placed upon rigor, formality, and machine readability of all project source materials.

If this is done, thorough, objective, complete reports on project status can be easily and automatically generated at critical points in the life cycle. These reports represent both the status of the project and inferences drawn from source materials. Verification of the soundness of efforts in a given development phase is then obtainable by a comparison of the inferences drawn from one phase to status summaries and inferences drawn from the previous phase.

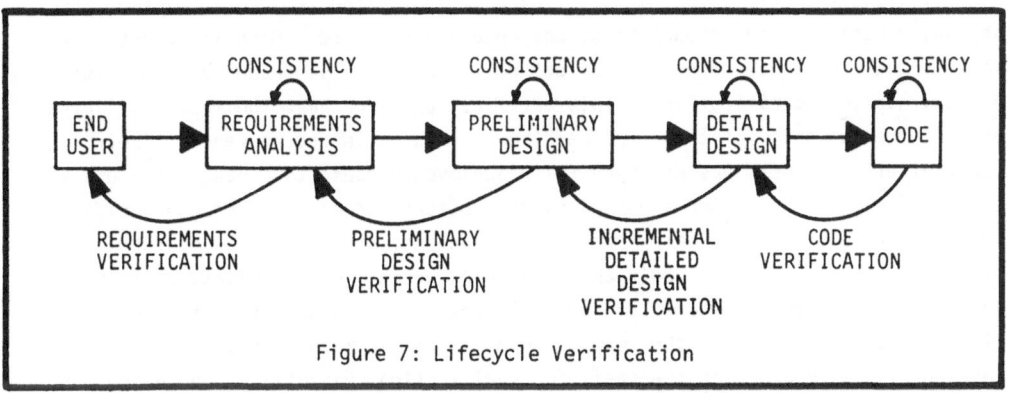

Figure 7: Lifecycle Verification

Figure 7 illustrates this idea and embodies the important principle that verification and testing are activities that must occur during every phase of the development and maintenance cycles. These incremental verification steps are exactly what are needed to assure that the software product is developing satisfactorily. Their purpose is to provide management (and project personnel) with the perceptions and insight needed to prevent drift, poor coordination, and misdirection.

Thus, for example, in Figure 7 we see that a verification of requirements back to the end user is dictated. This is supported by the creation of reports based upon the requirements as specified. The reports give the results of consistency cross-checks, and analyses of the interplay among requirements. Clearly this is most effectively done if the requirements are represented in a rigorous, unambiguous, machine readable format. More on this is presented in a later section.

Figure 7 also shows a verification of preliminary design to requirements. This verification would be supported by reports on the consistency of data flows and interfaces within the design. More important, however, is that functional effects and characteristics of the designed system are inferred from a rigorous, machine readable design representation. In comparing these inferred effects to the rigorous statement of required effects, a meaningful verification is obtained.

That verification can then serve as a basis for a management decision to proceed with the detailed design activity as planned. Here too, it is possible to verify that the effect of the detailed design specification achieves the functional capabilities and performance characteristics promised by the preliminary design, provided that both are in rigorous, unambiguous, machine readable format and that analytic tools are available. In actuality, we view design as a multi-stage hierarchical process with verification occurring at each incremental stage. This is described more fully in a later section of this paper.

Finally, Figure 7 shows a verification of the actual code to detail design. In this activity, the actual code is scrutinized by automated tools. Reports on the internal consistency and soundness of the code are produced. More important, however, is that inferences about the effect of the code can be drawn for comparison to detail design specifications. This verification is perhaps the most familiar because numerous tools of this type have been produced in recent years. Their potential effectiveness has not been fully achieved because they have not usually been coupled with the rigorous design specifications needed for thorough verification. Nevertheless, these early tools and techniques are extremely important to us. They serve as models of the tools and techniques needed for verification of the earlier phases of the software life cycle. Further, the weaknesses of these early efforts serve to underscore the importance of rigor and machine readability at all phases of the life cycle as the basis for verification, visibility, and hence manageability ([Brown 75a], [Osterweil 76c], [Osterweil 77]).

INTEGRATED VERIFICATION METHODOLOGY

In this section an overview of a verification methodology is presented. This verification methodology has been evolved previously for application to source code ([Osterweil 76a], [Osterweil 76c]). We have observed that it seems applicable, however, to any rigorous algorithmic or combinatorial expression of a problem and its solution. In this section the methodology itself is sketched; its applicability to the various life cycle phases is shown later.

Figure 8 shows the juxtaposition of the four major techniques used as components of the integrated verification methodology. As shown in Figure 8, incoming source representations (code, design representations, or requirements representations) are first scanned by a static analyzer. Static analyzers are capable of examining algorithmic representations for inconsistencies and certain errors without requiring actual or simulated execution. Systems such as the DAVE ([Osterweil 76b],

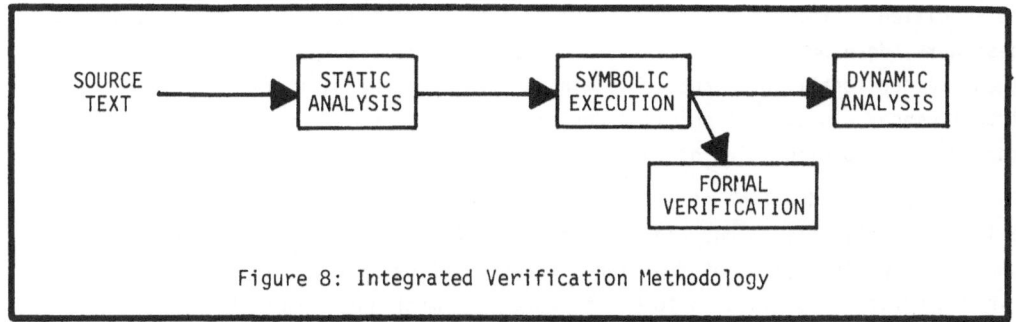

Figure 8: Integrated Verification Methodology

[Osterweil 76c], [Osterweil 77]) static analysis system have proven to be useful in this way.

DAVE is capable of inferring the nature of data flows both within and between modules of FORTRAN programs. The reports of these inference scans are useful documentation, providing visibility to project personnel and management. Further, instances of inconsistent data flow can be detected and reported as errors. DAVE can also demonstrate the absence of certain data flow errors such as uninitialized variable references and mismatched subprogram invocation lists.

DAVE's analysis is actually performed on a graph representation of the source program. Hence DAVE's basic analytic capabilities seem equally applicable to graph and algorithmic representations such as those available during design and requirements. This seems to be a common characteristic of most static analysis techniques. Hence static analysis of data flow and algorithmic consistency is the logical first step in providing visibility and verification at each phase of the software life cycle.

Dynamic analysis lies at the other end of the methodology pictured in Figure 8. In dynamic analysis, explicit inputs to an algorithmic process specification are used to explore the actual functioning of the process. This provides a different kind of visibility and enables different verification. Whereas static analysis was able to ferret general descriptions of data flows out of a general representation, dynamic analysis is able precisely to identify improper handling of specific input scenarios. With dynamic analysis the exact effect of a specified scenario can be determined. This is invariably the most important kind of visibility to project management and to a customer. Verification can be derived from this visibility by comparing observed execution effects to precise statements of intent.

Perhaps the most significant work in this area is the PET system ([Stucki 75], [Stucki 76]). The PET system and a prototype PL/1 Automated Verification System are designed to monitor, respectively, executing FORTRAN and PL/1 programs for adherence to specified statements of intent. The statements of intent are created by the designers, developers, and testers, and employ the full power of the predicate calculus either locally or globally within the program. Hence if the statements of intent embody a program's detailed design, these systems are capable of verifying the correct implementation of functions to handle expected input scenarios.

Careful consideration of this technique shows that this dynamic analysis capability is applicable to any algorithmic specification that has flow of control and contains representations of functional transformations for all modules. Hence dynamic verification is seen to be an extremely important capability applicable to the verification of designs and code. The approach can also be applied to simulated processes used to model early requirements and analyze their interactions.

Dynamic analysis techniques provide definitive visibility and verification for specific input data sets and scenarios, but general visibility can be difficult and expensive to achieve. Static analysis is capable of wide scope, but is less capable of specifics and details. In an important sense the two techniques are nicely complementary, but an important middle ground needs to be more fully addressed.

This middle-ground capability, specific detailed visibility and verification for classes of algorithmic scenarios, is supplied by a relatively new technique known as symbolic execution. Experiments in symbolic execution of source code have been carried out by Clarke [Clarke 76], Howden ([Howden 75], [Howden 76], [Howden 78]) and King [King 76]. These results have shown that this technique is capable of providing precise visibility into the functional effect of specific paths and classes of paths through a source program. Clarke and King have also shown that automatic constraint solving and theorem proving techniques can be coupled with symbolic execution to achieve verification. Their work shows that source code can sometimes be shown to adhere to specific statements of intent not unlike those employed by the PET system.

Work to date on symbolic execution shows that this technique is applicable to source code but is probably better applied to designs and requirements specifications. Symbolic execution is capable of portraying functional effect to whatever level of detail is specified by the input source text. The experiments on code indicate that too much detail is present in code. This results in excessively long and cumbersome expressions of effect and proves to be an obstacle to visibility, rather than an aid. Further, the excessive detail complicates automated verification. Higher level designs and requirements are inherently freer of detail and thus are more amenable to symbolic execution.

All of this is excellent justification for placing symbolic execution between static analysis and dynamic analysis, as shown in Figure 8.

This placement is further supported by observing that essentially the same statements of intent have been used as the basis for verification using both symbolic execution and dynamic analysis. Symbolic execution, however, has been shown to be effective only in some cases. This suggests that when verification is desired, symbolic execution should be attempted first because stronger, more general results are possible. Dynamic analysis might then be employed to verify specific cases for which symbolic execution verification attempts failed.

Experiments have shown that for actual source code, dynamic analysis is likely to be the more successful verification technique. In dealing with designs, however, it appears that the loss of detail will make symbolic execution more effective and dynamic analysis less effective. This shift in effectiveness should become more pronounced at higher levels of design. Finally in verifying requirements, it appears that symbolic execution shows much promise. It is important to note this implies that much important definitive verification will be achievable solely with symbolic execution early in the program development cycle. Accordingly, detailed verification emphasis should shift gradually to dynamic analysis as the coding phase is approached and begun.

Formal verification is the final technique contained in the integrated verification methodology. Formal verification is best viewed as the logical outgrowth of symbolic execution (although historically the reverse has been true). In formal verification the complete definitive, functional effect of an algorithmic specification is determined and compared to the complete, definitive statement of the program's intent. The determination of effect is made by symbolically executing every algorithmic path. This is the sense in which formal verification can be viewed as an outgrowth of symbolic execution, while the distinction between the two is based upon thoroughness and completeness.

Thus, as was the case for symbolic execution, the effectiveness and practicality of formal verification is expected to be greatest for higher-level designs. Formal verification of actual code is not expected to be effective at all because of the inundating effect of excessive detail. Interestingly, experience has shown this to be the case. Most researchers advocate the application of formal verification to high-level algorithmic outlines ([Elspas 72], [Good 75], [London 75]). Formal verifications of actual code, on the other hand, exhibit graphically the numbing effect of the detail contained in code ([Elspas 72], [Good 75]). Thus, formal verification is incorporated into our proposed methodology as an option that is expected to be most effectively exercised at the higher levels of requirements and design.

ARCHITECTURE OF A PROPOSED IMPLEMENTATION

The preceding section has described a methodology capable of providing visibility and verification at each phase of the software development cycle. It was shown earlier that these are critical capabilities needed to manage software development.

It was shown, moreover, that visibility and verification are equally necessary in the management of a successful software maintenance activity.

In this section, we present the general outlines of an architecture for a system capable of supporting the development and maintenance of software. The architecture dictates an integrated visibility and verification capability applicable at all stages of the development and maintenance cycles. Thus it supplies the basis for effective project management. It also incorporates editing, graphics, and file management capabilities necessary for conveniently accessing data and implementing decisions.

The heart of the proposed system is a data base containing all of the information needed for making and implementing management decisions about a given program. Thus the data base is to contain source code, object code, documentation, support libraries, and project utilities. In this respect it helps fulfill the librarian functions of the chief programmer team concept [Baker,F 72].

In addition, the requirements and design specifications for the program must also reside in the data base. This reflects the philosophy that a program is much more than code that executes on a computer. A program is a systematic, orderly plan for solving a problem. As such it must contain a clear expression of the nature of the problem as well as the solution to the problem. Hence, the program requirements and all available levels of design are integral components of the program and must reside in the program data base.

If all of these program components are placed in a centrally accessible data base, project personnel and management then have access to all of those materials required to effectively do their jobs. The architecture dictates user interface and internal structuring to facilitate access, as well as to restrict alteration of critical components. In this way, the data base management system serves as an extension and implementation of the project configuration management scheme. The data base also reflects our stress on management through visibility and verification, as it contains the reports produced by the components of the verification methodology. The data base management system must be designed to facilitate management access to these reports because the reports most effectively convey the project status.

The components of the integrated verification methodology might be viewed as part of the data base management system. They must be capable of producing analytical reports on appropriate source text within the data base. They must then leave their reports within the data base. By simplifying and placing the execution of analytic capabilities at the disposal of project management, a means is provided for gaining visibility when it is needed and in a variety of powerful ways. This provides a strong basis for decision making. As already noted, moreover, such data base manipulation capabilities provide a means for implementing certain decisions (e.g., reject or incorporate modules, retest or elaboratively continue testing other modules). Here too, we see that the data base management system implements many important configuration management and control functions.

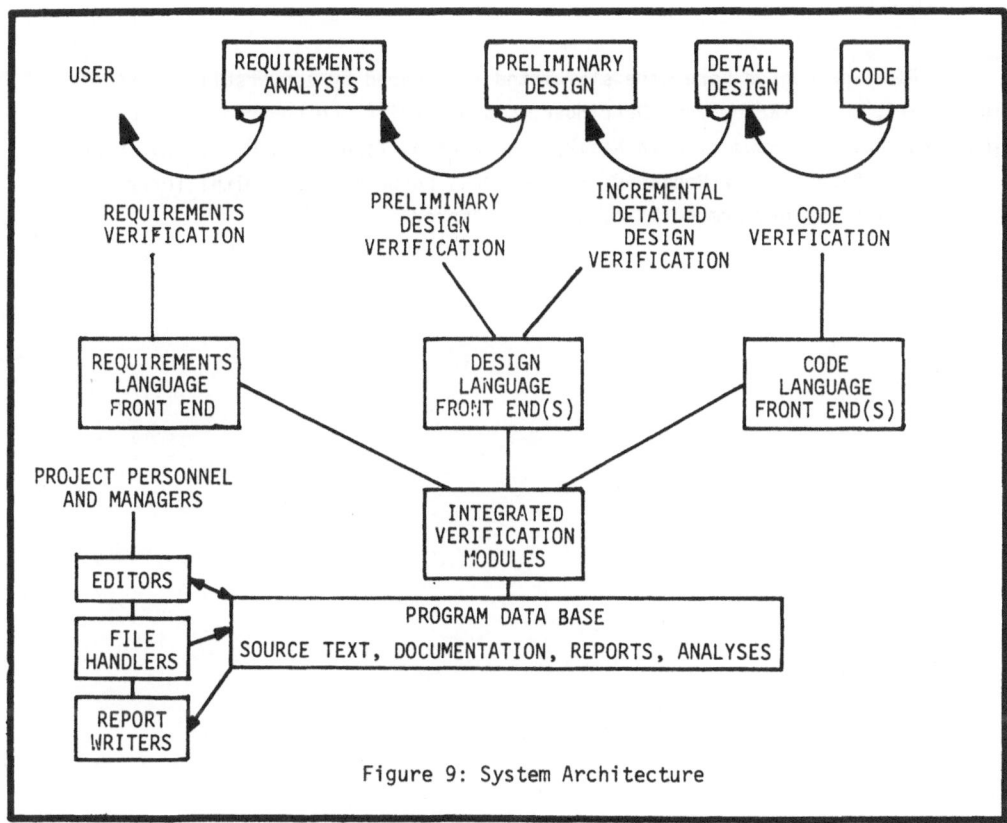

Figure 9: System Architecture

Figure 9 is a diagram of the architecture as just described. It is important to note that the verification processes pictured here are exactly those shown in Figure 7. Figure 9 shows, moreover, that all are supported by the same core of analytic capabilities represented in Figure 8. This is possible only if the requirements and design are captured and stored in rigorous unambiguous formats; if so, then syntax analyzers for each format (as well as for all code languages) could be created. These would then be used as front ends to produce standard representations for analysis by the modules of the integrated verification methodology.

Rigorous requirements and design notations are currently receiving considerable attention ([Alford 77], [Brown 77], [Ross 77], [Stephens 78]); thus these assumptions seem quite justified. Interestingly enough, early experience with them indicate that the discipline of representing requirements and design rigorously is highly beneficial in itself ([Brown 77], [Stucki 76]). The philosophy of compelling this is thus deemed an advantage rather than an obstacle.

ACKNOWLEDGEMENTS

   The ideas presented here were stimulated and shaped by conversations with Ted Biggerstaff, Lori Clarke, John Darringer, Lloyd Fosdick, Ed Foudriat, Bob Glass, Linda Hammond, Bill Howden, Dave Kasik, Sharon Lamb, Vern Leck, H. F. Lee, Larry Peters, Bill Riddle, Dick Robinson, Bill Rzepka, Ed Senn, Mark Smith, Terry Straeter, Dick Taylor, Armand Vito, and Roger Weber.

SOFTWARE TOOLS
AND THE
USER SOFTWARE ENGINEERING PROJECT

Anthony I. Wasserman

Section on Medical Information Science
University of California at San Francisco

Software tools are becoming an increasingly important aspect of systematic methods for software development. This paper describes some
general properties of tools, showing how they fit within an engineering
approach to software development. Then the use and development of
tools within the context of the User Software Engineering (USE) project
is described. The paper concludes with some cautionary notes about the
nature and use of software tools.

> "... the moment man first picked up a stone or a branch to use as a tool,
> he altered irrevocably the balance between him and his environment. From
> this point on, the way in which the world around him changed was different.
> It was no longer regular or predictable. New objects appeared that were
> not recognizable as a mutation of something that had existed before, and
> as each one emerged it altered the environment not for a season, but for
> ever. While the number of these tools remained small, their effect took
> a long time to spread and to cause change. But as they increased, so did
> their effects; the more the tools, the faster the rate of change."
>
> James Burke [Burke 78]

INTRODUCTION

A tool is defined by Webster's Third International Dictionary as "an instrument
used by a handicraftsman or laborer in his [sic] work" and as "an instrument by
which something is effected or accomplished." In that sense, tools are fundamental
to civilization and its technology, going back to the invention of the wheel and the
discovery of fire, if not earlier.

It is important to note from the outset, though, that a tool supports or facilitates an activity as a means to an end, rather than being an end in itself. In
some cases, the availability of a tool makes an activity physically and/or economi-
cally practical where it might not have been feasible in the absence of that tool.

This work was supported in part by National Science Foundation grant MCS 78-26287
and by the National Bureau of Standards contract NB79KACA1059. Computing support
for text preparation was provided by National Institutes of Health grant RR-1081 to
the UCSF Computer Graphics Laboratory, Principal Investigator: Robert Langridge.

(The ultimate example of such a tool is almost certainly the plough.)

A key notion concerning tools is that they should improve the productivity of their users. For example, a pocket calculator does not do anything that cannot be done by a human; it is just that it can perform calculations more rapidly and usually more accurately than can a human with pencil and paper. However, if the mathematical precision of the calculator is inadequate or if the size and spacing of keys leads to many errors in data entry, then the tool may be ineffective. In short, a tool may or may not be helpful in practice, and may be discarded if it fails to provide the desired assistance.

Next, a tool is typically developed in response to a perceived problem. Sextants, for example, were developed and improved because navigators and their ships were getting lost, with the attendant loss of people and goods. High-level programming languages were developed because the process of programming in assembler languages is tedious and error-prone. It is rarely the case that one invents a tool and then searches for a practical application of the tool.

Finally, the best tools are simple and address a specific problem, since they are easily used and are clearly appropriate for persons having such a problem. As Hoare has observed [Hoare 79], "All useful tools have limits. A saw is useful because it is *not* a screwdriver." A corollary to this observation is that a tool user may need access to an entire set of specialized tools during the process of performing a complex task.

A toolsmith, whose task it is to invent and/or develop new tools and to improve the utility of existing tools, must thereby have a solid understanding of the activities to be carried out by tool users *and* must be able to produce tools that can be effectively integrated into those activities so that they are relatively easy to learn and to use, are adaptable to changing user requirements or minor individual difference, and support the user carrying out a task.

In the remainder of this paper, we shall explore the notion of tools in support of software development activities, and the specific tasks of toolsmiths in such environments. Tools will be seen to have negative, as well as positive, characteristics, that will demand careful attention to their development and use in practice. The overall thesis, though, is that tools can be of substantial value when developed and deployed properly *within the context of a systematic approach to software development.*

The primary vehicle for this discussion will be the User Software Engineering (USE) project at the University of California, San Francisco. USE is an effort to develop a methodology, along with appropriate tools, for the design and development of interactive information systems, programs permitting computer-naive users to gain conversational access to data stored within a computer system. The tools of the USE environment will be built upon a collection of existing tools within a programming environment, namely the UNIX operating system ([BSTJ 78], [Ritchie 74]) and its (rather extensive) set of tools. It should also be noted that the process of inventing the USE methodology and programming environment makes use of a number of existing tools, so that the discussion will encompass tool creation, tool integration, and tool usage. Finally, although the primary concern is with automated software development tools, many useful tools involve no automation at all, but are just as necessary and as useful as the automated ones that they support.

SYSTEMATIC APPROACH TO SOFTWARE DEVELOPMENT

One of the most important considerations in developing high quality software systems is to follow a systematic approach to software development. The potential benefits of such an approach include:

- improved reliability,
- verifiability, at least in an informal sense,
- improved maintainability, including portability and adaptability,
- system comprehensibility, as a result of improved structure,
- more effective management control of the development process, and
- higher user satisfaction.

The unifying notion in this regard is that of *software engineering*. The term "software engineering" was invented in 1967 to suggest the need to follow an engineering type of discipline in the creation of computer software. Among the important engineering concepts are those of a "life cycle" and a "methodology" for production, as well as cost and performance prediction.

The software life cycle imposes an order on the steps by which the software is developed, based on the observation that software developers have a tendency to start by writing code, rather than with analysis and design, and on the further observation that development effort is improperly divided among the phases of software development.

Thus, one may identify a sequence of steps to be carried out in software creation, as follows:

- Requirements Analysis and Definition (leading to system specification)
- Architectural Design
- Detailed Design
- Coding
- Testing and/or Verification (Quality Assurance)
- System Evolution

We now elaborate on these terms, and indicate the activities that take place at each stage of the life cycle.

The first step in software development is to obtain a *complete understanding* of the problem and the user's requirement, and to document that understanding as part of the specification. The requirements definition is problem-oriented and describes the user's problem in complete and unambiguous terms. The requirements analysis includes not only a description of the functions that are to be carried out by the system, but also a description of the current operations of the (manual or automated) system. The requirements document can also include such things as constraints upon development, with necessary capacities, response times, mean times between failure, development costs, and operational costs.

The system specification is a description of what is to be built (as opposed to how to do it). While it is largely based upon the requirements definition, it may also include information on portability requirements, machine constraints, and so on. The specification is of use to the software designer and developer, who must create a program that does what is prescribed by the specification, and to the quality assurance organization, which must make sure that the program is in conformity to the specification. In addition, the specification often serves as the basis for an agreement between the development organization and the user organization, and must be understandable by both.

Next, architectural design involves the creation of the gross structure of the software system, the decomposition of the system into modules with the definition of the interfaces between the modules, and the assignment of specific functions to specific modules. During this stage, one may evaluate alternative designs, with the intent of developing a system structure that resembles the problem structure, and that will facilitate coding, testing, and system evolution.

Once it has been determined which steps will be carried out by which modules and how the modules will be related to one another, it is necessary to specify the algorithms that will be used in each module, the data items (including the data base) upon which the algorithms will operate, and similar detail. At the end of detailed design, all of the design problems will have been solved and the production of code will be straightforward. The two design stages, taken together, specify the modules for the system and the logic that is to be performed by each module.

After the design is complete, implementation can proceed. The programming language should support the construction of well-structured and comprehensible programs. The structure of the program should follow the structure of the detailed design as much as possible, so that the correspondence between stages of the development cycle is easy to trace.

The process of testing a program can begin as soon as the specification is written, since program testing involves the construction of a set of test cases that can reliably determine if an executing program is in conformity with its specifications.

The goal of program testing is to find errors and to repair them. Program testing is frequently divided into three stages: unit testing, integration testing, and acceptance testing. Unit testing is performed on individual modules, integration testing checks the interfaces between modules and various subsystems, and acceptance testing tests the system as a whole ready for delivery and operation.

It is clear, then, that errors introduced early in the development process, e.g., in the specification, are not uncovered until the latest phase of testing. Because of this situation, every effort should be made to review specifications and design before proceeding to the next stage, so that as many errors as possible can be detected and corrected at the early stages. If an error is first uncovered during acceptance testing, it is frequently necessary to go back to the specification, modify it, then correct the design and the code before performing all of the tests again; this situation leads to the unpredictably high costs that have characterized many software development projects over the years.

Any system that is put into use with the expectation that it will be used by a number of people over a period of time will certainly undergo change during its existence. Some of these changes (hopefully few) will be as a result of errors discovered during program use, while other will be enhancements to the present system. Evolution may also be caused by organizational changes, by new equipment, and by the need to interface with other systems.

The structure and comprehensibility of the original system, along with its documentation, are important factors in determining the ease with which the system can be modified to meet these new requirements. Since system evolution is frequently the most expensive aspect of software systems, it is important to carry out the original development with this need in mind.

In general, efforts to follow a systematic approach to software development involve putting increased effort into requirements analysis, specification, and design, with the expectation of lower costs for testing and system evolution, since the implemented system will represent a better fit to the user's needs and will operate more reliably than would otherwise be the case.

Not only should one follow the life cycle in carrying out system development, but one should also have a *methodology* for this process, using a set of tools for analysis, design, implementation, testing, and project control. The notion of "software engineering" implies that the developer will have a set of tools and procedures that can be applied to a large number of different projects. In short, when a development organization is presented with a problem which may require the development of a system, it should be able to follow this methodology from the original concept down through the release of the completed system.

A large number of software engineering techniques have been developed, addressing one or more of the various stages of the life cycle. In addition, many organizations have attempted to integrate some of these techniques, along with appropriate management structures and controls, in order to devise a system for the design and development of software systems. A survey of some of these techniques, along with an extensive set of references, is presented in [Wasserman 80a], and papers describing a number of these techniques have been collected in [Freeman 80].

AN OVERVIEW OF THE USE METHODOLOGY

USE is an approach to the specification, design, and implementation of interactive information systems. The project is based on a philosophy that combines principles of user-centered design with those of software engineering. The goal is to provide the designer of interactive information systems with a powerful set of tools that can make it possible to achieve the essential requirements of software reliability and usability.

USE attempts to span the software development life cycle, giving attention to various aspects of the system creation activity. The USE methodology combines tools and techniques developed by others with additional tools and techniques particularly applicable for interactive information systems.

Background

The USE project was undertaken in 1975 in recognition of a lack of suitable facilities for the design and construction of interactive information systems, particularly in the medical environment. Systems being built at that time were developed in an *ad hoc* manner, using woefully inadequate tools. Given the criticality of many applications in the health care setting, it seemed essential to build systems that were reliable, economical, easy to use, and suitable for the user's requirements. It became apparent, after an extensive study, that existing tools would not permit the creation of a suitable methodology that could be applied to system development. Hence, the effort to produce a methodology for the design and development of interactive information systems depended upon the development of new tools.

Attention focused first on programming languages, since it seemed that there were none that were well suited for transforming a design into an interactive

system of this kind. The observation that "the programming languages designed
explicitly for interaction do not [have the structure] for creating modular, well-
structured, reliable software" [Wasserman 74] led to design of the programming
language PLAIN (Programming LAnguage for INteraction). The idea behind PLAIN, then,
was to provide a tool for the construction of interactive information systems that
incorporates concepts of structured programming. PLAIN was also viewed as a possible
replacement for MUMPS [O'Neill 77], which was being used widely in the construction
of medical applications programs, despite its poor qualities as a programming
language.

The next focus of attention was the specification for interactive information
systems. At that time, specifications were largely written in narrative form, showing little or nothing about the system structure or about the way in which the user
would interact with the system. A specification method for interactive information
systems would have to serve both the need for showing a possible software system
structure and for explicitly showing the user interaction. In that way, the specification would be user-centered, and would thus encourage increased attention to
user needs at an early stage.

Little attention was given to the creation of new design tools, since there
appeared to be adequate tools in the form of Structured Design [Yourdon 79] for
architectural design, and program design languages [Caine 75] for detailed design.
In particular, the transaction model of Structured Design seemed appropriate and
integrated well with the specification concepts.

More recently, attention has been given to a tool that can assist with management of the development and evolution of system modules. This tool, named the
Module Control System (MCS), is intended to retain the history of module development, to maintain consistent names for modules throughout their specification,
design, and implementation, and to provide a form of version control at the module
level.

The USE project has been closely tied to the UNIX programming environment, since
UNIX is aimed at supporting interactive program development *as well as* the use of
interactive programs (not the same thing!). Furthermore, UNIX contained an impres-
sive set of tools for text processing, documentation, language implementation, and
file management. One can thus envision the USE techniques and tools, in conjunction
with those of UNIX, as providing a "workbench" [Ivie 77] for the engineering of
interactive information systems.

We now provide a little more detail on each of the USE tools: PLAIN, the specification aid, and MCS. Additional detail may be found in the cited references.

An Introduction to PLAIN

The design goals of PLAIN fall into two categories: those which support
systematic programming practices, and those which support the creation of interactive programs. In practice, these goals mesh in the process of language design,
but can be separated for the purpose of examining the design philosophy.

The design goals for systematic programming were:

- support for procedural and data abstraction,
- support for modularity,
- control structures to encourage linear flow of control within modules,
- visibility of data flow and data use,
- prevention of self-modifying programs,
- program readability, and
- limited language size.

Many of the features of PLAIN with respect to systematic programming are derived
from Pascal. However, a number of other modern languages, including LIS [HB 76],
CLU [Liskov 77], Euclid [Lampson 77a], and Gypsy ([Ambler 77], [Good 78]), have also
influenced the design. These goals, and the way that they are addressed in PLAIN,
are explained at greater length in [Wasserman 80b].

The design goals for supporting the construction of interactive programs were:

- support for strings and string-handling,
- facilities for exception-handling,
- availability of a rudimentary pattern specification and matching facility,
- features for data base management,
- appropriate input/output features, and
- rudimentary timing facilities.

With these features, PLAIN programs could be made resilient to user errors,
could facilitate user interaction with large data bases, and could be made flexible
in handling diverse forms of user input. Unlike the case with the systematic programming goals, there were few, if any, languages that had developed a satisfactory
solution for achieving the goals for reliable interactive programs. Accordingly,
much of the design effort went into the design of features for string handling,
exception handling, pattern-matching, and relational data base management.

String Handling in PLAIN

The key decision in the inclusion of string handling facilities was to permit the generalized use of variable length strings as well as the more traditional use of fixed length strings. It is permissible in PLAIN to declare a variable of type string, with no stated maximum length; as in Pascal, it is also permissible to declare arrays of characters for those instances where the variable-length facility is not needed.

Additional operators and functions were provided to support the use of this data type. The binary operations of concatenation, string contains, and string follows (lexical ordering) were introduced, along with functions for string insertion, removal, replacement, and extraction. It is also possible to convert between fixed and variable length strings.

The decision to permit variable length strings, with the necessary implementation overhead associated with heap management, was based on the assumption that string processing would not represent a significant bottleneck in PLAIN programs. Instead, it was felt that the majority of time would be spent either carrying out database and input/output operations involving secondary storage devices, or in waiting for user input. This decision also made it possible to generalize the Pascal array declaration facility to allow dynamic array (using the same heap management) declarations, thereby overcoming a common criticism of Pascal.

Exception handling in PLAIN

Events that occur during the execution of a program may cause an exception to be raised as the result of an exceptional condition, such as an arithmetic overflow. Without explicitly handling these exceptions, a program may fail. From the stand-point of the interactive user, such a program failure is *extremely* undesirable, since it may cause the user to lose some work. Instead, it is necessary to handle such situations gracefully. PLAIN incorporates a number of built-in exceptions and permits the programmer to define additional exceptions. All exceptions may be raised by using a signal statement, and the built-in exceptions may be raised auto-matically by the run-time system.

When an exception is raised, an exception handler is invoked. This handler is a PLAIN procedure, to which parameters may be passed. The handler may *clear* the active exception and provide for continued program execution, may clear the exception and provide for repetition of the statement that caused the exception to be raised, may notify the invoker of the module that received the exception signal, or may cause the program to fail.

The exception-handling mechanism makes it possible to trap exceptional conditions and to take actions that can prevent situations that may be harmful to the user. In short, it is possible to write extremely *robust* programs, capable of dealing with virtually every kind of user or software error situation. This exception-handling scheme is described at greater length in [Wasserman 80c].

Pattern specification and matching

The pattern matching facility of PLAIN permits patterns and pattern sets to be declared and used. Pattern matching operators are provided, along with pattern-directed input/output. The pattern declaration facility consists of patterns that are composed of string literals, pattern codes, repetition code, other pattern names, and pattern sets, each consisting of one or more patterns. The pattern codes designate commonly used groupings of characters, such as alphabetic characters or digits. Each pattern code (or group of pattern codes) is preceded by a repetition code, which may be definite or indefinite (0 or more, 1 or more). Pattern specifications are static, similar to those of MUMPS, and unlike the dynamic pattern specifications of SNOBOL4.

The binary pattern matching operations "?=" and "?" test a string to determine whether or not it conforms to a pattern. The keywords match and contains are available for pattern sets to determine if a string matches any one of the patterns in a pattern set. In each case, the former operation tests for an exact match between the target string and the pattern, while the latter looks for any occurrence of the pattern in the string.

The programmer may specify any context-free grammar using this facility. Thus, in the construction of an interactive information system, all of the valid user inputs, such as command strings, may be specified in patterns, and the user input string may be compared with various patterns, with appropriate action taken depending on whether or not the string matches a given pattern.

Data Base Management

A complete set of relational data base management facilities are part of PLAIN. A relation is a built-in data type, and may be seen as a set of records whose storage persistence is separate from the execution time of the programs accessing them. Relations from one or more data bases may be *imported* into the execution environment of a PLAIN program to carry out the desired data base management operations.

One can routinely create and manipulate relations in PLAIN programs. The data

base operations in PLAIN are aimed at providing the programmer with some control
over the sequence of data base operations, and therefore at incorporating a set of
features that permits the programmer to improve the efficiency of the program's
data base management. The data base management facilities of PLAIN include:

- formation of data base expressions using the following relational
  algebra-like operations:
    - selection of a set of tuples satisfying a certain constraint,
    - projection on some attributes,
    - joining two relations on attributes of the *same* type,
    - set operations: union, intersection, and difference,
- assignment of a data base expression to a variable,
- individual tuple operations:
    - associative access using key-attribute values,
    - insertion/deletion of tuples,
    - modification of non-key attribute values,
- iteration through the set of tuples by means of a foreach clause, and
- aggregation operations count, sum, min, max, and avg.

These operations, along with some examples, are described further in [Wasserman 79a].

It is really the synthesis of these features, rather than any one of them alone,
that makes PLAIN a powerful tool for the construction of interactive information
systems. For example, the ability to use relations as a representation mechanism
in the declaration of a module (which provides data abstraction facilities) permits
one to encapsulate a set of data base operations that might correspond to a "transaction."

As a more compelling example, consider the scenario of a user of an interactive
information system: the user issues commands that are either inquiries on a data
base, or modifications to the data base, using a simple language designed specifically for this application, with appropriate diagnostic messages provided in the
event of user or system errors. From the programmer's standpoint, the main program
is a loop that reads user input, branches according to the input, calling the appropriate procedures and terminating if and when the user issues the command to quit.
The legal syntax for the various commands are each specified as patterns, and the
patterns are collected into a pattern set. The user input is matched against the
pattern set to branch to the appropriate case, including the "illegal command" case.
The procedures that are thereby invoked contain data base operations using the data
management facilities of PLAIN. Any execution time errors result in the signalling
of an exception, so that a handler procedure can handle the exceptional condition
without causing the program to crash, instead generating an appropriate message and
carrying out any necessary recovery activities.

Unless the programming language has facilities for string handling, pattern

matching, exception handling, and data base management, it would be extremely difficult to write programs that conform to this extremely common scenario. It is precisely for this reason that PLAIN was designed: to provide the application programmer with an appropriate tool for this important class of software systems. This is
not to say that PLAIN is not well-suited for other kinds of applications, but simply
to observe that PLAIN is addressed to a type of application that is not well treated
by other programming languages.

The USE Specification Aid

Similarly, existing specification tools seemed to have serious shortcomings from
the standpoint of specifying interactive information systems, particularly with
respect to tying the user input to specific actions. Among the goals that one seeks
in a specification method are completeness, consistency, unambiguity, writeability,
testability, implementability, modifiability, and, perhaps most important, comprehensibility. Achievement of these diverse goals is difficult, since some of them
entail a significant amount of formalism, while others are less suited for the use
of formalisms. Accordingly, some blending of formal and informal specifcation
techniques is necessary.

From a specification standpoint, an interactive information system may be seen
as consisting of three major components: the user interface, the operations upon
the data objects, and the data base (or files). We use an informal narrative notation for our informal specification, but couple it to a more formal transition diagram scheme to provide consistency and to eliminate ambiguity.

The user interface of an interactive information system provides the user with
a language for communicating with the system, and the normal action of the program
is determined by user input. The program may respond in a variety of ways, including the printing of results, requests for additional input, error messages, or
assistance in the use of the system.

The critical observation, though, is that the semantics of the system are
driven by raw or transformed user input. As with programming languages, the user
language in its runtime context determines the semantic actions to be performed;
the resemblance between such a user language and an interpreted programming language
is quite strong. Accordingly, an effective specification technique for programming
languages can be used effectively for specifying user interfaces.

We have chosen to use transition diagrams [Conway 63] for this purpose. A
transition diagram is a network of nodes and directed paths. Each path may contain
a token, corresponding to a character string in the primitive alphabet (such as
ASCII), or the name of another diagram. If the path is blank, it will be traversed

as a default case, i.e., if all other paths leaving a given node fail. Scanning of
the diagram begins at a designated entry point and proceeds until reaching an exit
node or a dead end (no successful match on the paths from a given node and no
default). A semantic action may be associated with any path; traversal of the path
causes the action to occur.

The next aspect of the specification is to define the data base, since the
operations in the interactive information system are generally tied to the logical
structure of the data base. We follow the ANSI/SPARC framework [ANSI 75], focusing
primarily upon the external model(s) defined in relations. We design a separate
external model for each user class, thereby providing a separate view of the data
base, typically determined by a different set of operations, thereby producing a
number of user view specifications.

The final step of the specifications is to create a tie between the semantic
actions of the transition diagrams and the operations upon the data base. Each
semantic action must be specified and the method of specification may be chosen from
a variety of alternatives. Our preference is to first use a narrative form, and
then to use a more formal approach. Any of a number of specification languages, in
combination with some specification of data base operations, such as the relational
calculus, is appropriate.

The specification of the semantic actions in this way is a powerful tool for
several reasons:

- Each of the semantic actions is relatively small, since it is associated
  with the traversal of a single arc of a transition diagram. Thus, an
  effective decomposition of the system is produced in this way.

- One may continually rework the individual semantic actions, beginning
  with a prose description and proceeding through a specification
  language, a program design language, and finally code. Comparison
  and tracing from one stage of the software life cycle to another is
  simplified in this way.

- The relational data base definition and the syntax of the paths on the
  transition diagram are extremely well-suited to implementation in PLAIN,
  so that the transformation from the specification of an interactive information system to its realization in a PLAIN program is relatively
  straightforward.

It can be seen that the specification tool works in harmony with PLAIN, in that
the content and notation of the specification method blends well with the features
of PLAIN. Furthermore, the structure of the semantic action specification encourages the use of a program design language at the detailed design stage. In this
way, the USE methodology spans the heart of the software development life cycle.
An example showing the specification method and a sample implementation is presented
in [Wasserman 79b].

The Module Control System

The design and development of interactive information systems requires the
specification, design, and development of a sizeable number of modules, and typically results in the generation of a large amount of documentation. Furthermore,
the use of a system over a number of months or years results in changes to the
system and the need for multiple versions or releases of the system. Some machine
assistance is essential for managing all of these different pieces of text and ᶠor
managing the software development activity that has produced them.

The goal of MCS is to provide a means for handling all of the required documen-
taion and linking together all of the documents related at both the system level and
the module level. It is intended to be used in both a horizontal (timewise) and
vertical manner. Thus, one can examine, for any given module, the specification,
design, code, and test data as it existed on any given date. Alternatively, one can
link together the object versions of a number of modules as they existed on a given
date to produce a linked, executable version of the system.

While PLAIN and the specification tool are intended to support the technical
activities associated with the development of interactive information systems, MCS
is aimed more directly at the managerial and organizational issues in software
creation. Information concerning the status of every module can be maintained online so that it is possible to monitor project progress and to identify problems.
Furthermore, various members of a project team have access to the information, so
that some of the traditional communication and interface problems between members
of a group can be overcome. These three tools, PLAIN, the specification aid, and
MCS, are the innovative contributions to the USE methodology. As noted earlier,
though, these tools have to be integrated into a workbench environment for the application development team, and must therefore be implemented in that environment.
We now describe some of the aspects of that implementation.

THE IMPLEMENTATION ENVIRONMENT FOR USE

As noted above, the UNIX time-sharing system was selected as the best environment for the developer of interactive information systems, with the idea that PLAIN,
the specification aid, and MCS would be added to that environment, thereby giving
the application programmer the best possible set of tools.

UNIX was selected for a number of reasons, including the following:

- It was developed to run on relatively small systems, and variants of
  UNIX, Mini-UNIX and LSX [Lycklama 78], had been developed to run on even
  smaller systems. Small systems seem much more appropriate for a

development setting, even if the interactive information system will eventually be used on a larger system.

- UNIX already possessed a good collection of tools that would assist not only the eventual application developer, but would also assist in the construction of the USE tools. Among the most useful of the UNIX tools are:

    - the text editor (ex), with the vi option to provide full-screen editing

    - the nroff and troff formatting programs, for typewritten and phototypeset output respectively

    - the tbl package for producing tables, and usable in conjunction with both nroff and troff

    - macro packages (me and ms) to simplify the formatting of text, and to permit the standardized formatting of various documents

    - a fully hierarchical file system, which permits distribution of the various specification, design, and code files into a number of directories

    - a systems programming language (C) that includes a type checking package (lint) and a source code debugging package (sdb)

    - a lexical analyzer generator (Lex)

    - a parser generator (YACC)

    - a standard I/O library that could be used to implement the I/O operations of PLAIN

    - the "shell" which permits one or more UNIX commands to be packaged (in a macro-like way) and executed as if it were a single command

    - a program (make) for combining a number of files and preparing them for execution

    - an excellent collection of games, including chess, bridge, and adventure, to occupy the developer during less productive interludes

- The UNIX command language (shell commands) are very easy to learn, and the user of the application programs, as well as the application programmer, would not have to learn a complicated operating system command language; indeed, most of the features of UNIX could be made completely invisible to the end user

- UNIX was in widespread use so that the USE tools could be exported to other organizations.

Initial attention was given to the implementation of PLAIN. It was decided to separate the task into two parts: the translator and the data base handler. This choice was made for several reasons:

- it provided a natural decomposition of the task,

- it would make it possible for PLAIN programs to interface to an existing relational data base management system,

- it would make it possible to provide interfaces to the data base handler by means other than PLAIN programs, and

- the technology of writing translators is quite different from that of writing data base management systems.

It was next decided to follow an intermediate language approach in the construction of the PLAIN interpreter. The original plan was to generate P-code, the intermediate language of the Pascal compiler, and then use existing P-code software and/or hardware for program execution. After some deliberation, though, it was decided to use EM-1 instead. EM-1 (Experimental Machine - 1) ([Tanenbaum 78], [Tanenbaum 80]) is a machine architecture for a hypothetical stack-oriented machine, and had been used as the intermediate language in the Pascal compiler developed at the Vrije Universiteit, Amsterdam, for the PDP-11 using the UNIX operating system.

The EM-1 architecture assumes a monitor that provides a number of low-level functions, corresponding closely to those functions required by the runtime system of a programming language processor. The available EM-1 software included an EM-1 optimizer, an interpreter for EM-1, and an EM-1 to PDP-11 assembler translator, making it possible to either interpret or generate executable PDP-11 object code from EM-1. In short, once a PLAIN-to-EM-1 translator was built, much of the remaining lower-level and runtime procedures were already available, thereby reducing the implementation effort substantially.

It was also decided to build a relational data base management system explicitly for use with PLAIN. Initial consideration was given to interfacing with an existing data base management system, INGRES [Stonebraker 76], but INGRES at that time was too large and too inefficient to permit effective experimentation with PLAIN. Instead, the PLAIN Data Base Handler [Kersten 79] was designed to be extremely compact and highly modular so that it could serve as a research vehicle in the area of DBMS performance. The interface between the PLAIN translator and the Data Base Handler was defined and the resulting interface language, named Troll [Kersten 80], is sent by the translator to the Data Base Handler. Troll resembles a low-level query language, and it also suitable as the intermediate language for some other form of data base interface, such as a non-procedural query language.

The separation of these two software pieces appears to have been a good decision, since the size of the language processor is such that a division would have been needed anyway. Furthermore, the separation enhances the overall modularity of the PLAIN inplementation, and makes it feasible to use PLAIN in a distributed environment, with the eventual possibility of implementing the Data Base Handler on a "data base machine."

The existing UNIX tools played a significant role in the implementation of PLAIN. Of course, all of the code and documentation was entered with the text editors. The lexical analysis phase of the translator was written using Lex. The parser for PLAIN programs and the parser for Troll were both written using YACC. The semantic actions of the PLAIN translator and the Data Base Handler were written in C, and the C program checker, Lint, was used to ensure that good programming practices were used in the implementation. Make was used to link together the various object files to produce an executable version of the translator.

Automated support for the specification aid is also under development. The transition diagram can be specified in a table, showing, for each node, each of the possible exit paths, the target of the path (a node), the token of diagram that must be matched to cause the arc to be traversed, and the name of the semantic action (typically a procedure) to be carried out if the arc is traversed.

This information can be encoded in a form similar to that used by the YACC parser generator, using one of the text editors. Then a Transition Diagram Interpreter (TDI) can use that table as input and can carry out two important tasks:

- it can check the diagram(s) for consistency, making sure, for example, that there is a path from each node (checking to see that there is a path from entry to exit becomes an exponentially large problem as the number of nodes increases), and
- it can be used to provide a "mockup" of the actual user/system dialogue simply by making the semantic actions into dummy statements.

This latter use is extremely valuable in the specification of interactive information systems. First, it lets the eventual user interact with "the system" at a very early stage in the life cycle and provides a "feel" for the character of the eventual system. If the user has little or no prior experience with information systems, this process helps the user to think about what the system will actually do, and therefore to gain a better idea of the requirements and to see how usable the interface will be.

Without such a tool, the information system remains too abstract for the user, who will not then get to interact with it until it has been built. In such a case, the user might be expected to request a large number of changes based on initial usage. As noted above, the cost of evolving the system to accommodate these requests is typically much higher than the cost of meeting the requirements the first time. Hence, the payoff from the TDI is improved user understanding of the interactive information system, giving the user the ability to assist in modification of the requirements and specification at an early stage in the development life cycle.

The Module Control System also relies heavily on the UNIX tools. The program developer enters the MCS system, and can issue a number of commands that control a number of different functions, including:

- definition of a system, for which the system will establish a directory to hold information about the various modules that comprise the system, along with other administrative information.
- definition of a module, for which the system will create files to store a specification, design, source code, object code, and test data for that module,
- editing of a file to create or modify some aspect of the information

stored concerning a module; the old version will be saved and the new version will be saved as a set of changes to the old version (except in the case of an object module, where the newest is saved and older versions must be specifically recreated),

- definition of a version, consisting of a named set of object modules and associated date,

- linking together of a set of object modules to produce an executable load module for UNIX, and

- display of statistics concerning the system and the development effort associated with various phases of the system or with specific modules.

To a very large extent, MCS will be implemented using UNIX shell scripts, so as to make it possible for MCS to make use of a wide variety of existing UNIX facilities, including the text editor, the loader, file renaming and copying commands, and language compilers. It should be noted that MCS is not in any way restricted to PLAIN programs, but could serve equally well for programs written in C, for example.

In summary, the existing UNIX tools greatly aided the development effort. These tools, combined with PLAIN, MCS, and TDI, will then form the programming environment for the PLAIN application developer. In this way, it can be seen that the UNIX tools have been valuable throughout the USE project, and then will be of further use to persons making use of the new tools.

THE NEED FOR FUTURE TOOLS

The three USE tools described here are seen as having a significant favorable impact on the development of interactive information systems. Yet this observation should be viewed with caution for two reasons:

- there is, as yet, very little actual experience with PLAIN and TDI, and none with MCS; their design and development was based on a perceived need and it will be some time before any kind of experiment can be conducted to demonstrate convincingly that these tools increase the productivity of programmers or improve the quality of the resulting software (it is even conceivable that they do not!), and

- it may be necessary to create additional tools, or to modify these tools, in order to gain the potential benefit; USE, for example, does not directly address the key area of program testing.

If these tools are successful, then various additional tools would be particularly valuable. The most overriding need seems to be for some kind of graphic tool to help illustrate the structure of the system and to aid the construction of transition diagrams. There already exist several powerful graphics packages in the UNIX environment, and such a tool could take advantage of those facilities.

The next set of necessary tools are in the data base area. Although the PLAIN Data Base Handler collects some statistics on storage and use of various relations, including the number of disk accesses required for various operations, more sophisticated tools can help to reorganize the data base and to enhance the performance of programs using the data base facilities. This need goes hand-in-hand with the need for data base design aids.

Next, although the design of PLAIN has been very deliberate and many sample programs have been written, it will almost certainly be necessary to make some revisions to the language, based on more widespread use.

Finally, the implementation of the existing tools will have to be improved. While an initial language translator can be implemented using Lex and YACC, it will almost certainly be necessary to rewrite the lexical analyzer and parser for a production version of the translator. The newer implementation would be more compact and would execute more rapidly than does the initial version, and would be able to produce a better set of diagnostic messages. While the generality of Lex and YACC is extremely useful for the initial construction of the PLAIN translator, it is not at all clear that they will be satisfactory in the long term.

Similarly, the use of Troll as an interface between the PLAIN translator and the Data Base Handler introduces an extra stage of inefficiency for the availability of a more general interface. In the present version, the Troll input must be parsed and mapped into the various data base functions; a more efficient implementation would have the PLAIN translator call the data base functions directly. Such an alternative was not available in the initial version, since the functions and their calling sequences were not frozen.

In short, support of the USE methodology will require ongoing attention to the development of new tools and to the improvement of existing tools.

SOFTWARE TOOLS: SOME GENERAL OBSERVATIONS

The discussion has proceeded to this point on the implicit assumption that software tools are inherently good and that, furthermore, there is some agreement as to what constitutes a good tool. Yet neither of these assumptions are true. As noted elsewhere [Wasserman 78a], the use of languages, operating systems, and other tools requires an investment on the part of their users, who must learn (and remember) their particular notations and idiosyncrasies. Furthermore, these tools must be maintained and enhanced just as other software products must. Thus, some effort is taken away from producing end products (applications software, for example) and diverted to tool building and maintenance, on the premise that the net effect will be more economical and timely development of high-quality end products.

Unfortunately, hard data in support of that premise is difficult to find, and is just now beginning to be generated. What is needed is a *coherent* set of tools that not only work together, but also support a particular methodology for software development, so that system developers will tend to use the same set of tools in much the same way on a number of projects.

One of the primary obstacles to developing such a set of tools is that designers and programmers often disagree as to what features they want in their tools. Even if one considers such well-understood tools as programming languages and text editors, the lack of consensus is startling. There are new programming languages being developed at a rapid rate, many of which will see extremely limited use, but each of which is developed with the desire to provide some features or capabilities that appear to be missing or unwieldy to use in other languages.

The situation with text editors is equally complex, even though the task of editing text seems inherently simpler than writing programs. Efforts to develop a "standard" text editor have invariably met with failure. Indeed, text editors seem to be subject to strong variations depending upon personal taste and the device on which the editing is done. It is not uncommon for there to be three or more different (perhaps similar) text editors available in a given development environment. Frequently, text prepared with one editor cannot then be edited with one of the other editors!

The examples of programming languages and text editors simply illustrate how difficult it will be to develop suitable programming environments with appropriate automated tools, and then to determine the extent to which such tools improve programmer productivity. The point at which agreement can be reached on a common set of tools, such as envisioned by the U.S. Department of Defense [DoD 79], still appears to be some time in the future. (Of course, a set of standards can be imposed in an organization by administrative fiat, but such an approach is quite different from agreement.)

In short, the state of the art of software tools is still quite primitive, except in a few restricted areas, and there is a need to understand what tools are needed and how the existing ones are presently used, in an attempt to build more effective tools in the future. Beyond that lies the problem of organizing the tools into "tool kits" appropriate for a development methodology, with the concomitant problem of determining the degree to which the development methodology should enforce the use of particular tools or a specific style of usage of a given tool. These issues remain open research problems, and we may expect to see a number of alternative methodologies supported by automated tools that claim to represent an engineering approach to the development of software with the benefits of more efficient development and higher quality software.

Indeed, USE may be viewed in that context, as an attempt to build upon a well-understood set of tools (UNIX) by adding some new tools (PLAIN, TDI, and MCS) that can aid the developer of interactive information systems. At the same time, the present state of USE can be seen a little more than a first step toward the longer term goal of a software development methodology with a coherent set of tools whose benefits are real and quantifiable. This longer term goal represents the future direction of the USE project.

One of the areas of potential consensus in the topic of software tool integration is the universality of the software life cycle. While not all projects follow the life cycle in all its details, most can be mapped onto some variant of the basic form. The basic life cycle passes through the following phases:

- Requirements Analysis
- Preliminary Design
- Detailed Design
- Implementation
- Validation & Verification
- Operation & Maintenance

The discussion centered on tools and techniques useful for performing the tasks implied in the first four phases of the life cycle, and methods for integrating and unifying those tools into a more formalized development system.

It was acknowledged that three unifying threads ran through all phases of a software project life cycle: user interaction, developer progress, and testing requirements. User interaction is vital throughout all phases of the life cycle, particularly during the requirements analysis phase when an agreement must be reached between user and developer as to the product to be produced. Some people felt that this definition of the requirements is a continuous process with numerous iterations, at various phases, between user and developer. However, it was recognized that in some cases, iteration could lead to contractual hassles. Generally the user does not know exactly what he wants, and the difficulty lies in communicating those ill-defined desires to the developer in terms that the developer can use. It is thus helpful for a first prototype of the requirements to be carefully specified so that only minor modifications need be made to that prototype as the project progresses through the life cycle.

In the preliminary design phase of the development cycle, the developer describes the main conceptual organization of the system. Some of the participants felt that the user need not be informed of any details concerning the user interface or implementation at this stage, while others felt that the user should, even at this stage, be told some aspects of the user interface. Most agreed that throughout all phases, the user should be kept informed to give the developer the benefit of user feedback. There is no reason to build a development support system in such a way that the user cannot use the system to "look around" during any of the various phases of development.

It was generally agreed that even though validation and verification is commonly listed as a separate phase, it is important that some verification and testing be performed throughout the development cycle. Further, the most important part of independent testing is the concept of "independent," that is that the test is performed by knowledgeable people not involved in the development.

Much of the remaining discussion was focused upon several questions raised by Paul Zeiger:

- How universal is the software lifecycle model? Are other models possible?

- There is often need for more than one kind of specification (to meet the needs of different readers). How can this need be met without duplication and resulting inconsistencies?

- Many descriptive techniques have been developed, along with software tools to support them. Is this a new Tower of Babel? Might there be a universal language for requirements analysis?

- How can performance constraints be integrated into all phases of the development cycle, so that earlier warnings of failure with respect to these constraints may be generated?

- Does the nature of the formal system description change from phase to phase, or does the description continue in the same formal language, merely accumulating detail?

- Which forms of analysis and verification are useful at each stage?

- Can we accomplish what is needed with current technology, or are new advances required?

- Who does what; that is, what is the appropriate social organization for the production of high-quality software systems?

Further focus for the discussion was provided by Ray Houghton, who pointed out that there are:

several successes and shortcomings for requirements analysis specification. If the shortcomings are scrutinized carefully one can find a recurring theme. For example, Structured Systems Analysis (SSA) requires the knowledge and use of four different notations, the Structured Analysis and Design Technique (SADT) requires considerable training and experience to become a skilled SADT author, the Problem Statement Language (PSL) has a very complex syntax, the Software Requirements Engineering Methodology (SREM) is a very complex methodology that is not cost-effective for small and medium systems, and Use Specification Aid requires knowledge and use of three different notations. It can be seen from these examples that all of these systems require skilled knowledge and experience with one or more possibly complex notations. A recent publication [McNurlin 79] has found a similar situation for program design techniques.

Because of this situation, any commercial enterprise or government agency that adopts one of these methodologies will do so with a great concerted effort and will make the technique a standard throughout the organization. To do otherwise would not let the technique take hold in the organization, and would allow programmers and managers to fall back to their old methods. Once a method has been adopted by an organization and found to be beneficial, there will be extremely strong resistance to change, no matter how many faults may appear with the methodology. This situation is similar to the adoption of certain programming languages by organizations in the past and has been one of the major deterrents to acceptance of new and better languages.

Houghton also indicated that:

As software development systems become more automated, the view of the software life cycle [presented by Osterweil] may very well become reality. Documentation and test scenarios will become by-products of the development process and will be developed automatically along with the rest of the system. Maintenance or enhancements of the system will mean reloading of the data base with information about the current system and then backing up the refinement process as far as required to make the necessary changes.

Finally, Houghton raised several issues that are of particular concern within the government:

- *Standards Checking* An area of obvious interest is the application of tools to software standards. Software development tools can enforce, encourage, or at least identify non-adherence to the standards of a development methodology. For example, deviations from structured constructs or exceeding maximum complexity could be automatically flagged by a compiler.

- *Documentation* Much of the software that is developed for the government is developed by a contractor where the government will be the end-user. Software development tools should provide various diagrams (using graphic techniques) with supporting documentation that can be readily understood by both technical and non-technical people.

- *Portability* The government has a tremendous investment in computer
  systems developed by a large number of manufacturers. This situation has developed for the most part by purchasing the best equipment for the lowest cost through competitive procurements. For a
  software tool to be useful to the government it must be transferable
  from one system to the next.

Carl Hewitt pointed out that the preliminary design and detailed design phases of
software development do not generally produce well-defined documents as do the requirements and coding phases, although they consume a good deal of time. Consequently,
it frequently happens, especially in a research laboratory environment, that the project progresses directly from the requirements phase into the implementation phase to
produce an initial implementation which elicits a good deal of feedback from the user
cheaper and faster than progressing through the design phases. One benefit is that
the immediate feedback on user requirements results in requirements changes early in
the project development. Since every project has two kinds of specifications, behavioral and performance, "building it quick" allows a better opportunity to more
accurately pinpoint those specifications, especially performance. John Buxton agreed
that prototyping is a necessary and important part of the initial steps of real system development, not merely an add-on extra.

The discussion then turned to the nature of the formal descriptive medium throughout the development cycle and its relation to the issue of integration independence
of tools. Previous presentations and discussions had illustrated two extremes:
1) the CADES system where the data base is the unifying concept and numerous tools
for management control are wired into the development system, and 2) UNIX, where if
a data base exists, the developer must build it himself using a collection of loosely
coupled independent tools with very little management control. The distinction between the integrated and independent approaches is related to both the formal descriptive media and the generation of documentation throughout the development cycle.
It reduces to the questions: do we want to change descriptive media as we go along?
or do we want several descriptive media to use in parallel, as for example, both
textual and structural representations? or should only one notation be used throughout the development cycle?

There was universal agreement at this point that there should only exist one
user modifiable form of the formal descriptive medium. Thus, the "Pingree Park
Principle" from Chapter III was resurrected.

Dick Fairley pointed out that according to the life cycle model, the specification phase describes "what" without implying "how" and the design phase focuses on
"how." This difference implies that the descriptive medium has to change, as for
example, algebraic specifications differ from structural design charts. Paul Zeiger
disagreed, stating that the formal descriptive medium ought to remain consistent

across the whole development cycle. Carl Davis then warned of the potential of abuse in this approach, i.e., deciding "how" before deciding "what." It was agreed that the whole problem reduces to language and data base design.

Another problem with a single descriptive medium is the fact that many specification techniques are not applicable to distributed systems. It was felt that distributed systems require specifications of sequences of events and what they mean with a separate set of specifications for what sequences should be allowed. Algebraic specifications, for example, define meaning for the sequences but cannot be used to define the relevancy of the sequences.

Dave Pearson then discussed a problem he sees with the entire life cycle discussion, i.e., the assumption that the life cycle approach works after the first release of the software product. He believes this assumption is erroneous. In its earlier years, the CADES system attacked the whole life cycle up to the first release of the product to the customer, with no thought given to the next phase, the handling of bugs found at several sites or the enhancement of the product. CADES suffered degradation because it contained no mechanisms to carry continuity from initial development through subsequent development after the first release. Bob Snowden commented that they have learned it is essential to recognize the continuation of the system life cycle (enhancement of old to create new, multiple versions, debugging, etc.). The current CADES system handles these problem. Carl Hewitt suggested that networking may help with this type of problem by providing "snapshots" of the whole system when bugs occur.

The discussion then turned to Ray Houghton's issue, openness to change. An example was in the area of requirements analysis tools. The shortcomings of these tools relate to their complexity and the amount of training required for their effective use. He noted that those organizations which adopt these techniques became resistant to change; he concluded that standardization of program design methods is difficult and expensive. Dick Fairley remarked that any new methods require five to ten years to become commonly used in industry, but that does not necessarily imply resistance to change. Examples are the acceptance of new and better programming languages and computing hardware.

It was pointed out that software is not like hardware in possessing a measurable life span. Many corporations are resistant to the conversion of software upon changing hardware, partially because even programs written in so-called transportable languages like COBOL do not necessarily produce transportable data files. However, designing a system to be transportable from the beginning can simplify the task.

A question was asked about the NBS position on Ada. Houghton pointed out that Ada may become a *defacto* standard of the Department of Defense. John Buxton added that Ada is one of the available standard Department of Defense languages but will never be the only standard.

Chapter V. Procedural Description Techniques

The topic of notational tools for use during pre-implementation phases was the subject of two sessions at the workshop. This chapter reports on the first of these sessions and focuses upon notations that are procedural in nature, having a strong heritage in programming languages.

In the first paper, Burt Leavenworth describes a language that augments PL/I with data abstraction capabilities. This language was developed in order to assess the impact of these new capabilities upon the maintainability and modifiability of software. Leavenworth reports on the rationale behind developing the language, gives an example of its use, and relates some preliminary assessments.

Bill Riddle's paper provides a classification of various pre-implementation description techniques and delineates a number of similarities and differences. He then focuses on the procedural class and argues that, for the purpose of modelling, which is the major pre-implementation activity, it provides the currently best basis for aiding practitioners during the pre-implementation phases of development.

In his remarks, discussant Steve Zilles offers a number of comments on Riddlle's classifications and conclusions. His alternative characterizations provide important insights on what notational tools are needed and how different ones relate to each other.

The subject of modelling is the focus of discussant Carl Hewitt's remarks. He gives a cogent argument that evolutionary modelling is an important approach to system development and discusses some of the aspects of, and problems with, this approach.

The discussion's general focus is upon modelling and addresses: different modelling approaches, the relationships between modelling approaches and modelling notations, the different roles and purposes of modelling, and information retention facilities needed to support modelling during pre-implementation development activities.

THE USE OF DATA ABSTRACTION
IN PROGRAM DESIGN

B. Leavenworth

Computer Sciences Department
IBM Yorktown Research Center

This paper proposes a design language based on PL/1, called extended
PL/1, which supports the notion of data abstraction. Some of the features of the language are described such as parameterized data types,
generic procedures, and an external structure mechanism which defines
the interconnection logic of modules. The use of the language and the
data abstraction methodology in a design context are illustrated by considering a telegram analysis problem.

INTRODUCTION

The design process requires a methodology and a formal language supporting that
methodology. The lack of a formal language in the past has been a severe handicap
to the design process. In general, program design has been carried out using a combination of English text and flowcharts. Two serious problems with this approach
are: 1) English is ambiguous, and 2) the programmer has had to contend with two
levels of specification, the design language and the executable language. Not only
has it not been possible to assure that these were equivalent, but it has been extremely difficult in practice to keep the two specifications up-to-date.

The basic principles espoused in this paper are the following:

- The design language should be a vehicle for communication between de-
  signers and programmers.
- It must be mappable to an executable language.
- It must allow suppression of detail to whatever degree required.
- It must allow consistency checking of the design.
- The design language modules must interface with the executable
  modules.

In this paper, we propose a design language based on PL/1, called Extended PL/1
[IBM 78]. It satisfies the above principles and is open-ended with respect to the
abstractions which the designer will find useful in specifying his application.
This language is being developed at the IBM Yorktown Research Center as part of a
project studying the use of data abstractions in the software development process.

A major emphasis of the project is on modifiability and maintenance of software, and we plan to rewrite a kernel of VTAM in order to prove the usefulness of the approach. In addition to this experiment in the structuring of operating systems, we will also study the use of these techniques in applications programming. A preprocessor which supports the language described in this paper is being written.

PROCEDURAL AND DATA ABSTRACTIONS

The notion of procedural abstraction has been the cornerstone of language extensibility since the dawn of programming. If we consider a subroutine at the point of call, we can think of it as a black box which either returns a value or performs some state change on the underlying machine. At this level, the subroutine has some observable effect but we do not care how it is accomplished. There has been nothing comparable in the area of data definition until fairly recently ([Liskov 74],[Liskov 77]), and the programmer has been restricted to the fixed set of data types supplied by a particular language.

A data abstraction or abstract type is characterized by a set of operations that can be performed on all objects of that type, and is supported by a program called a *capsule*. The users of the data abstraction need not be aware of the representation of the objects nor of the implementation of the operations. Even if users are aware of the implementation, they are allowed to manipulate the objects only by invoking the operations supported by the capsule and not by directly accessing the implementation. Just as the procedure defines an abstract operation without the caller understanding the internals of the procedure, so also a data abstraction defines a class of data objects that can be manipulated by operations without the user understanding the details of how each data object is represented or how the operations are implemented.

FEATURES OF THE LANGUAGE

The language is strongly typed, not only with respect to the primitive types, but also the new types that are defined by the programmer. This means that type consistency can be automatically checked by the machine. We have found this feature to be extremely valuable in the programs we have already written.

The language has parameterized data types and generic procedures, which are analogous concepts for data and procedure abstractions respectively. Generic procedures enable the designer to specify a class of procedures which can work with a variety of data types, thereby achieving reusability and commonality of modules. Examples of both generic procedures and parameterized data types will be given in the example to follow.

The language has an *external structure* mechanism, which allows the designer to specify the interface properties of the modules. This component allows the independent compilation of individual modules whereby external references within the module can be checked for consistency.

To complete this brief overview, there are two types of modules supported: procedures and capsules. Procedures are like conventional procedures except that they accept abstract data objects as parameters and (optionally) return abstract data objects as values. Capsules allow the definition of abstract types. That is, capsules are containers for internal data representations which are shared by the operations on the representations. Both the data representations and the operations are hidden from users of the data type. We will not discuss the internal definition of capsules in this paper, but rather their external behavior as seen by the user.

DESIGN METHODOLOGY

In order to best convey the design methodology and application of the language in a design context, we will use an example which has been extensively studied in the literature ([Gerhart 76], [Henderson 72], [Jackson 75], [Ledgard 73]). First we will give a paradigm for data transformation which will be the basis for the design methodology used in the paper. However, we should stress that the design language described here is by no means confined or restricted to any one design methodology; the design problem is in general too difficult to yield to any single strategy. Since the language satisfies the principles stated at the beginning of the paper, we expect that it will mesh smoothly with any reasonable design approach.

Paradigm for Data Transformation

1. Define input and output data.
2. Find one-to-one relationship between components of these data.
3. Find mapping function for a typical source/target pair.
4. Replicate.

Step 4 is a consequence of the fact that it is not usually possible to find a single relationship, but rather a sequence of transformations will be defined. This is the Jackson Design Methodology [Jackson 75].

AN EXAMPLE

The problem is to process a stream of telegrams which are contained in an input file. The telegrams are to be printed on an output medium together with the number of words in each telegram and the number of overcharge words (greater than 12 characters), if any. A word in the input file is a sequence of one or more nonblank characters delimited by one or more blank characters. A telegram is a sequence of words followed by the word 'ZZZZ'. The file ends with the blank telegram (zero words followed by the word 'ZZZZ'). The problem is interesting because of a property called a *structure clash* which means that a one-to-one correspondence between input and output seems not to exist. However, a sequence of correspondences giving rise to data transformations will be found naturally by our apporach.

We describe below such a sequence of transformations giving a description of the mappings to be performed.

T1 - The input file is converted to a sequence of characters.

T2 - Each word is identified as a sequence of nonblank characters and converted to a string, so that we now have a sequence of strings.

T3 - Each telegram is identified as a sequence of strings ending with 'ZZZZ' so that we now have a sequence of a sequence of strings.

T4 - For each sequence of strings representing a telegram, we will construct an abstract object called a telegram which will hide its internal structure consisting of a sequence of strings, a word count and overcharge count. At the same time, we will construct a sequence of telegrams.

T5 - Finally, we will iterate through the sequence printing each telegram.

We will now describe the procedural and data abstractions relating to this problem and then define the transformations based on these abstractions.

Sequence Abstraction

The primitive types of Extended PL/1 are INT (integer), CHAR (character), BOOL (boolean), STRING, and NULL. A basic abstraction that is necessary for both design and programming is that of a sequence. We will list below some operations associated with sequences and strings that are relevant to what we will be doing. They will be shown in the format used by the External Structure.

```
TYPE SEQ [T:TYPE]
  DEFINES
   (CREATE()    →  SEQ[T]
    CONS(T,SEQ[T])  →  SEQ[T]
    FIRST(SEQ[T])  →  T
    REST(SEQ[T])  →  SEQ[T]
    EMPTY(SEQ[T])  →  BOOL
    LENGTH(SEQ[T])  →  INT  )
```

The specification of T as a TYPE in square brackets in the definition of SEQ indicates that the SEQ type is parameterized, so that we may form a sequence of any other type.

For example, we could have SEQ[INT] (sequence of integers), SEQ[SEQ[CHAR]], etc.

Sequences and Streams

Streams are similar to sequences except that they are not necessarily homogeneous. For example, a function may be applied to a sequence of type T and return a collection of elements where the FIRST is not of type T. The treatment of streams in [Burge 75] exploits the fact that the elements of a stream are accessed one at a time and no physical sequence may in fact exist. Our use of streams here has been inspired by [Burge 75] but has been influenced by the following requirements: to keep the type specifications consistent, and to produce the entire sequence after each data transformation in order to provide a convenient testing capability. However, we do not rule out an alternative implementation of streams where the creation of the next element is delayed until it is actually needed. A stream can be characterized by the specification:

```
TYPE STREAM  [T1:TYPE,T2:TYPE]
  DEFINES
   (MAKE(T1,T2)  →   STREAM[T1,T2]
    FIRST(STREAM[T1,T2])  →  T1
    REST(STREAM[T1,T2])  →  T2
    EMPTY(STREAM[T1,T2])  →  BOOL    )
```

A function which operates on a sequence to produce a stream is typically used to apply some mapping to the prefix of the sequence. It therefore returns a stream whose FIRST is the mapping, and whose REST is the remainder of the sequence. For example, consider the WHILE function which has the following type definition (where we use the abbriviation SC to represent SEQ[CHAR]):

```
WHILE (PROC(CHAR) → BOOL,SC) → STREAM[STRING,SC]
```

The above function has two parameters: the first is a predicate from CHAR to BOOL, and the second is a sequence of characters. This function produces a string from the prefix as long as the predicate is true.

We will now define a function called GETWORD which will produce a string representing a word as the FIRST of a stream (after the leading blanks have been eliminated).

```
GETWORD:  PROC(S:SC)  RETURNS  (STREAM[STRING,SC]);
      DCL X    SC;
      DCL Y    STREAM[STRING,SC];
      Y  =  WHILE(SPACE,S);
      X  =  STREAM[STRING,SC]¢REST(Y);
      RETURN(WHILE(LETTER,X));
  END  GETWORD;
```

A procedure is defined with one parameter S of type SEQ[CHAR] which returns a stream as shown. First, declarations are established for X and Y. Then Y becomes the stream whose FIRST is a string of leading blanks, where SPACE is a predicate which is true if its CHAR argument is a blank and false otherwise. X becomes the REST of Y. Finally, the WHILE function is applied to X and returned as the value of GETWORD. The predicate LETTER is true if its CHAR argument is a letter and false otherwise. The notation STREAM[STRING,SC]¢REST(Y) indicates STREAM is a parameterized type and REST is an operation on an object of this type. An obvious advantage of this notation is that the same operation name can be used for different abstractions.

We also need a function called REPEAT which will apply GETWORD repeatedly to a sequence until it is exhausted. REPEAT will return a sequence of the values resulting from the repeated application of GETWORD. The type definition is

    REPEAT (PROC(SC) → STREAM[STRING,SC],SC) → SEQ[STRING]

Now, if INSTREAM is a function from a file to a sequence of characters, the first two transformations of our problem can be specified:

```
DCL INF FILE;
DCL T1 SC;
DCL T2 SEQ[STRING];
T1 = INSTREAM(INF);
T2 = REPEAT(GETWORD,T1);
```

Telegram Abstraction

It only remains to add the telegram abstraction to the External Structure.

```
WORDS  :=  SEQ[STRING]
TYPE  TELEGRAM
 DEFINES
  (MAKE(WORDS)  →  TELEGRAM
   PRINT(TELEGRAM)  →  TELEGRAM  )
 USES
  (SEQ
   OUTSTREAM  )
```

The notation WORDS := SEQ[STRING] is an equate statement and indicates that WORDS is a shorthand for SEQ[STRING]. The telegram abstraction has two associated operations, MAKE and PRINT. MAKE takes a sequence of strings and produces a telegram. It is not necessary to know how this is done in detail, and in fact at the design level we do not want to be bothered by this information. PRINT prints a telegram, and again we are interested in the behavior of the print operation and not in a further level of detail. Finally, the specification indicates that the telegram abstraction uses two other abstractions: SEQ and OUTSTREAM.

The remaining transformations can now be given.

```
DCL T3 SEQ[WORDS];
DCL T4 SEQ[TELEGRAM];
DCL T5 SEQ[TELEGRAM];
T3 = REPEAT(ENDZ,T2);
T4 = MAP(TELEGRAM¢MAKE,T3);
T5 = MAP(TELEGRAM¢PRINT,T4);
```

The function ENDZ as shown above is needed to recognize the end of telegrams.

```
ENDZ:  PROC  (S:WORDS)  RETURNS(STREAM[WORDS,WORDS]);
       RETURN(UNTIL(ENDWORD,S));
END  ENDZ;
```

where ENDWORD is given by

```
ENDWORD:  PROC  (S:STRING)  RETURNS(BOOL);
       RETURNS(S  =  'ZZZZ');
END  ENDWORD;
```

and UNTIL differs from WHILE in that WHILE only adds an element if the predicate is true, whereas UNTIL adds an element until the predicate is true.

The REPEAT function has the type definition

```
REPEAT(PROC(WORDS) → STREAM[WORDS,WORDS],WORDS)
       → SEQ[WORDS]
```

The MAP function applies its functional argument to each element of a sequence to produce a new transformed sequence. Its use eliminates explicit loops.

It is clear that, in general, the REPEAT and MAP functions used above take different types as arguments and return different types as values. In order to preserve type correctness, we must either use a different name for each different usage, or define generalized functions which can subsequently be instantiated for customized usage. We will follow the second approach.

Generic Procedures

Type definitions for REPEAT and MAP can be given as follows:

```
REPEAT[T1:TYPE,T2:TYPE](PROC(T1) → STREAM[T2,T1],T1)
       → SEQ[T2]
```

```
MAP[T1:TYPE,T2:TYPE](PROC(T1) → T2,SEQ[T1])
       → SEQ[T2]
```

The last four transformations of the telegram problem can now be correctly written using appropriate instantiations.

```
T2 = REPEAT[SC,STRING](GETWORD,T1);
T3 = REPEAT[WORDS,WORDS](ENDZ,T2);
T4 = MAP[WORDS,TELEGRAM](TELEGRAM¢MAKE,T3);
T5 = MAP[TELEGRAM,TELEGRAM](TELEGRAM¢PRINT,T4);
```

If desired, the program can be made more readable by using equate statements to substitute mnemonic names for instantiations. For example:

```
MAPWORD := MAP[WORDS,TELEGRAM]
```

Figure 10 shows an example of the transformations performed on two simple telegrams.

CONCLUSIONS

An attempt has been made to give the flavor of Extended PL/I as a design language without enumerating the full set of facilities which it provides. The major attributes that it possesses as a design language can be summarized as follows:

> It facilitates the description of the abstractions which are relevant to the problem.

> It enables the designer to suppress unnecessary detail to whatever degree required.

> It caters to modularity and encourages the specification of module interfaces.

> It follows the principle of "information hiding" [Parnas 72] which is a prerequisite for the maintainability of programs and design specifications with minimum disruption.

> It allows the integration of design methodology with the formalism of a programming language, and enforces constraints which make for greater security and integrity.

Not only can one provide a library or data base of frequently used abstractions which have been found useful in other design contexts, but individual designers can define their own set of facilities by extension.

ACKNOWLEDGMENTS

I would like to thank Jerry Archibald, Andy Black, and Les Belady for their careful reading of the paper and their many helpful comments.

T1 - Input file converted to SEQ[CHAR]

(H,E,L,L,O, ,D,O,L,L,Y, ,Z,Z,Z,Z, ,S,E,N,D, ,M,O,N,E,Y, ,Z,Z,Z,Z)

T2 - Each word identified and converted to a string
yielding SEQ[STRING]

(HELLO,DOLLY,ZZZZ,SEND,MONEY,ZZZZ)

T3 - Each SEQ[STRING] ending with 'ZZZZ'
identified as telegram yielding SEQ[WORDS]

((HELLO,DOLLY,ZZZZ),(SEND,MONEY,ZZZZ))

T4 - Each SEQ[STRING] representing telegram converted
to TELEGRAM object yielding SEQ[TELEGRAM]

(telegram,telegram)

Figure 10: Example of Telegram Transformations

PROCEDURAL APPROACHES
TO
SOFTWARE DESIGN MODELLING

William E. Riddle

Department of Computer Science
University of Colorado at Boulder

Several approaches to modelling a software system during its design are
discussed. Existing software design modelling techniques are categorized
and it is concluded that the category of procedural techniques, which
utilizes many of the same concepts as programming languages, offers the
most promising opportunity for providing an effective design support
system as an integrated collection of tools.

INTRODUCTION

In developing a software system which appropriately realizes a solution to a
problem, one must pass through many levels of conceptualization of the system. During
the initial stages of development, these conceptualizations are oriented toward the
user or customer community. Gradually, during development, the conceptualizations
change to an orientation toward the environment in which the system will execute.

At every conceptual level, the system is abstractly described so as to record
what is known about the system, allow the recognition of what remains to be determined about the system, and provide the ability to answer questions for the purpose
of assessing the validity and applicability of the system. Therefore, these abstract
descriptions are each, in the full sense of the word, a model of the system.

Software system development is thus a process of model construction and elaboration. The ease with which this may be done depends primarily upon the modelling
"materials" provided to software development practitioners and the tools provided
these practitioners to aid in both the formulation of models using these "materials"
and the assessment of the models. The development process is further facilitated by
providing a support environment in which the model formulation and assessment tools
are highly integrated, complementing each other and easily usable in tandem.

In this paper, we discuss several software design modelling formalisms, i.e.,
approaches to providing modelling "material" to software system developers during
the design phase of development. We then focus on one particular formalism, characterize a number of existing techniques for bringing this formalism to design practi-

tioners, and argue that it provides the best opportunity, of the formalisms discussed here, for the provision of an integrated collection of tools.

MODELLING DURING SOFTWARE DESIGN

By *design* we mean that activity during development which follows an initial phase of specification (also known as requirements definition) and precedes the implementation phase. Thus, the system's required capabilities have been detailed and recorded before the design activity starts and this record serves to define the design's acceptance criteria. Also, specific details of the data processing and organization will be developed after the design phase. The intent during design is therefore to transform the system's overall requirements into specific, detailed requirements for the system's components.

The goal during design is the preparation of a gross, conceptual blueprint, or schematic, for the system. One task is therefore to modularize the system and demarcate its major processing and data repository components. Another task is to define the interfaces among the components. The final task is to describe the components' interactions.

It is through the description of the interactions that the purpose of design, the transformation of system requirements into component requirements, is primarily achieved. The interactions are an embodiment of strategies that the designer has chosen for the component cooperation necessary to achieve the policies set forth in the system's specification. Thus the interaction description may be vague as to the algorithmic data manipulation that must be performed in support of the information exchange required by the strategies. But it must be specific as to the actual information exchange so that it can be determined that the strategies actually achieve the required policies and so that the requirements for information preparation and transmission levied against the components can be determined.

Because the individual components' processing capabilities and their interactions are the aspects of interest during design, the system description prepared during the design phase should explicitly describe the functionality of the system's modules. Focusing upon the explicit description of functionality generally precludes the simultaneous, explicit description of other system characteristics; but these other characteristics should be able to be easily derived from the description. (This sometimes requires that additional information, not necessarily pertinent to the functional characteristics, be provided in the model.)

SOFTWARE DESIGN MODELLING FORMALISMS

We have established that the goal of the design phase of software development is
to model the system's modularity and the interactions among the modules. The aspect
of primary interest is functionality and the audience is primarily the designer but
some part of the design is eventually presented to the implementors as a definition
of the functional capabilities of the components which they must prepare. Also,
there is an assessment task, namely to assure that the system as designed has some
chance of producing the required overall system capabilities. Another secondary
audience is therefore composed of those persons, perhaps identical to the designers,
who will assess the design with respect to the system specification. Before review-
ing existing techniques for software design modelling and making several observations
concerning the various ways in which they satisfy this goal, we introduce, in this
section, some general modelling terms which will help in classifying and commenting
on existing software design modelling techniques.

A model is a description prepared according to the rules of some *modelling formalism*. A modelling formalism, itself, consists of three parts. First there is a *basic
vocabulary* of concepts which are primitive, i.e., well-defined and (usually) not
definable using the modelling scheme. Second, there is a set of *composition rules*
which define the ways in which models may be validly constructed. Finally, there is
a set of *derivation rules* by which the effect of composing the primitive concepts in
the ways allowed by the composition rules may be determined -- these rules allow the
derivation of the overall properties of a model itself.

As one example of a modelling formalism, consider a traditional, sequential
programming language. The base vocabulary consists of the concepts of variables,
constants, data types, operations, assignment, etc. -- the base vocabulary is roughly
related to the lexicographic micro—syntax of the language. The composition rules
are closely related to, but not identical with, the language's syntax; they include
the rules by which execution flow may be controlled, structures of data may be composed, elements may be selected from data structures, etc. Finally, the derivation
rules are related to, but again not identical with, the language's semantics. Very
roughly, they allow one to determine the effect of the model in terms of the changes
in the values of variables over time.

As indicated, the concepts of base vocabulary, composition rules and derivation
rules are akin to, but distinct from, the seemingly similar concepts of lexicographic,
syntactic and semantic rules for a language. The distinction is that the modelling
concepts relate to the approach that is used to capture the system being modelled
whereas the language concepts pertain to the statement of the model in some well-
defined description technique. We are thus making a distinction between the "world
view" which is captured in the modelling formalism and a description technique which

provides one way, probably of many, to state models using this "world view."

To clarify this distinction, consider a Newtonian formalism for modelling a gas. This formalism has a base vocabulary consisting of the concepts of moving and stationary objects, composition rules governing the containment of a collection of moving objects within an organized and structured collection of stationary objects, and derivation rules provided by the principles of Newtonian motion and two-body interaction. This modelling formalism is quite distinct from the many "languages" which may be used to represent models in the formalism, languages which range from English to graphical techniques to mathematical formalisms.

In the remainder of this paper, we use the term *modelling technique* when referring to a language by which models may be represented using some modelling formalism. We emphasize that there are many modelling techniques corresponding to a particular modelling formalism, just as there are many Algolic languages.

The composition and derivation rules provide the opportunity to check the validity of a model. The validity of the model's "form" may be checked by assessing its adherence to the composition rules -- alternatively, anything constructed using solely the composition rules is a legally formed model. Considering programming languages, an example of this type of check is assuring that the type restrictions upon operations and assignment are not violated. The derivation rules permit a different type of check, namely one that relates to aspects concerning the effect of the model. An example from the domain of programming languages is the check that subscript selection values are within range. While the distinction between violations of the composition rules and violations of the derivation rules is not precise, the major difference is that the composition rules relate to static properties while the derivation rules relate to dynamic properties.

While the composition and derivation rules allow the determination of the validity of the model with respect to the rules for the proper formation of models, they do not, by themselves, allow one to assess the correctness of the model as a representation of the modelled system. For this purpose, it is necessary to have an *interpretation* which relates the characteristics of the model to those of the modelled system. It is through the interpretation that a model has meaning with respect to the system being modelled, and it provides a "window" into the model that relates some of the characteristics of the model to some of the characteristics of the modelled system. The interpretation is therefore determined by three things: the modelling formalism, the modelled system and the characteristics of the modelled system which are of interest.

It is common to use a higher-level modelling formalism to represent the system characteristics which are of interest, in which case the interpretation may be captured as a mapping between models, relating the characteristics of the lower-level model to those of the higher-level model, and thus the modelled system. In terms of the previous programming language example, the higher-level modelling formalism could be that for which the language of predicate calculus may be used as the modelling technique. In this case, the interpretation consists of the rules of verification-condition generation which allow a model in the higher-level domain to be extracted from one in the lower-level domain. For the previous non-software example, a higher-level modelling formalism for gases is provided by thermodynamics and the interpretation is provided by statistical mechanics.

When an interpretation is captured as a mapping between modelling formalisms, the role of the interpretation, namely to allow the verification of the correctness of the model with respect to the characteristics of the modelled system, is achieved in a two-step process. First, the formally defined interpretation rules are used to transform the model from the lower-level formalism to the higher-level formalism, thus inferring the modelled system's characteristics as they are represented by the model. Then the composition and derivation rules of the higher-level formalism are used to check the validity of the higher-level model. Thus the question of correctness of the model is reduced to the question of the validity of another model.

TYPES OF EXISTING DESIGN MODELLING FORMALISMS AND TECHNIQUES

Using these concepts, it is possible to categorize existing modelling formalisms and techniques and comment on some of their differences and similarities. In this section, we form a rough categorization of some existing approaches to software design modelling to illustrate some of the possibilities which have been tried. We then focus upon one category, procedural modelling formalisms, and subdivide it so as to be able to make some observations about various techniques that have been used. Our observations concerning the various techniques appear in the next section and our categorizations are graphically presented in Figure 11.

A dichotomy of existing software design modelling formalisms can be made on the basis of the formalism's basic vocabulary. One broad category of formalisms, called *event-based formalisms*, relies upon the idea of significant events which occur during system operation and the use of sequences of events to relate system behavior. These formalisms are reviewed elsewhere [Shaw,A 80].

The other broad category of existing formalisms, called *decompositional formalisms*, uses the concepts of information manipulation and storage components, and control and accessing relationships among them. These formalisms are quite natural for the modelling of software systems as they use concepts similar to well-defined ones from the implementation phase -- in some instances the techniques have been obtained by the generalization of programming languages.

This category may be refined by considering the primitive concepts used to denote the coupling among the entities in the system. One set of formalisms, which can be

134

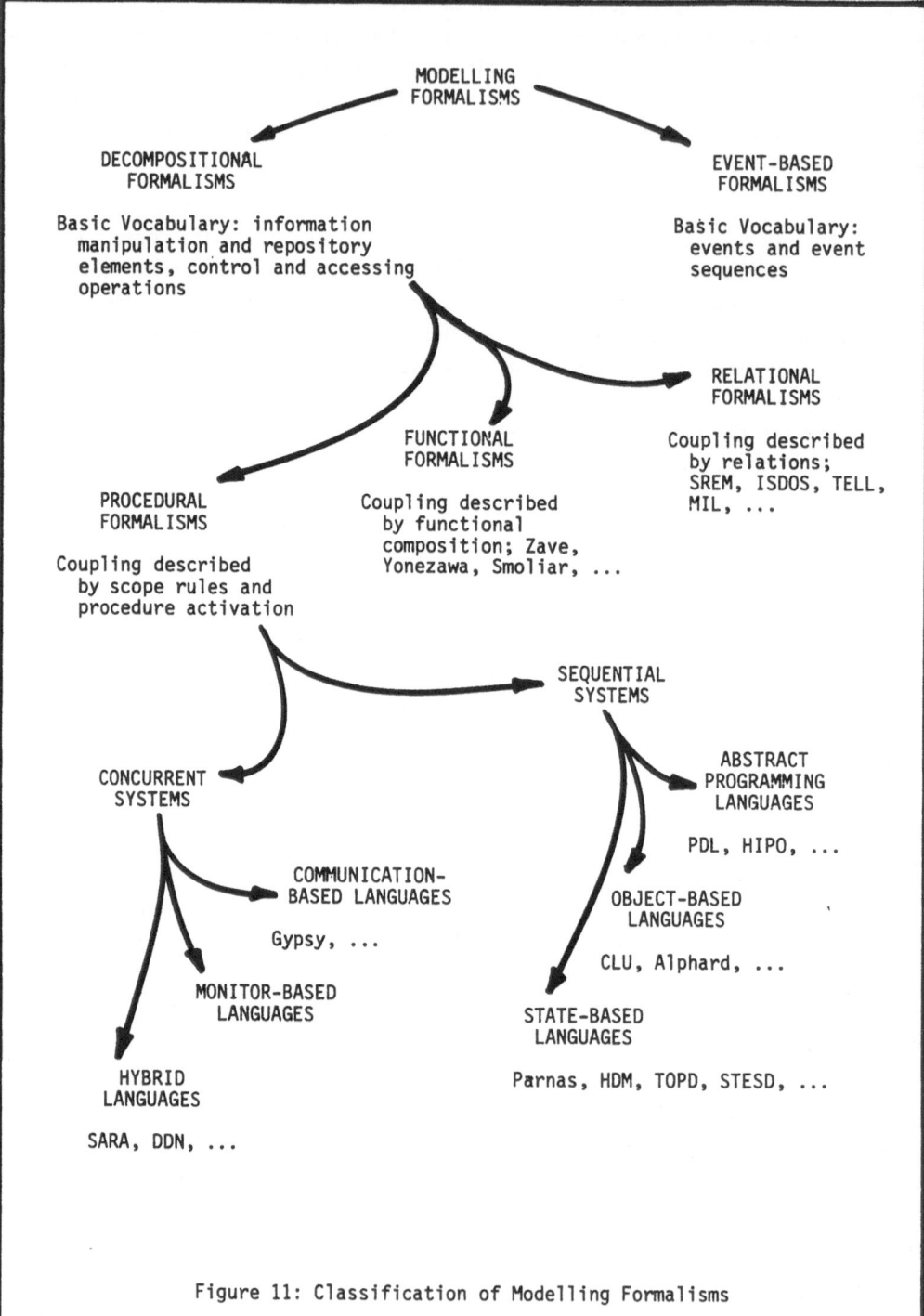

MODELLING
FORMALISMS

DECOMPOSITIONAL
FORMALISMS

Basic Vocabulary: information
manipulation and repository
elements, control and accessing
operations

EVENT-BASED
FORMALISMS

Basic Vocabulary:
events and event
sequences

FUNCTIONAL
FORMALISMS

RELATIONAL
FORMALISMS

Coupling described
by relations;
SREM, ISDOS, TELL,
MIL, ...

PROCEDURAL
FORMALISMS

Coupling described
by scope rules and
procedure activation

Coupling described
by functional
composition; Zave,
Yonezawa, Smoliar, ...

SEQUENTIAL
SYSTEMS

ABSTRACT
PROGRAMMING
LANGUAGES

PDL, HIPO, ...

CONCURRENT
SYSTEMS

COMMUNICATION-
BASED LANGUAGES

Gypsy, ...

OBJECT-BASED
LANGUAGES

CLU, Alphard, ...

MONITOR-BASED
LANGUAGES

STATE-BASED
LANGUAGES

Parnas, HDM, TOPD, STESD, ...

HYBRID
LANGUAGES

SARA, DDN, ...

Figure 11: Classification of Modelling Formalisms

called *relational formalisms*, uses the formal notion of a relation to describe the data usage, data organization and control interactions among the components of a system. Some of these formalisms (e.g., ISDOS [Teichroew 77] and SREM [Davis 77]) were developed for use during the specification phase of software development. But they allow the system's modularity and interactions to be exposed and so are equally useful during the design phase. Others (e.g., TELL [Hebalkar 79] and MIL [DeRemer 76]) were developed expressly for the purposes of design. Regardless of their genesis, these techniques all require that the interrelationships among the entities in the system be modelled by the use of (predefined or user-defined) relations such as *contains*, *uses*, *activates*, *causes*, etc.

A second subcategory, called *functional formalisms*, relies upon the concept of function composition in order to denote coupling. Entities are considered to be represented by functions and system modularity, both of a physical and logical nature, is represented by the composition of these functions. Some techniques falling in this subcategory are described in [Smoliar 79], [Yonezawa 77], and [Zave 79]; most of them are based upon the same general principles as those underlying the Lisp programming language.

The third, and last, major subcategory, called *procedural formalisms*, is similar to the second but utilizes the concept of procedure activation to reflect component interactions, and hence coupling. These are perhaps the most natural for use by designers who are experienced programmers. Techniques falling in this category are currently the most numerous and are the ones of interest in the remainder of this paper.

One major class of techniques useful for this formalism subcategory are oriented towards the modelling of sequential programs. Some of these are notations which may be used to highlight the control flow (e.g., PDL [Caine 75]) or the data flow (e.g. HIPO [Katzen 76]) through the system. These generally consist of a small "programming" language which retains the pertinent constructs from traditional, sequential programming languages but allows the designer to express processing details in English.

Other techniques falling in this class are based on the concept of data abstraction. These force the designer to structure the model into collections of procedures which serve, as a unit, to define an abstract class of objects (i.e., data type) in terms of the operations that can be performed upon it and the effect of these operations both in isolation and in conjunction with each other. Many of these techniques (e.g., CLU [Liskov 77] and Alphard [Wulf 76]) have been developed as extensions to traditional programming languages, but have resulted in the elevation of these languages to the realm of design because they allow the focus of attention to be directed toward the interactions between modules and away from processing details.

The third set of techniques within this class are closely related to the second since they, too, rely upon the notion of data abstraction. But these also include the concept of the state of the system's components. This additional concept makes these techniques less like programming languages and more clearly modelling languages. Some of these (e.g., Parnas' method [Parnas 72] and HDM [Robinson 75]) recognize a dichotomy of procedures into those which change the state of objects and those which merely inspect the state of objects -- these are quite similar to traditional programming languages. Others (e.g., TOPD [Henderson 76b] and STESD [Baker,J 78]) incorporate the additional notation of state transitions in order to allow the direct description of pre-conditions and post-conditions upon procedure invocation and the effect of procedure invocation itself.

The other major class of techniques falling within the procedural modelling formalism subcategory are those which are oriented toward the description of concurrent systems. This orientation requires that the techniques provide for the description of synchronization among asynchronous components as well as the sharing of data repositories. (Provision of constructs for the modelling of shared data is theoretically not necessary as it can usually be modelled by use of the synchronization interaction constructs; but less obscure models generally result from the inclusion of constructs specific to the description of shared data.) The basic vocabulary of these techniques (e.g., DREAM [Riddle 78a], SARA [Campos 78] and Gypsy [Ambler 77]) generally include the concepts of processes and monitors, or concepts very similar. The most popular means of describing synchronization interactions is by message communication and this is a primitive concept in most techniques. Some include the concept of collections of processes so that entities which are capable of internal parallelism may be directly represented.

It is interesting to note that, until recently, this last class of techniques were clearly for the purposes of modelling as they used a synchronization mechanism, namely message transmission, which was sometimes inefficient for use in the actual system. But, recent proposals ([Andrews 79], [Brinch Hansen 78], [Feldman 79] and [Hoare 78]) for concurrent programming languages useful in the domain of distributed systems have used many of the same notions and thus it is no longer as clear where modelling stops and programming begins.

SOME OBSERVATIONS CONCERNING
PROCEDURAL MODELLING FORMALISMS AND TECHNIQUES

Having categorized various formalisms for software design modelling and very roughly classified some techniques in terms of the basic vocabularies of the procedural modelling formalisms upon which the techniques are based, we turn to some observations concerning the nature of procedural modelling techniques.

The first is that what is good for modelling is not necessarily good for programming. Given recent developments in programming languages, it is perhaps more accurate

to say that what is good for modelling may be good for programming but that usefulness for programming is not an important goal when developing a modelling technique.
Instead, there are two more important goals which are often in conflict with those
goals present during the development of programming techniques. One of these goals
is that the models be projective representations of the modelled system. A basic
attribute of a model is that it is abstract, meaning that it suppresses some details
in order to highlight other details. Thus, it is important that a modelling technique
utilize a set of primitive concepts that allows the succinct and natural expression
of the details which are to be highlighted and the suppression of unnecessary details.
As an example, non-determinism is an important concept in the modelling of software
systems, but is generally held to be an anathema with respect to programming techniques.

Another goal is that the modelling technique permit descriptions which are non-
prescriptive with respect to the details of the modelled system. This is generally
hard to achieve for procedural modelling techniques, because many of the basic
concepts have strong connotations in the realm of programming. Take, for example,
the use of message transmission to represent synchronization within concurrent systems.
The recent proposals for distributed system programming languages indicate that this
synchronization mechanism is one which can plausibly and profitably be used in the
actual system implementation. But it may also be used to represent synchronization
which is perhaps more effectively accomplished, during implementation, by other
mechanisms such as semaphores.

Because of the fact that there are differing goals for modelling and programming,
the use of concepts and constructs in a modelling technique which are similar or
identical to those found in programming languages results in a confusing similarity
between the model and the system it models. This confusion is, however, in the eye
of the beholder and can generally be clarified by consideration of the differing aims
of modelling and programming. On the other hand, the confusion can be capitalized
upon, as done in HDM and, to some extent, in Gypsy so that the act of model construction results in the development of control algorithms to be used, verbatim, in the
eventual system.

Another observation is that there is a difference between the organization of
the model's description and the organization of the model (and the modelled system)
itself. Algolic languages suffered from the lack of this distinction with respect
to variable accessibility and hierarchical organization of program text using
begin...end blocks. Recently, languages (such as Mesa [Geschke 77]) have been
developed in which the hierarchical structure of the text implies nothing about the
accessibility of the variables declared at various levels of the hierarchy.

The goal in developing a modelling technique for use during software design
should be to allow hierarchically organized descriptions that can be easily prepared

incrementally. The hierarchical structure of the textual description tends to foster an approach to design which relies upon the gradual evolution of the model. The ability to incrementally develop the text supports the general, and natural, tendency to "jump around" the system during design. Taken together, the result is the ability to prepare an organized description as a result of a somewhat disorganized process.

For procedural modelling formalisms, however, there seems to be general agreement that the technique, and the formalism which it represents, should permit the development of hierarchical models. In some cases, for example HIPO, there is the restriction that the model hierarchy coincide with the hierarchical structure of the text of the model description. In most cases, however, there is some provision for organizing the model itself differently from the organization of the model's textual description. There is also general agreement that the organization of the model should coincide with the organization of the modelled system -- which is reasonable given that the intent is to capture the modularity of the system.

A final set of goals that can be extracted from considering existing software modelling techniques concern the ability to perform assessment during design. First, the modelling technique should be based upon a well-defined, unambiguous, underlying formalism so that the rules for composition, derivation and interpretation are well formulated. For procedural modelling techniques, this is relatively easily achieved because of the similarity to programming languages and thus the ability to utilize simulation and analytic techniques already developed for the validation and verification of programs. But other underlying formalisms exist and have been used in some techniques, for example SARA and DREAM.

Another goal related to the ability to perform analysis is that the procedural modelling technique should be closely related to some higher-level modelling technique so that questions concerning the correctness of the model can be handled by "reducing" them to questions concerning the validity of a higher-level model obtained algorithmically from the model expressed in the procedural technique. Most of the procedural modelling techniques cited above are related to higher-level, usually event-based, formalisms.

MODELS, TOOLS AND METHODS

Modelling formalisms and their associated representational techniques form a basis for a variety of software design tools:

- *bookkeeping* tools provide aid in preparing, augmenting and modifying a model's description,
- *supervisory* tools enforce design methods, principles and guidelines which are deemed beneficial,

- *management* tools allow the assessment of the extent of progress
  and the determination of how best to allocate design team efforts
  so as to speed progress,
- *decision-making* tools help designers determine the validity and
  applicability of design decisions as well as identify, and rank
  order, decisions yet to be made.

In addition to their purpose, tools may vary according to the extent to which
they incorporate knowledge about the details of the modelling technique and the
modelling formalism upon which they are based. A text manipulation bookkeeping tool,
for example, may be independent of the modelling technique and formalism and view
descriptions solely as unstructured sequences of characters; or the tool could be
highly dependent on the technique and formalism and utilize knowledge of the organization of models and their descriptions to guide or monitor the text manipulations.
Note, however, that some tools cannot be defined independently of the modelling
technique and formalism - the above list of tool types is arranged in terms of
increasing dependence of the tools upon the modelling techniques and formalism.

Variance among tools may also stem from the *design method*, i.e., the approach
used to elaborate a model's textual description. Supervisory tools generally, as a
class, exhibit a high degree of dependence upon the design method as they typically
are the embodiment of the method. But a supervisory tool which enforces the information hiding design principle [Parnas 71] is totally independent of the design method.
Similar variance may be found in the other tool classes defined above.

Finally, there is a variance among tools stemming from the *design methodology*, or
approach to model construction, which they reflect. The "rules" which constitute the
methodology, such as "check the validity of each model elaboration before proceeding
to the next elaboration," not only place specific capability requirements upon the
tools but also generally require that there be certain interrelationships among these
capabilities.

TOOL INTEGRATION

Collections of tools may be characterized according to the breadth of their
collective coverage of the spectrum of functional capabilities and the extent to
which they are collectively dependent upon a particular modelling formalism, modelling technique, design method, or design methodology. Before assessing the effectiveness of the procedural modelling formalism for allowing the development of a highly
integrated and effective collection of design tools, we demarcate two major categories
of tool collections and comment on the quality of the aid which can be delivered by
collections in these categories.

In the *toolbox* category, major emphasis is placed on achieving a breadth of functional capabilities with little or no dependence upon any particular approach to modelling or to design. Collections in this category are akin to operating systems in that they are able to support a variety of languages, and therefore modelling techniques and formalisms, and place very few restrictions upon the sequence in which the various tools may be used.

In the other broad category of tool collections, called *support systems*, there is a high degree of dependence of the tools upon a specific approach to modelling or design, or both. In this type of collection, one particular language is emphasized, namely the language of the modelling technique. If the support system is additionally dependent upon a particular design method or methodology, there are also restrictions upon the manner in which the tools may be used either in isolation or in tandem.

These categories are not exhaustive of the possibilities. Instead, they roughly represent the end-points of a spectrum defined by the degree of relationship between the tools in the collection and the modelling or design approach being supported.

Toolboxes are relatively easier to prepare because of the high degree of independence of the tools; because the tools are not oriented toward any particular modelling or design approach, each may be a "stand-alone" module. This allows the toolbox to be organized relatively loosely and means that the command language which allows the user to activate the individual tools may be relatively simple.

Support systems, on the other hand, are harder to prepare because of the need to account for the modelling or design approach in both the system's organization and its command language. The payoff for this increase in effort is higher quality help to the users. While toolboxes can be utilized according to some modelling or design approach which the users impose upon themselves, in a support system there can be tools specific to the modelling or design approach being used and these can provide effective help more directly related to the tasks being performed.

The point is that while the restrictions which are part of the particular modelling formalism or design methodology complicate the task of developing a support system, they also facilitate the preparation of a design and thus enhance the aid provided by the collection of tools.

CONCLUSION

We have discussed the strong relationship between software design and software modelling, developed a framework for discussing alternative software design modelling formalisms and techniques, used the framework to roughly categorize existing software design modelling formalisms and techniques, and made some general observations about the nature of one particular modelling formalism, the procedural modelling formalism. We then turned to the issue of providing an integrated collection of software development tools, noting the dependencies of the tools upon both the modelling formalism and the design methodology and arguing that higher quality help can be provided, at the cost of additional effort, by a support system where the orientation of the collection of tools is toward a particular modelling formalism or design methodology. The question addressed in this final section is: What modelling formalism is best to adopt as the basis for a software design support system?

The answer is that, *at this point*, the procedural modelling formalism seems best suited to providing high-quality support systems. The major reason is that more techniques upon which to base tools are available because of the similarity of procedural modelling formalisms to programming formalisms. This does not necessarily hold with respect to bookkeeping tools because of the relative independence of this type of tool from the underlying formalism even in the case of support systems. But for supervisory tools, the extensive body of knowledge concerning the rules by which clear, succinct, modifiable descriptions should be evolved can be utilized directly in controlling the preparation of procedurally-defined design models. And in the realm of decision-making and management tools, both analytic and simulation techniques which have been developed for the assessment of programs may be used for the assessment of designs. For none of the other formalisms discussed here are both the rules governing good structure of a model or its description and the techniques for assessment as extensively developed.

A second reason is that the procedural formalism provides a set of primitive concepts which are quite natural for describing system modularity and module interactions.

It also appears that this conclusion is not just an artifact of the current state of the art. Because the procedural formalism has a direct and obvious relationship to detailed, program-level description formalisms and there are well-defined techniques for interpreting procedural models in terms of characteristics of interest, these formalisms appear best suited for use in stating descriptions which fall "midway" between user-oriented specifications and machine-oriented programs. The other formalisms discussed here perhaps admit easier interpretation but are "further away" from the realm of programming and thus not as easily related, algorithmically or non-algorithmically, to the eventual program which is the product of design.

We venture the summary conclusion, therefore, that the procedural modelling formalism is, and will continue to be, the most adequate basis for effective design support systems.

ACKNOWLEDGEMENTS

I would like to acknowledge the beneficial comments, during discussions of this material, by Jack Wileden and the students in my graduate-level software engineering courses.

During the presentation of their papers, Burt Leavenworth and Bill Riddle concentrated primarily on the modelling of software systems and the value of modelling.
Leavenworth discussed an experiment underway at IBM T.J. Watson Research Laboratories which is intended to test the hypothesis that a system which has a hierarchical
structure of successively more detailed models can be more easily and more cheaply
maintained. To obtain well-structured initial products which exhibit a hierarchy-
of-models structure, a system is programmed in an "extended subset" of PL/I using a
design method which relies on data abstraction to enhance the localization of code,
system modularity, and information hiding. The conclusions drawn from work-to-date
are that: 1) data abstractions enhance program modifiability by catering to
modularity and allowing the suppression of unnecessary detail, and 2) data abstraction concepts permit the integration of a design method which facilitates modification with a formal programming language.

The focus of Bill Riddle's comments was upon the need to use modelling during
software system design in order to record the system's modular structure and define
the strategies governing module interaction. Noting the current proliferation of
modelling languages, and the current lack of a firm understanding of the relationships among and the relative value of these languages, Riddle suggested a morato-
rium on modelling language production until current ones have been assessed and the
development of new languages can be guided by knowledge of what is needed and useful.

Both speakers indicated that there is an education and training problem created
by the use of modelling oriented languages. Bill Riddle pointed out that the task
of modelling is different from the programming task and that the similarity of procedural modelling languages to programming languages can inhibit the learning of how
to effectively use modelling languages for software design. Burt Leavenworth
reported that learning the extended subset of PL/I was a high anxiety situation for
many people.

Following the presentations, Carl Hewitt introduced a somewhat different view
of software system modelling. Whereas Burt Leavenworth and Bill Riddle perceived
models as forming "horizontal" abstractions, each providing visibility into the
details of the system to some depth, Hewitt proposed that models should form a
series of successively more sophisticated prototypes, i.e., versions of the system.
Hewitt called the process of producing this sequence of models *evolutionary program-*
ming and argued in favor of this approach to development as follows:

The documentation, implementations, and runtime environment of

useful software systems evolve asynchronously and continually. This
is particularly true of large systems for applications such as reser-
vations, programming environments, real-time control, data base query
and update, and document preparation. Implementations change because
of the development of new hardware and algorithms. Documentation
changes to keep up with other changes. Runtime environments change
because of changes in legislation and other unforseen events rearrange
the physical environment.

Neither fully automatic program synthesis nor fully automatic
program proving have been very successful so far in dealing with large
software systems. We believe that it is necessary to build environments to interact with software engineers in the course of the *co-
evolution* of the partial interface specifications and implementations
of a system. Realistic software systems impose the requirement that
the interface specifications of modules must be allowed to evolve
along with the implementations. This situation makes it correspondingly more difficult to ever construct a fully automatic programmer
for such systems. In case of inconsistency between the partial interface specifications, runtime environment, and implementation of a
large system, it may be desirable to modify *any* of them. It is naive
to believe that complete interface specifications can be laid down
once and for all time in a large software system and the implementations of the modules derived by top-down, stepwise refinement.

It is important to realize that the co-evolution of implementations and interface specifications is an entirely natural and fruitful
process. In most applications it is fruitless to delay implementation until complete and final interface specifications have been provided.

The history of the development of text editors on interactive
systems provides a good illustration of the co-evolution of implementations and interface specifications. In the late fifties when
text editors were first being developed, it would have been completely
impossible to have developed interface specifications or implementations for current generation text editors. It was necessary for users
and implementors of text editors to evolve the systems over a long
period time in context of an evolving hardware base in order to reach
the current state of development. Furthermore, it seems rather clear
that interactive text editors will continue to evolve at a rapid pace
for quite some time in the future.

Exploration of what it is possible to implement provides guidance

on what are reasonable partial interface specifications. As experience accumulates in using an implementation, more of the real needs
and possible benefits are discovered causing the partial interface
specifications to change. An important consideration in a proposed
change is the difficulty of modifying the implementation and documentation. Conversely, implementors attempt to create systems that have the
generality to cope with anticipated directions of evolution. Partial
interface specifications in large systems change gradually over a long
period of time through a process of negotiation.

Hewitt proposed a development method incorporating the idea of evolutionary
programming and consisting of the following three phases: definition of a design
for a prototype version, implementation and use of this version, and transfer of
the ideas to a follow-on version or obsolescence of the system. Hewitt emphasized
that the intent to have the first version be a "toy" ("not a full blown dinosaur")
should be explicitly and emphatically stated as a design goal so as to keep frills
out of the system. He also pointed out that a pipeline-style development situation
results, in which the last tools produced are used to aid in the production of the
next set of tools. He reported a good deal of success at MIT in using this development method, indicating that another contributing factor was that the development
team was small (six-eight people) and stable (no attrition over the approximately
four-year period spent on one iteration). He also mentioned that the definition of
a design for a prototype had been best done when carried out over dinner at a
Chinese restaurant, preferably around 2-4 am in the Boston area.

The topic of prototyping was also addressed by Steve Zilles who pointed out that
the two modelling approaches are complementary but apply to different kinds of problems. In particular, for those situations where similar systems have previously
been constructed — situations of a less research-oriented nature — prototyping is
not as necessary. However, this does not mean, as Vic Lesser pointed out, that
there are not tools which are equally important in both prototype-oriented and non-
prototype-oriented development environments. Chuck Bradley added a warning against
choosing prototyping for the wrong reason — because it is more fun to write code
than to write specs — and that this error was far more common than the error of
writing specs when attention should have been directed toward building a prototype.

Zilles endorsed modelling as an important activity during software design and
emphasized the need to have a multiplicity of formalisms:

> I see the structure of the space of modelling formalisms somewhat
> differently [than Riddle's view]. The important properties of a
> modelling formalism as I see them are:
>
> • What aspects of the system can be modelled: function,
>   performance, packaging?

- What types of model building blocks are covered: activities (or processes, or procedures), data, control?
- What level of detail can be modelled well: the decomposition of the system into parts, the interfaces, the functions performed, ...?
- What is the form of the description language: relational (e.g., input/output specifications), functional (e.g., data flow languages), procedural (e.g., algol-like languages)?

These short characterizations are not meant to be exhaustive, but rather suggestive of the dimensions of the space of modelling formalisms. For example, a given formalism might best be used for describing the packaging aspects of the decomposition of a system into activities and data in terms of the relationships among the pieces.

With this view of the modelling space, one can see I do not subscribe to the view that a single modelling language is best used in all phases of the design. This is not to say that the notation used (the modelling formalism) should not have a unifying structure. What is being said, however, is that there are several useful ways to look at and even enter/create the design; the formalism (or integrated set of formalisms) should allow all these to be used. For example, engineering drawing has different kinds of projections (all using the same geometric medium) that illustrate different aspects of a machine part. No one of these projections (drawings) is sufficient to adequately describe the whole design, but the combination is. This is true even though there is redundant information in the projections. The implication of this for software design is that we should choose a set of formalisms, few in number, that completely cover the design space without being forced. For example, I would suggest a relational model at the level of system decomposition and interfaces, but would choose a procedural or input/output approach at the level of individual pieces.

Zilles went on to talk about a graphics-based development system, TELL [Hebalkar 79], which provides a variety of formalisms for describing different properties at different levels of detail. His description gave a convincing argument that an effective, people-oriented development support system based on a multiplicity of useful formalisms could, in fact, be prepared.

Another topic during the discussion was the use of models in the detection of errors. Carl Hewitt expressed a strong skepticism concerning the value of simulation, pointing out that the analytic models requisite to assessing performance do not exist — this was an additional argument for his evolutionary programming approach to development.

Steve Zilles took issue with Bill Riddle's feeling that procedural description techniques were more useful because they permit execution-based approaches to error analysis:

> ... there is a difference between executable and procedural. Given the current state of the art, it is possible to achieve the effect of (that is, execute) non-procedural specifications such as input/output assertions or equational data type definitions. The "execution" of these definitions may not be efficient but it can be used to check functional properties of the modelled entity. Given this, I am not convinced that procedural modelling is the kind which can be given the most effective support most easily. Certainly analysis is simpler on a more descriptive approach than it is on an operational approach.

The final topic addressed during the discussion was the management of the information base formed by the system models. The problems of maintaining consistency and keeping track of the relationships among the models were mentioned but no solution approaches were identified. To cope with the necessity of handling incomplete, partial description which evolve over time, Carl Hewitt suggested the development of a programmers' apprentice [Hewitt 75]:

> A primary goal of the Programmers' Apprentice is to make explicit how each module depends on the partial interface specifications of other modules, how each implementation of a module meets its partial interface specifications, and how each implementation depends on the knowledge of the runtime environment. The proposed Programmers' Apprentice will gradually make the above dependencies explicit through a process of *symbolic evaluation*. Symbolic evaluation consists of executing the implementation of a module M on abstract input using the partial interface specifications of modules it uses. An important purpose of symbolic evaluation is to make explicit exactly how the partial interface specifications of M are satisfied. Symbolic evaluation ensures that a module M only depends on the partial interface specifications and the knowledge of the runtime environment of the modules which it uses and does not depend on idiosyncratic properties of particular implementations. It establishes and maintains an interface between users and implementors of a module. An explicit record of dependencies is necessary for the successful creation and co-evolution of the documentation, implementations, and knowledge of runtime environment of a large software system.

Hewitt acknowledged that the problem of organizing the knowledge obtained from the user through inquiries driven by the symbolic evaluation tool is a severe one and offered the opinion that current artificial intelligence work could help in finding a solution.

Chapter VI. Non-Procedural Description Techniques

The second workshop session concerning notational tools focused upon those which do not have their heritage in traditional programming languages. These non-procedural notational tools are the subject of this chapter, with reports on two radically different approaches and a summary of the discussion which primarily concerned the value of non-procedural notations over procedural ones.

Alan Shaw's paper provides an extensive review of a number of alternative notations, all based on the concept of regular expressions, for describing the effect of a system's operation without describing the system's operational detail. Shaw offers a number of observations on the value of these notations, provides extensive examples of their use, and suggests several topics that need attention in the future.

In their paper, John and Diane Smith discuss a data base-related approach to the description of what a system does without specifying how the system operates. They review different data base-related modelling techniques and give a number of examples of a particular technique, called semantic data base modelling. They show the applicability of this technique to the modelling of software by providing example descriptions of a number of data types including stacks and symbol tables.

Discussant Jack Wileden provides several insights into the value of non-procedural notations and discusses the issue of the naturalness of the techniques overviewed in the papers. The focus of discussant Pamela Zave's remarks is also upon the value of non-procedural techniques, concerning primarily upon their value when persons who are not sophisticated computer scientists are involved in a development project.

Alan C. Shaw

Department of Computer Science
University of Washington

The behavior of a software system can be modelled in terms of sequences of
events, flows, or operations that may occur during execution. To support
this approach, a number of non-procedural description languages based on
regular expressions have been proposed. These include event expressions,
flow expressions, and the many variations of path expressions. The purpose of this paper is to survey and assess these notations, and to suggest
some directions for future research.

INTRODUCTION

   Regular Expressions (RE's) have been used as a design and modelling tool for a
broad variety of computer system elements, including sequential circuits, lexical
analyzers, communication system protocols, command languages, and programs. Since
the early 1970's, the RE notation has been adapted, embedded, and/or extended to describe some of the more difficult aspects of sequential and concurrent software, especially the latter. The result is a new set of software specification languages.
The purpose of this paper is to survey and assess the developments in RE-based description schemes, including some of my work in the area, and to suggest some directions
for future work.

   Historically and logically, the expression notations can be divided into two
classes. One class originated in the research of Riddle, first reported in 1972
[Riddle 72a], in defining and applying *message transfer expressions* (MTE's), later
called event expressions (EE's) [Riddle 79b]. The EE notation is a pure extension of
RE's with interleaving operators to model concurrency and with synchronization symbols; the language denoted by an EE is interpreted as a set of event sequences char-
acterizing the behavior of some part of a system. *Flow expressions* (FE's), the language I devised starting in 1975 ([Shaw,A 75] [Shaw,A 78]), is similar to EE's but
with a different synchronization method. The other class is the *path expression* (PE)
notations introduced by Campbell and Habermann in 1974 [Campbell 74] and further developed by them, Lauer, and others. Most of the work in this class is aimed specifically at specifying constraints, given by PE's, on the order of execution of operations in encapsulated data or resource objects. While PE's also consist primarily of RE's,

This work was supported in part by the Institut für Informatik, ETH, Zurich, where
the author was on leave during 1978-1979.

they have more of a programming "flavor" than the EE and FE schemes, and do not use explicit synchronization symbols.

Despite differences in motivation, syntax, and interpretation of symbols in expressions, both classes of description methods have many similarities. For example, any of the notations could be viewed as representing flows, paths, or events, and some formal relations between the schemes have been established. Most, but not all, of the applications may be described with any of the methods, the choice being a matter of taste and convenience.

In the next three sections, I review the RE formalism and its applications in software description; present and compare EE's, FE's, the various reported forms of PE's, and some related proposals; and describe applications of each. The final section contains a general assessment and some ideas for future work. An index of symbols and abbreviations is included at the end of the paper. The presentation is informal and the reader is referred to the literature for more precise definitions and statements of formal results.

There is a natural connection and overlap between non-procedural description techniques, such as the ones discussed here, on the one hand, and procedural methods, analysis and verification tools, and implementation methods, on the other side. Thus, one will find RE ideas being used in all of these areas. I will emphasize the purely descriptive aspect of the notations, but will also, on occasion, mention these latter applications since they follow directly from the former.

REGULAR EXPRESSIONS AND LANGUAGES

The underlying idea behind the use of RE's is that the permissible behavior or the constraints of a system can be described by a language, each sentence of which is interpreted as a permissible "trace," "path," "flow," or sequence of "events." The basic symbols or atoms of the language are viewed as indivisible or atomic behavioral descriptors.

RE's are formed from the basic symbols and operators for:

- concatenation, indicated by juxtaposition of expressions,
- union or selection, denoted by ∪, and
- indefinite repetition, represented by the Kleene star * (e.g., [Minsky 67]).

Thus, a b means a followed by b, a ∪ b means either a or b, and a* means zero or more repetitions of a.

Example 1:

Let Insert and Remove be atoms. Then the RE's:

Insert , Insert Remove , Insert ∪ Remove , and Insert*

describe the languages (sets of strings):

{Insert}, {Insert Remove}, {Insert,Remove}, and {λ,Insert,
Insert Insert,Insert Insert Insert,...}

respectively, where λ is the symbol for the null or empty string.

Parenthesis are used for grouping, so that quite elaborate expressions may be constructed.

Example 2:

The permissible operations on a particular data base may be described by
the RE:

Open (Read ((Update Write) ∪ Print))* Close

which represents the sequences (using O for Open, R for Read, U for Update,
W for Write, P for Print, and C for Close):

{O C, O R U W C, O R P C, O R U W R P C, O R U W R U W C, ...}.

The intended interpretation is that an Open operation (command, message,...)
is followed by zero or more (Read Update Write)'s and/or (Read Print)'s, and
finally terminated by a Close.

In addition to being a simple and convenient notation, RE's have a well-developed
theory and their languages can be implemented, i.e., recognized, by relatively simple
finite automata or finite-state machines. Figure 12 presents a state diagram

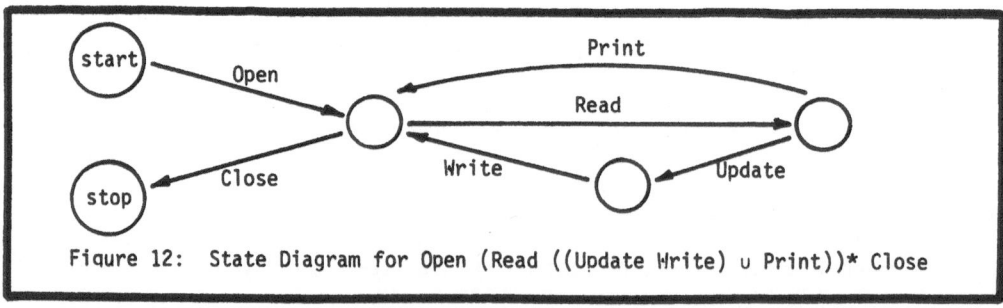

Figure 12: State Diagram for Open (Read ((Update Write) ∪ Print))* Close

for recognizing the language of the RE given in Example 2; the circles represent machine states and a labelled edge is a path to the next state that is entered if the
next input symbol is equal to the label. The significance for software design is
that RE descriptions can be readily used for simulation, analysis, and implementation.

The basic symbols used in the RE's may stand for a variety of entities, depending on the particular aspect being modelled. For example, the symbols of the RE (a (b ∪ c)) * may denote any of the following:

1) message transmissions: a, b, and c are types of messages, such as an end-of-file message, a resource request or release message, or a job log-in message. The RE states that a message of type a must or may be followed by either one of type b or one of type c, and that transmissions of a must occur between b and c.

2) procedure or operation executions: a, b, and c are procedures. The RE expresses the constraints that the execution of a must precede that of b or c and that b and c cannot be executed in sequence without an intervening a.

3) control points: the symbols identify program control locations, such as statement or module labels. In this context, the RE says that control passes from point a to either b or c repeatedly.

4) input language symbols: the RE may describe some part of the user (interactive) input that drives the software. Here a, b, and c could be input lexical items; for example, the RE could be (MOVE (BOX ∪ TEXT))*.

5) resource flows: the symbols name the particular system component, such as a process or a user, that has been allocated a specific resource, for example, a processor, tape unit, file, or table. The RE states that either component b or c may have the resource after it passes through a, and that a must have it between allocations to b and c.

The above list is not exhaustive but it covers most of the reported software description applications where RE's are used in their pure form. Hierarchical or structured descriptions are easily produced by assigning names to expressions.

EVENT AND FLOW EXPRESSIONS

The Shuffle Operators

Both the EE and FE works rely on an *interleaved* model to describe concurrencies in systems. The intuitive idea is that the effect of the concurrent execution of two components, say p_1 and p_2, is the same as that obtained by interleaving or shuffling the execution history of p_1 with that of p_2. To describe this interleaving, the RE notation was extended with a shuffle operator and its closure, here denoted ● and ●, respectively.

The expression ($S_1 \circledcirc S_2$) represents* the shuffle of all elements of S_1 with those of S_2. $S^{\circledast}$ means zero or more shuffles of S; it can be used to specify an unbounded or variable degree of concurrency.

Example 3:

1) Read ⊚ Write describes the language {Read Write, Write Read}.

2) (a b) ⊚ (c d) produces the set of strings {a b c d, a c b d, a c d b,
c a d b, c d a b, c a b d}

3) (a b c)⊛ stands for λ ∪ (a b c) ∪ ((a b c) ⊚ (a b c)) ∪
∪ ((a b c) ⊚ (a b c) ⊚ (a b c)) ∪ ...

I will use the term *shuffle expression* (SE) to mean an RE extended with the ⊚ and ⊛ operators. (Aside on history and notation. A shuffle operator similar to ⊚ was earlier defined in [Ginsburg 66] and also appeared in [Ginsburg 65]. Riddle used † and Δ, instead of my ⊚ and ⊛, in his EE work which preceded mine. The main argument for ⊚ and ⊛ is that because they are meant to be interleaved/concurrent analogs of the sequential concatenation and * operators, respectively, it is convenient to have them similar in appearance.)

Example 4:

Let Read($r_1,\ldots,r_n$) denote an SE describing the elementary activities involved in reading a data base, where $r_1,\ldots,r_n$ are the atomic operations of the read. Similarly, let Write($w_1,\ldots,w_m$) stand for an SE for the flows through the data base write operations, where $w_1,\ldots,w_m$ are the elementary write activities. Then, the standard reader-writer problem constraints, stating that Read's may proceed concurrently, Write's must proceed sequentially, and a Write may not overlap a Read, can be expressed by the SE:

(Read($r_1,\ldots,r_n$) ⊛ ∪ Write($w_1,\ldots,w_m$))*

Example 5:

Consider the SE:

(Put Get)⊛

The language described is:

L = {λ, Put Get, Put Get Put Get, Put Put Get Get, Put Get Put Get Put Get,
Put Put Get Get Put Get, Put Put Get Put Get Get,...}.

L has the interesting property that for any string α = $\alpha_1\alpha_2$ in L, where α_1 is

---

*) Precise, formal definitions of these operators appear, for example, in [Riddle 79b] and [Shaw,A 78]. It is hoped that the examples will clarify any problems related to my deliberately informal definitions.

any initial substring of α , the number of Put's in α_1 is always greater or equal to the number of Get's in α_1. This SE can model the operation constraints on a data type where retrieval of a data element (Get) is only possible if it can be matched with a preceding insertion (Put), such as an unbounded queue (Put = Insert, Get = Remove), an unbounded stack (Put = Push, Get = Pop), or a general semaphore initialized to zero (Put = V, Get = P).

Theoretically, RE's augmented by only the ⊚ operator are no more powerful than RE's ([Ginsberg 66], [Riddle 79b]); i.e., the resulting languages can still be described by RE's. However, from a practical viewpoint, the recognizing automata are much more complex [Ogden 78]. However, the further addition of ⊛ does increase the expressive power beyond that of RE's [Shaw,A 78]; for example, the language of Example 5 cannot be described by an RE. The exponential parsing algorithm in [Shaw,A 79] provides some insight into the practical complexity of parsing general SE's.

The interleaved model of concurrency has attracted some criticism because the "events" comprising concurrent activities become ordered under the shuffling operations whereas they may be truly parallel and asynchronous if, for example, there is no global clock in a system; it has also been argued that shuffling introduces unnecessary details into descriptions compared with a notation based on *partial orders* [Greif 77]. I will discuss this point further in the last section. It should be noted, however, that true simultaneity can be handled in SE's by bracketting the relevant entities with start and finish symbols and omitting the rest of the activities [Riddle 79b]; for example, if $start_i$ and $finish_i$ denote the beginning and end of activity i, the SE

$$(start_1\ finish_1)^* \circledcirc (start_2\ finish_2)^*$$

indicates that activity 1 is sequenced, activity 2 is sequenced, and activities 1 and 2 may proceed in parallel.

One unanticipated product of the interleaving research was the discovery of some new and interesting applications in command language description. While a language design tool is not the same as a software design tool, it is nevertheless the case that the design of language processors is strongly influenced by the language specification technique used. Welter first suggested that the shuffle ⊚ may be useful as an extension to BNF for command languages [Welter 76]. Applications of FE's in textual and graphics command language specification were demonstrated in [Shaw,A 78] and [Shaw,A 79]; some required the full power of SE's (⊚ and ⊛), as well as the synchronization facility of FE's.

RE's and finite state machines are the most commonly used formal schemes for defining command languages and their parsers. However, RE's are not convenient and/or adequate for some of the desired properties of interactive textual and graphics languages. Some of these properties that can be handled by SE's and FE's are the following.

First, it is often immaterial in which order a command and its parameters are entered, and at different times during an interactive session, different orderings may be convenient.

Example 6:

To take a simple case, computing the sum of two numbers x and y could be specified in at least three ways:

x + y , + x y , and x y +

Depending on the ways in which x, y, and + can be designated (e.g., pointing on a display, rotating a dial, typing, ...), all three may be desired. These options are described by an SE:

<+> ⊕ <number> ⊕ <number>

Second, several different command languages may be active at the same time, especially in graphics applications. At the extreme, each textual or graphical object may have its own language (e.g., [Ingalls 78]).

Example 7:

A text editing and placement language T is often used in conjunction with a drawing language D. (Let D define the operations for drawing and manipulating a box, and T be the means for specifying the text inside a box.) If T_1, T_2, ..., T_n are the possible commands of T and D_1, D_2, ..., D_m are those of D, then the FE:

$$(T \odot D)^* = ((T_1 \cup T_2 ... \cup T_n)^* \odot (D_1 \cup D_2 ... \cup D_m)^*)^*$$

is a reasonable description that maintains the separation of the languages yet indicates that the commands may be interleaved.

Third, in a manner similar to the last property, it is occasionally convenient to interleave several commands or sequences of commands from the *same* language. Several instantiations of the same command sequence may also be desirable.

Example 8:

Consider the file processing FE of Example 2 as a command language:

Open (Read ((Update Write) ∪ Print))* Close .

If one wishes to view and manipulate several files concurrently, the command language would be

(Open (Read ((Update Write) ∪ Print))* Close) ⊕

This FE reflects, for example, part of a program design system, where each procedure or module is a separate file and several partially defined procedures may be displayed and edited at the same time. Of course, each instantiation resulting from ● must be uniquely identified at some point.

An application related to the above that I am developing is the description of interactive document generation systems. Here, the "abstract syntax" of a document— its structure and components — has been defined as a combination of ordered and un-ordered sets of document objects, each of which can be similarly decomposed. I am using SE's and FE's to describe this abstract syntax.

Event Expressions

EE's were originally invented to specify the message transmission behavior among a set of interacting processes; for this application, the notation was called message transfer expressions (MTE's) and the basic symbols denote message types [Riddle 72a]. However, the scheme is completely general and can be used in other areas. The name "event expression" reflects this broader view. The basic symbols of EE's denote *events* — a general term for entities that may be partially or totally ordered by time (e.g., [Greif 77], [Lamport 78], [Reed 79]). Thus, any of the symbol interpretations mentioned at the end of the previous section are "events."

EE's are SE's with the addition of a synchronization mechanism. The idea is to impose some restrictions on shuffling so that in an interleave such as $(S_1 \bullet S_2)$ only a subset of the possible shuffles are in the language; the objective is to describe critical sections, message passing, and other synchronization constraints.

A point "in time" is marked in an EE with one of the special synchronization sym-bol pairs $(@, \overline{@})$, $(@_1, \overline{@}_1)$, etc. For example:

$$S_1 = (P\ @\ )*$$
$$S_2 = (\overline{@}\ C\ )*$$

The symbols are interpreted so that each $@_i$ must be matched with its "inverse" $\overline{@}_i$ and that the time points marked by each $@_i \overline{@}_i$ pair are forced to be identical. Taking the shuffle of S_1 and S_2, defined above, gives:

P @   P @   P @   P @   . . .
 1   2   3   4
@̄ C   @̄ C   @̄ C   @̄ C   . . .

The matched pairs at points 1,2,3,... cause the shuffling to be restricted to P (P ⊙ C)* C .

Critical section locking is specified by surrounding an expression with synchro-nization symbols for entry and exit.

Example 9:

$$(a \; @_1 \; b \; c \; @_2 \;) \odot (\; @_1 \; d \; e \; @_2 \;) \odot (\; \overline{@}_1 \; \overline{@}_2 \;)*$$

produces matching @ symbols in two possible ways (solid and dotted lines):

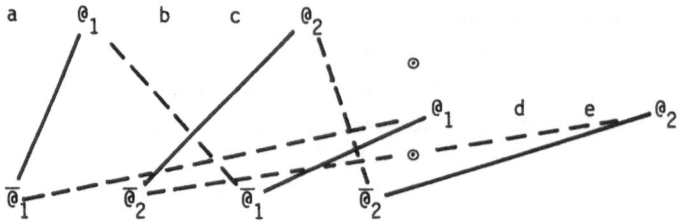

The EE describes the strings:

{a b c d e , a d e b c , d a e b c , d e a b c}.

bc and de are thus indivisible with respect to one another, and only four of the possible 10 shuffles of (a b c) and (d e) are in the language.

Example 10:

Let the events comprising a data base read, update, write, and print be defined by the EE's:

```
Read   = startread doread endread
Update = startupdate doupdate endupdate
Write  = startwrite dowrite endwrite
Print  = startprint doprint endprint
```

The EE:

$$(\; @_1 \; Read \; @_2 \; (\; (\; Update \; @_1 \; Write \; @_2 \;) \; \cup \; Print \;) \;) \overset{\bullet}{\bullet} \odot (\; \overline{@}_1 \; \overline{@}_2 \;)*$$

describes the behaviors or constraints:

1) Any number of (Read Update Write)'s and (Read Print)'s may be in execution concurrently (●).

2) Read's and Write's are mutually exclusive; neither can overlap other
   Read's or Write's $(@_1, @_2, \overline{@}_1, \overline{@}_2)$.

The synchronization method is quite elegant and its meaning can be expressed concisely: Treat the EE first as an ordinary SE and generate the language. Apply the transformations

$$@_i \; \overline{@}_i \rightarrow \lambda \; \text{and} \; \overline{@}_i \; @_i \rightarrow \lambda$$

for all synchronization symbols to each sentence repeatedly; this cancels out matched pairs. The language described by the EE is just those resulting sentences that have *no* remaining (uncancelled) synchronization symbols.

Example 11:

Treated as an SE, the expression (a @) $\overset{\bullet}{\,}$ ($\overline{@}$ b) $\overset{\bullet}{\,}$ describes the language:

$$\{\lambda,\ a\ @,\ \overline{@}\ b,\ a\ \underline{@\ \overline{@}}\ b,\ a\ @\ a\ @,\ a\ a\ @\ @,\ \overline{@}\ b\ \overline{@}\ b,\ \overline{@}\ \overline{@}\ b\ b,\ a\ \underline{@\ \overline{@}}\ b\ \overline{@}\ b,$$
$$\ldots,\ a\ a\ @\ \underline{@\ \overline{@}\ \overline{@}}\ b\ b,\ldots,\ a\ a\ a\ @\ @\ \underline{@\ \overline{@}\ \overline{@}\ \overline{@}}\ b\ b\ b,\ \ldots$$

The matched pairs that may be cancelled in the next step are underlined. After cancelling symbols, the resulting set is:

$$\{\lambda, a\ @, \overline{@}\ b,\ a\ b,\ a\ @\ a\ @,\ a\ a\ @\ @,\ \overline{@}\ b\ \overline{@}\ b,\ \overline{@}\ \overline{@}\ b\ b,\ a\ b\ \overline{@}\ b,\ \ldots,$$
$$a\ a\ b\ b,\ \ldots,\ a\ a\ a\ b\ b\ b,\ldots\}.$$

The elements with synchronization symbols still remaining are removed to give the final language, the one described by the EE, as:

$$\{a^n\ b^n : n \geq 0\}.$$

Example 12:

Consider a producer-consumer problem where a cyclic producer process fills a single-slot buffer and a consumer process empties the buffer. Let:

    ProducerProcess = (Produce Put)*
    ConsumerProcess = (Get Consume)*

We would like an EE that, on the one hand, describes the possible concurrencies among the events comprising Produce, Consume, Get, and Put, and that, at the same time, restricts the Put's and Get's to the behavior (Put Get)* defining the allowable operation sequences on a one-slot buffer. This behavior is specified by the EE:

$$(\text{ Produce } @_1 \text{ Put } @_2)* \circledcirc (@_3 \text{ Get } @_4 \text{ Consume })* \circledcirc (\overline{@}_1\ \overline{@}_2\ \overline{@}_3\ \overline{@}_4)*$$

The interactions among the three subexpressions are illustrated below:

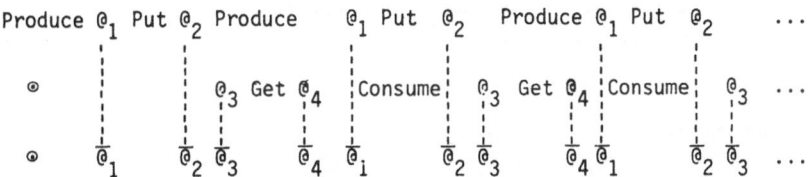

The synchronizing expression $(\overline{@}_1\ \overline{@}_2\ \overline{@}_3\ \overline{@}_4)*$ ensures the (Put Get)* constraint.

The EE scheme is deceptively powerful. In fact, it is descriptively universal; any language that can be recognized by a Turing machine or a computer with unbounded storage or that can be generated by an unrestricted (type 0) grammar, can be described by an EE ([Ogden 78], [Riddle 79b]). However, if the ⊚ operator is eliminated from EE's, the resulting notation is equivalent only to RE's [Riddle 79b]. While theoretically sufficient for any descriptive task, EE's are sometimes inconvenient when compared with other methods (and vice versa) on particular problems; specific comparisons are made in subsequent sections.

An elaborate set of axioms and rules of inference for manipulating EE's have been devised ([Riddle 72a], [Riddle 79b]). These are of potential value in proving equivalence of descriptions and deriving performance measures from EE's.

One major application of EE's has been in Riddle's software design methodology where EE's are the medium for behavioral specification and analysis. As outlined in [Riddle 79c], a software system with concurrently operating subsystems is modelled by a "Program Process Modelling Scheme" (PPMS) resembling a programming language but concerned only with message generation and transmission activities. There is a procedure for translating a set of programs (processes) given in the PPMS modelling language into an MTE that specifies the message transmission sequences generated by the system. Related work is reported in [Wileden 78] where a variant called constrained expressions can be derived from a dynamic process modelling scheme (DPMS).

Another application is the design notation DDN that is part of an interactive software design system currently under development ([Riddle 75], [Riddle 77], [Riddle 78a], [Riddle 78b], [Riddle 79a]). In DDN, internal system events are defined in terms of system state transitions, and the desired behavior is specified by a notation similar to EE's.

The PPMS model and derived MTE's have also been studied for performance prediction and analysis ([Sanguinetti 77], [Sanguinetti 78]). Message generation times and conditional branching probabilities associated with PPMS statements are mapped into time parameters and selection probabilities in the associated MTE's. In principle, the MTE's are then "evaluated" to produce performance measures such as the distribution, expected value, and variance of completion times. As in many of the RE-based applications presented in the paper, this approach appears promising but requires more development and experience before it can be used as a practical tool.

Flow Expressions

FE's were developed to describe the flows of computer system entities, such as resources, messages, jobs, commands, and control, through sequential and concurrent software components such as programs, procedures, processes, monitors, data types, and modules. The basic symbols of FE's are interpreted as atomic activities rather than events as in EE's, but this distinction may be academic since either notation may, in principle, be used for the same description task. However, the extensions to SE's are different and result in differences in specification convenience.

While the * operator is retained in FE's to express indefinite and usually finite repetition, a new *cyclic* operator ∞ is used to characterize the infinite repetitions that appear in cyclic processes and languages with non-terminating sentences ([Shaw,A 78], [Shaw,A 79]).

Example 13:

The producer-consumer example given in the last section might be more accurately described (excluding synchronization):

(Produce Put) $^{\infty}$ ⊚ (Get Consume) $^{\infty}$

The ∞ operator is primarily of descriptive value and appears to be difficult to handle analytically.

The synchronization scheme in FE's has a more direct programming connection than that in EE's, and is the major distinguishing difference between the notations. An FE can be *locked* for shuffling by bracketing it with lock symbols [,] , $_1$[,]$_1$, $_2$[,]$_2$, ... Flows inside the brackets are then treated as indivisible when interleaving other flows with the *same* lock brackets; e.g., ([a] ⊚ [b c]) describes the language {a b c , b c a}.

Example 14:

1) The EE of Example 9 has the equivalent FE:

(a [b c]) ⊚ ([d e])

b c and d e are "critical sections."

2) Example 10 may be rewritten as an FE:

([Read] ((Update [Write]) ∪ Print))$^{●}$

Example 15:

A high-level (gross) description of user job flows in an operating system may be:

($_1$[InputSpoolJob]$_1$ RunJob $_2$[OutputSpoolJob]$_2$)$^{●}$

Any number of jobs may be executing concurrently, only one InputSpoolJob and one OutputSpoolJob may proceed at a time but they may overlap each other, and RunJob's can proceed in parallel.

The second and more complex FE synchronization mechanism is a wait and signal facility similar to <u>binary</u> semaphores. The symbols $\sigma,\omega,\sigma_1,\omega_1,...$ are introduced into FE's, where σ_i is the analog of a "send signal i" (Dijkstra V) and ω_i corresponds approximately to a "wait for signal i" (Dijkstra P). A string is in the language described by an FE only if every ω_i can be matched (cancelled) with a preceding closest σ_i. For example, treating (a ω b) ● (d σ) as an SE, yields the strings:

a ω b d σ a ω d b σ a d ω b σ d a ω b σ d a ω σ b

<u>d a σ ω b</u>   <u>d σ a ω b</u>   <u>a d σ ω b</u>   a ω d σ b   a d ω σ b

Only the underlined strings have ω matched with a preceding σ. The FE then just describes the language {d a b , a d b}. The synchronization defined by this example is informally given by the following diagram:

Locks are definable using the σ/ω facility; for example, ([a] ⊙ [b c]) is equivalent to σ ((ω a σ) ⊙ (ω b c σ)) . However, locking appears so often in descriptions that it is convenient to have the separate [,] notation, both for brevity and to specifically distinguish this use. Locks are also useful in the command language application, discussed previously, when one wants to selectively prohibit shuffling.

In EE's, the paired symbols are symmetric - both @ $\overline{@}$ and $\overline{@}$ @ are legitimate, and the synchronization symbols must be adjacent (or eventually adjacent after cancellation of intervening symbols). By contrast, the FE scheme is asymmetric - an ω preceding a σ does not lead to a legitimate sentence, and the symbols need not be adjacent; a σ is capable of "action at a distance" so that a σ b c ω d yields the string a b c d . In addition, unconsumed σ's are lost but do not affect the resulting sentence while unmatched ω's, like uncancelled @'s or $\overline{@}$'s, do not result in sentences.

In the critical section (locking) case, these differences lead to easier FE descriptions, that is, fewer symbols are used. The opposite is true for describing some other strings as shown by the next example.

Example 16:
An FE for the language $\{a^n b^n : n \geq 0\}$ (Example 11) is

$$((\sigma_1 a \omega_2)^* (\sigma_3 b \omega_4) ^*)^* \odot (\omega_1 \sigma_2 \omega_3 \sigma_4)^\bullet$$

The equivalent EE $(a@)^\bullet (\overline{@}b)^\bullet$ is much simpler. The following diagram shows how aabb is generated from the FE:

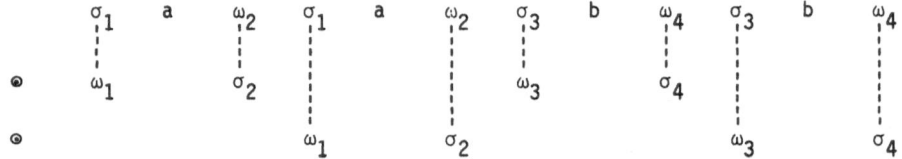

Example 17:
The producer-consumer example (Example 12) with cyclic processes and synchronization is given by the relatively simple FE:

$$\sigma_1 ((\text{Produce } \omega_1 \text{ Put } \sigma_2)^\infty \odot (\omega_2 \text{ Get } \sigma_1 \text{ Consume })^\infty)$$

Example 18:
A reader-writer problem (Example 4) is treated in more detail. Let a read operation be decomposed into two FE's, one designating a read request and the

second denoting the actual read:

Read = ReadRequest ActualRead.

Similarly, let Write = WriteRequest ActualWrite.

Example 4 can then be restated as:

((ReadRequest ActualRead)$^{\circledast}$ ∪ (WriteRequest ActualWrite))*

In these terms, the FE may be overly restrictive in that it does not provide for either:

- the overlap of WriteRequest's with ActualRead's and ActualWrite's, or
- the overlap of ReadRequest's with ActualWrite's.

It may not be restrictive enough in that it permits the overlapping of Read-Request's with each other. To allow overlapping as indicated above and, at the same time, make the requests mutually exclusive, synchronization symbols and locks are added as follows:

$$([\text{ReadRequest}] \; \omega_{R_1} \; \text{ActualRead} \; \sigma_{R_2} \quad)^{\circledast}$$

$$\circledast \quad (\; [\text{WriteRequest}] \; \omega_{W_1} \; \text{ActualWrite} \; \sigma_{W_2} \;)^{\circledast}$$

$$\circledast \quad (\; (\sigma_{R_1} \; \omega_{R_2} \;)^{\circledast} \cup (\quad \sigma_{W_1} \; \omega_{W_2} \;) \;)*$$

Some formal properties of FE's are given in [Shaw,A 78]. FE's that do not contain either $\circledast$ or ∞ are equivalent to RE's. It was conjectured in [Shaw,A 78] that EE's were more powerful than FE's but that apparently is false since proofs (e.g., [Araki 78a]) are being circulated that FE's are indeed universal also.

The analysis and verification possibilities appear to be identical to those of EE's ([Riddle 79b], [Shaw,A 78]). Some of these can be stated as general questions such as:

- Does a system exhibit a given behavior?
- What are the deadlock and starvation possibilities?
- Can a resource request or request sequence be serviced without violating any systems constraints?

In the FE context, these questions become:

- Membership problems: Is some string in the language described by an FE, or is it a prefix of some sentence in the language?
- Equivalence and inclusion problems: Are the languages described by two

FE's identical, or is one language included in the other?

● Emptiness problem: Is the language given by an FE empty?

These questions are either undecidable or unacceptably complex to answer (compute) for the general FE or EE case; instead one is forced to deal with restricted subsets or specific applications, much the same way as is done in the PE work.

In [Shaw,A 78], small examples illustrating a large number of software description applications were presented. These included modelling of sequential and parallel program control constructs, mappings between programs and FE's, descriptions of multiprogramming systems with centralized and distributed control, and specification of synchronization constraints in reader-writer, bounded and unbounded buffer, and resource priority scheduling systems; in addition, the application to command language definition was first developed. My most recent FE work has been concerned mainly with the new applications of interleaving to command language definition. FE's are also being used to describe and verify some design and research ideas for single-user, single-language distributed systems.

PATH EXPRESSIONS AND RELATED SCHEMES

The term "path expressions" denotes a number of notations all based on the scheme introduced by Campbell and Habermann [Campbell 74]. PE's were designed to describe execution sequences of operations or procedures, and the notational variations are meant to either simplify or handle some aspects of the description, analysis, and/or implementation of the constraints on operation executions. The PE orientation can be contrasted with that of EE's and FE's which are proposed as more general notational tools. PE's have been embedded directly in data type definitions and have also been used as an abstract "programming" language for systems of processes and resources. After presenting most of the PE notations, I will discuss these two applications in some detail and mention some other PE-related work in protection and graphics.

Path Notations

I will first discuss PE's that use RE's only. Then several parallel operators are introduced. Finally, schemes for conditional paths, priorities, and counting are described.

A PE is given by the syntax

path expr *end*

where expr describes execution sequences that may be indefinitely repeated. The *path end* is thus interpreted as * bracketting the expr.

Regular PE's (RPE's) are those that consist only of RE's.

> *Example 19:*
>
> *path* (Insert Look* Remove) ∪ Look *end*

This RPE may specify the restrictions of the operations Insert, Remove, and Look of a particular one-slot data type. The constraints are that all operations are sequential (mutually exclusive), two Inserts cannot occur without an intervening Remove, each Remove must be preceded by an Insert, and Look's can proceed at any time.

The PE literature employs the symbols ";" and either "+" or "," for concatenation and selection, respectively, but I will stay with the RE symbols of the earlier sections. Restrictions on the RPE's, such as no repeated procedure names, or limited or no use of the interior *, have been proposed to simplify implementation or analysis ([Campbell 74], [Campbell 76], [Lauer 75b]).

When *more* than one PE is permitted for a description of the same set of operations, the notation becomes more powerful ([Campbell 76], [Habermann 75a], and [Lauer 75b]). The interpretation is that operation histories must be compatible with *all* of the PE's in the *multiple* path specification. Multiple paths implicitly provide for some parallelism; if a relative ordering between two operations cannot be derived from the description, then the operations may proceed in parallel.

> *Example 20:*
>
> Consider the two RPE's
>
> *path* Fetch Print *end* and *path* Fetch Store *end*

The first expression states that Fetch's and Print's must alternate while the second one specifies alternating Fetch's and Store's. This is interpreted to mean that between two successive Fetch's there must be both a Store and a Print, between two successive Store's there must be a Fetch, and between two successive Print's there must be a Fetch. These constraints are roughly equivalent to these in the single SE

> (Fetch (Print ⊚ Store)) *

The difference is that Print and Store *could* be executed truly in parallel according to the RPE's. Because the RPE's give no constraints on the relative orderings of Print and Store, any or *no* ordering is permissible.

Possible parallel instantiations are specified with brackets { }. Thus {expr} describes zero or more parallel instantiations of expr; {expr} is approximately equivalent to the SE expr*, *except* that non-interleaved parallelism is also included in the former.

> *Example 21:*
>   The reader-writer constraints presented in Example 4 are re-expressed as a RPE with { }:
>   *path* { Read } ∪ Write *end*

The { } construct, RE's without *, and a mechanism for describing finite, parallel execution are the components of *Open Path Expressions* (OPE's) ([Campbell 76], [Campbell 79a]); OPE's use a different semantics than the other RE-based schemes. Finite, bounded parallelism is specified by the notation:

>   n : (expr)

where n is an integer and expr is an OPE. The meaning is that up to n simultaneous executions of the procedures specified by expr are possible, provided that any surrounding constraints are also satisfied. The semantics are such that, for example, the simple OPE's:

>   *path* p *end* and *path* a ∪ b *end*

each specify *no* restrictions whatever on the execution of p, a, or b; they essentially just declare the existence of p, a and b. However, the OPE:

>   *path* a b *end*

states that *each* b must be preceded by a matching a and contains no constraints on how many a's might be executed; it is therefore equivalent to {a b}.

> *Example 22:*
> 1) The OPE:
>   *path* 1: (Insert Remove) *end*
>   is equivalent to the RPE
>   *path* Insert Remove *end*
>   because it states that only one simultaneous execution of the sequences in parentheses is possible.
>
> 2) The OPE:
>   *path* 1: ({Read}∪Write) *end*
>   gives the same permissible executions as the RPE in Example 21; "1:" distributes through to {Read} and Write.

3) The OPE:

   path 3: (1: (Insert) 1: (Remove)) *end*

permits up to three parallel instantiations of Insert Remove sequences, but Insert's are mutually exclusive and Remove's are mutually exclusive.

OPE's are also of interest because there exists an implementation ([Campbell 79a], [Campbell 79b]). The range of describable behaviors is, however, not evident.

An explicit parallel operator has been defined for PE's ([Andler 79], [Campbell 76], [Habermann 75a]). A form of interleaving, called a "connected path" has also been proposed [Habermann 75a]. Neither of these operators seem to be used to any extent in the published PE examples but they could be employed for some of the same tasks as the SE ⊛.

Conditional paths ([Campbell 76], [Habermann 75a]) and predicate paths [Andler 79] offer a still finer control over the selection of path elements. As an alternative to the PE selection a ∪ b ∪ ... ∪ c, conditional paths permit a Boolean expression B_i (with no side effects) to be attached to each element i of the selection*:

  if B_a *then* a *else* *if* B_b *then* b ... *else* *if* B_c *then* c
 or
  if B_a *then* a *else* *if* B_b *then* b ... *else* c

In [Campbell 76], the semantics of the conditional elements is similar to Dijkstra's guarded commands.

Example 23:
  Consider a bounded stack of maximum size bound, with operations Push, Pop, and Top, and a data element count that contains the current number of elements in the stack. The operation constraints are given by the PE with conditional elements:

    path if count = 0 *then* Push
    else if count = bound *then* (Pop ∪ Top)
    else (Push ∪ Pop ∪ Top) *end*

In Andler's proposal for predicate paths [Andler 79], Boolean expressions (predicates) may be attached to any path element, and may use only constants and event counters that are associated with path elements; the predicate PE's also follow a guarded command semantics.

Priorities may be specified in the selection part of a PE using the comparison

---

*I am again taking liberties with the syntax of the published notations, as is done throughout the paper.

relations > and > instead of ∪ ([Campbell 76], [Habermann 75a]).

Example 24:

   Suppose the three operations on a memory resource are GetSpace, FreeSpace, and GarbageCollect. Then the PE with priorities

   path FreeSpace > GarbageCollect > GetSpace *end*

reflects the scheduling policy that FreeSpace requests have priority over GarbageCollect's, and GarbageCollect's have priority over GetSpace requests.

A counting facility, called a numeric path element, is used in [Flon 76] with the general form $(a - b - \ldots - c)^n$. This has the meaning $(a \cup b \cup \ldots \cup c)$ with the constraint that the relation $\#(a) \geq \#(b) \geq \ldots \geq \#(c) \geq \#(a) - n$ remains invariant, where $\#(x)$ means the number of executions of x.

Example 25:

   path (Insert - Remove)^{15} *end*

This describes the selection (Insert ∪ Remove)* with the restrictions that $0 \leq \#(\text{Insert}) - \#(\text{Remove}) \leq 15$, thus modelling, for example, operations on a bounded buffer with 15 slots. An equivalent SE is quite lengthy:

$$(\overset{15}{\underset{i=0}{\cup}} \ (\text{Insert Remove}) \ ⊙^j)*$$

where $a⊙^0 = \lambda$, and $a⊙^{i+1} = (a⊙^i ⊙ a)$ for $i \geq 0$.

Several other variations and additions have been suggested. By selecting "options" appropriately, one can easily produce many hundreds of different path notations.

The most "popular" path notations appear to be the following:

1) the original PE's introduced in [Campbell 74]. These consist of RE's without the internal * and the parallel { } without nesting. A procedure name (basic symbol) can only appear once in an expression,

2) RPE's and their restrictions,

3) multiple PE's with each individual PE being an RPE or a restricted RPE, and

4) OPE's.

The semantics of some of the notations have been defined more precisely so that implementations, analysis, or verification are possible. The definitional methods include:

1) relatively informal implementation-oriented descriptions. It is shown how the procedure constraints contained in a PE can be directly mapped either into Dijkstra P and V operations that are inserted before (prologue) and after (epilogue) the procedure or into more complex prologues and epilogues involving path "state" testing. The former techniques are used in defining the original notation [Campbell 74] and for OPE's ([Campbell 76], [Campbell 79a]) while the more complex scheme appears necessary for RPE's [Habermann 79a].

2) Petri net transformations. RPE's and their restrictions, and multiple PE's, have all been defined by exhibiting transformations that map the expressions into corresponding Petri nets ([Campbell 76], [Lauer 75b], [Lauer 78a]). The Petri nets define the PE's in the sense that the set of procedure execution sequences accepted or described by a PE is the set of event sequences generated by the corresponding net.

3) others such as axioms or invariants for program execution sequences constrained by PE's [Flon 76], partial ordering of events generated by program computations [Andler 79], and formal denotational and axiomatic techniques [Berzins 77].

The descriptive power of PE's is difficult to establish once one goes beyond RE's. The principal technique has been to relate PE classes to different classes of Petri nets ([Lauer 75b], [Lauer 78a]). This has also permitted the use of net theory to investigate properties such as deadlock and starvation, (e.g., [Lauer 78a], [Lauer 78b]).

Object Definitions

The intended application of PE's is in data type specifications. Instead of distributing synchronization primitives throughout the operations of software objects, it is proposed that each object centrally contain PE's that declare the required synchronization constraints on its use. This kind of data object has the form:

```
type <object name>
    <data declarations>
    path <expr> end
    operations
        procedure <procedure name and definition>
        procedure <procedure name and definition>
                 :
        procedure <procedure name and definition>
end type
```

The <expr> in the PE specifies the restrictions on the executions of the procedures declared in the object.

Example 26:

```
type OneSlotBuffer;
    frame:  message ; /* frame is a variable of type message.*/
    path Put  Get end;
    operations
        procedure Put(x:  message) ; /* Insert message into buffer.*/
        begin frame := x end ;
        procedure Get(x: message) ; /*  Remove message from buffer.*/
        begin x := frame end ;
end type
```

The PE describes the standard restrictions; that is, Get and Put are critical sections and must follow in sequence. It is not necessary to either surround calls of Get and Put by synchronization operations or to distribute those operations through Get and Put.

The idea of removing synchronization specifications from operations and user programs, and inserting them as PE's in object declarations is extremely attractive. This approach is contrasted with the use of monitors where each procedure is implicitly a critical section and synchronization primitives (wait and signal) are distributed through the procedures. However, while PE's embedded in data types provide elegant solutions to many synchronization problems, it is not evident that they are powerful enough to handle *all* such problems; it appears that one may eventually be forced to extend PE's to a universal-programming or description language or provide some "escape" to express synchronization outside the PE mechanism. These remarks apply primarily to systems where the PE is part of the *programming* language as opposed to the *specification* language.

The literature contains many examples of object (type) definitions with PE's used as above, including ring buffers (bounded buffers), Dijkstra P and V, stack, alarm clock service, disk scheduler, message passing, and various other resource allocators; for example, [Andler 77], [Campbell 74], [Campbell 76], [Campbell 79b], and [Habermann 75a]. PE's in abstract data types also appear to simplify verification, primarily because (when) the invariants derived from the PE may be almost identical to the invariant to be proven ([Andler 78], [Flon 76]).

There exist two programming implementations of data types with PE's. OPE's have been included in the Path Pascal system recently described in [Campbell 79a] and [Campbell 79b]. This system extends Pascal with processes, OPE's, and encapsulated data objects. There is also an implementation reported in [Andler 79] which introduces types into Algol68 [Andler 77]. RPE's plus predicates, called predicate path expressions (PPE's), are used. The implementations are important to test the practicality of the PE ideas for a *system programming* language; they are also of great

potential value in design *simulation* and for determining the benefits and limitations
of PE's in larger contexts.

Some PE Related Work

Some other recent related proposals are also of interest. In the PE work, the
operations of the data type may be executed by *any* process provided the PE is not
violated. It is often the case, however, that some selectivity is desirable to ensure
that users employ the type properly.

> *Example 27:*
>
> Suppose a data object has operations Startread and Endread constrained to
> execute in sequence by the PE
>
> > *path* Startread Endread *end*
>
> A Startread might be executed by a user U_1 followed by the execution of End-
> read by a different user U_2. While this sequence may be acceptable in some
> applications, there are many where it would be incorrect; only the user that
> executes Startread should be able to subsequently execute Endread.

RE's called *access right expressions* (ARE's) are suggested in [Kieburtz 78] to
handle the above kind of situation. A set of ARE's is given in the definition of an
object. When a user program U declares an *instance* of the type, it also specifies a
subset of the object's ARE's. U can then only execute operations according to the
sequencing declared in its instance. Thus, in the example above, *each* user could get
an instance of the ARE (Startread Endread)*.

A variation of PE's has also been suggested in a completely different domain —
the specification of logical graphics input devices ([van den Bos 78], [van den Bos 79a],
[van den Bos 79b]). The sequences of input events comprising a logical device are
described by a PE-like notation, an *input expression* (IE), that appears as part of
the device definition. The device definition, a data object, contains code that is
invoked whenever an input sequence satisfies the expression in the IE. These ideas
have recently been implemented as an extension of the C language under the UNIX system [Plasmeijer 78].

> *Example 28:*
>
> *input* (Key("+") Key(CR)) ∪ Button(6) ∪ Pick("menu",5) *end*

The above IE describes three simple input event sequence alternatives:

1) a '+' followed by a carriage return (CR) entered through a keyboard,

2) the single event corresponding to depressing button number 6, and

3) the single event corresponding to pointing (on a display screen) at item number 5 of the segment named "menu."

The IE is satisfied if any of these sequences occur; the code associated with the IE would then be executed.

The IE's are RE's plus prioritites, a parallel operator, and conditional elements. The basic symbols denote either input primitives with parameters, or higher level logical devices defined previously. This approach has some similarities with my work on command languages mentioned previously.

System Descriptions: Path and Process Expressions

Another major class of applications employs PE ideas to describe both the flow through the procedures of each process in a (sub) system *and* the constraints on the procedure executions ([Campbell 76], [Lauer 75b], [Lauer 78a], [Lauer 78b], [Torrigiani 77]). The latter PE's are essentially abstractions of data type definitions, i.e., resource objects, and may consist of multiple PE's; the process paths approximate the control flow of processes.

Example 29:

> *begin path* lock unlock *end*
> p_1: *process* compute1 lock CS1 unlock *end*
> p_2: *process* compute2 lock CS2 unlock *end*
> *end*

The path specifies a locking mechanism (binary semaphores), restricting the lock and unlock calls to the sequences described by (lock unlock)*. p_1 and p_2 are cyclic processes with cyclic execution sequences given, for example, by the RE's:

(compute1 lock CS1 unlock)$^\infty$ and (compute2 lock CS2 unlock)$^\infty$

The process flows are constrained by the path declarations so that CS1 and CS2 are mutually exclusive (critical sections); compute1 may proceed in parallel with any of the operations of p_2 and analogously for compute2.

A program in the basic path/process notation is then a collection of paths followed by a collection of processes. The multiple paths are interpreted as in RPE's and the processes are independent entities with execution sequences subject to the constraints of the paths. RE's and restricted RE's are used for the path and process notations. The semantics of the path/process languages are described by Petri nets

and are related to various classes of nets. One aim of this work is to use net
theory as a basis for proving properties of the languages and programs written in the
languages. Much emphasis has been placed on the notion of "adequacy;" this is a type
of correctness, defined in net theory, that implies freedom from deadlock.

The basic path/process notation is extended to permit the definition of classes
of paths and their instantiation ([Campbell 76], [Lauer 75b], [Lauer 78a],
[Torrigiani 77]). The most recent development is the COSY language which contains a
macro facility with elaborate path/process generators ([Lauer 78a], [Torrigiani 77]).

Example 30: (from [Lauer 78a])
Below is a COSY program:

```
begin array DEPOSIT, REMOVE(n)
       [path DEPOSIT(i) REMOVE(i) end i̅ /1,n,1]
       [ process ∪(DEPOSIT) end i̅ /1,m,1]
       [ process ∪(REMOVE) end i̅ /1,k,1]
end
```

The path declaration "macro" expands to n paths:

path DEPOSIT(1) REMOVE(1) *end* ... *path* DEPOSIT(n) REMOVE(n) *end*

The array declares each DEPOSIT(i) and REMOVE(i), i=1,...,n as a separate
distinct operation. The notation ∪(DEPOSIT) is an abbreviation for

DEPOSIT(1) ∪ DEPOSIT(2) ... ∪ DEPOSIT(n)

The first process then expands to m processes, each a copy of

process DEPOSIT(1) ∪ ... ∪ DEPOSIT(n) *end*

Similar expansions hold for the second process. The COSY program then defines
m+k processes, subject to restrictions given by n paths. It models an n-slot
buffer that permits a process to DEPOSIT into an empty slot and REMOVE from a
full one (one that had been previously DEPOSIT'ed).

The COSY notation has been used to describe many small systems including buffering programs with different disciplines, extended (and bounded) semaphores, and a
simple spooling system ([Lauer 78a], [Lauer 78b], [Shields 78], [Torrigiani 78]).
Some suggestions are given in [Shields 79] for extending the notation to handle unbounded elements, for example, unbounded counters. As in the other PE notations,
COSY does not have the full power of a general programming language (Turing machine).

172

ASSESSMENT AND FUTURE DIRECTIONS

Many regular expression based schemes have been proposed as design aids for
describing sequential and concurrent software. The numerous specification examples
appearing in published reports demonstrate, at least on a small scale, that convenient
and tractable descriptions can be produced with these notations; in particular, standard, and difficult, synchronization problems, such as those involving critical sections, reader-writers, producer-consumers, buffering, and priority scheduling, have
surprisingly simple descriptions. In addition, the notations have resulted in some
new approaches in systems analysis and programming.

I believe that the principal contributions, and novel and useful ideas of those
works are the following:

1) The behavior of a system should (can?) be modelled in terms of sequences of
   events, flows, or operations that may occur during execution. Much of systems design is concerned, directly or indirectly, with the specification of
   permissible sequences.

2) Given 1), RE's are a natural notation on which to base a nonprocedural design language.

3) Shuffling operators can express concurrent and interleaved behaviors, and
   are a natural extension to RE's.

4) Given 1), path expressions are an attractive way to describe synchronization constraints on operations in resource objects.

5) The resulting EE, FE, and PE notations have theoretical properties and
   underlying models of computing that are interesting in their own right.

The EE and FE notations are similar in that they both use the same shuffling
operators (SE's); however, they have different synchronization schemes, and a distinction is made between indefinite repetition (*) and cyclic or infinite repetition (∞)
in FE's. Examples can be found where either scheme provides a simpler specification
than the other. It is difficult to compare the analysis possibilities of the two
notations, but software analysis applications have been more extensively investigated
in the EE case.

PE's, as a general class of notations, have several properties that distinguish
them from EE's and FE's. The extension of RE's that appear in PE's are completely
different than the synchronization mechanisms of EE's and FE's. The parallel
operator { } can be modelled by $\circ$ but interleaving is not the same as potentially
asynchronous concurrency; multiple paths also have parallelism by default. In both
cases, the total orderings of elements in FE and EE descriptions are replaced by

partial orderings. None of the PE schemes are universal while EE's and FE's are capable of describing *any* computable constraint. The specific interpretation of PE elements as procedure executions and the programming language flavor of some of the extensions, e.g., conditional elements, also permit some descriptions that are not easy to formulate in EE's or FE's. While FE's and EE's are not meant to be implemented in programming languages, PE's are used in both the design and programming stages of software development.

Research with all of these schemes has led to some notational issues that should be further analyzed:

1) bounded vs.unbounded parallelism. Should unbounded parallelism be expressible in a software design notation? Is an operator such as ⊛ or { } necessary? Bounded schemes are more tractable theoretically (e.g., Petri net models) but unbounded methods appear to be more natural when exact numbers of resources or processes are not known, or when they may vary dynamically.

2) interleave vs.concurrency. Interleaving is an adequate model for concurrency in most applications but it can well be argued, at least philosophically, that it does not always capture the notion of concurrency, especially for distributed asynchronous systems. Parallel operators such as the PE { } are one solution but they appear to be difficult to formally manipulate. Notations based directly on partial orderings of events offer another possible approach that might be developed further into a description notation ([Greif 77], [Lamport 78], [Reed 79]). Here, for two events a and b, either a precedes b (a→b), b precedes a (b→a), or neither (a↛b and b↛a); in the last case, the events are concurrent.

3) limited power. How descriptively powerful should a design notation be? One apparent reason for each proposed extension of PE's is the discovery of a new problem that requires the extension; this is inevitable unless the notation is universal. However, a design notation does not necessarily have to be universal, especially if it describes most practical behaviors conveniently and precisely, and provides reasonable approximations to others.

Design notations are only useful if they facilitate the analysis and implementation phases of software development. I have referred to some of the work in these other phases but it is fair to say that the new notations have not yet been used as practical tools. On the other hand, they do provide a precise software specification language that can be clearly independent of implementations as compared with procedural design languages.

The many examples and theoretical results show that the RE-based notations are promising. Some practical experiences in software design and development would seem to be the next logical step. The experiences obtained with the several implementations should be of value in further assessing the notations ([Andler 77], [Campbell 79b], [Plasmeijer 78], [Riddle 78a]).

There are also some new description applications worth pursuing. The problems of distributed systems and message communication patterns within them are still being formulated, and the RE description notations may be useful for problem and design specifications. Coroutines have been recognized as a fundamental control structure for both simulating concurrent activities and for naturally interleaved tasks; FE's and EE's, which can describe coroutine-like interleaving, should be studied as a design notation for coroutine-based software. The uses of interleaving in command language specifications ([Shaw,A 78], [Shaw,A 79]) and PE's in input processing ([van den Bos 79a], [van den Bos 79b]) are still relatively undeveloped. Finally, there are some protection applications, such as the ARE proposal [Kieburtz 78], where constraints on sequences of operations, messages, and other entities are required; two of these are access control lists for files — who can use a particular file and how — and limitations on process operations such as those expressed by capabilities.

INDEX TO SYMBOLS AND ABBREVIATIONS

The entry for each item indicates the page where the item is defined.

Symbol or Abbreviation	Meaning	Page
ARE	access right expression	169
EE	event expression	155
FE	flow expression	158
IE	input expression	169
MTE	message transfer expression	155
OPE	open path expression	164
PE	path expression	162
RE	regular expression	149
RPE	regular path expression	163
SE	shuffle expression	152
∪	RE selection	149
⋆	Kleene star	149
λ	empty string	150
⊚	SE shuffle operator	152
●	closure of ⊚	152
$\theta, \overline{\theta}$	EE synchronization symbols	155
∞	FE cyclic operator	158
[,]	FE lock	159
σ,ω	FE signal and wait	159
{ }	PE simultaneous execution	163

John Miles Smith
Diane C.P. Smith

Computer Corporation of America

A data base is a *simulation* of some real-world phenomena that is *repre-sented* on a computing machine. A long-standing goal of data base technology has been to *specify* the semantics of the simulation while suppressing all details of its computer representation. To meet this goal, a variety of specification languages called *data base models* have been developed. These models are oriented towards applications where large quantities of intricately interrelated data are manipulated by multiple users.

These applications are, in some ways, more exacting than the systems programming applications which have motivated most other specification languages. A rich typing structure, which includes higher-order types, subtypes and component types, is necessary. A flexible attribute structure, which allows types to have attributes, must also be provided. Data sharing and side-effects must be handled in a simple and natural way. This requires a powerful predicate language for identifying individuals on the basis of their structure. A data base approach can therefore bring a different perspective to software specification.

INTRODUCTION

A data base is a *simulation* of some real-world phenomena that is *represented* on a computing machine. A long-standing goal of data base technology has been to *specify* the semantics of the simulation while suppressing all details of its computer repre-sentation. To meet this goal, a variety of specification languages called *data base models* have been developed. These models are oriented towards applications where large quantities of intricately interrelated data are manipulated by multiple users.

These applications are, in some ways, more exacting than the systems programming applications which have motivated most other specification languages. A rich typing structure, which includes higher-order types, subtypes and component types, is neces-sary. A flexible attribute structure, which allows types to have attributes, must also be provided. Data sharing and side-effects must be handled in a simple and natural way. This requires a powerful predicate language for identifying individuals on the basis of their structure. A data base approach can therefore bring a differ-ent perspective to software specification.

The important ideas in data base models have been obscured from those outside
the data base community by two factors. First, the jargon of data base models has
developed separately from that of programming languages and software engineering.
Second, data base models have often had both a *specification* aspect and an *implemen-*
tation aspect. Unfortunately, these two aspects are not always carefully separated
and much confusion has resulted. To overcome these problems, in the next section we
provide a historical review of the specification aspects *only* of data base models,
and introduce a consistent, programming language oriented terminology. The reader is
forewarned that the usage of terms when discussing a particular data base model may
be different from the usage traditionally associated with that model.

The most recent data base models, which are collectively referred to here as
semantic models, consider only specification aspects. The differences among these
models, while often significant, mainly concern which semantic aspects should be
included and how. One such model, called the *semantic hierarchy model*, is described
in detail in the third section. This model represents the authors' perception of
which semantic aspects are important and not a consensus of data base researchers.
This model has the advantage of being quite simple and easy to present formally.
Short examples are given to illustrate how various features of the model can be used
in the specification of commercial applications. Several important features of the
semantic hierarchy model are not discussed -- these are general constraint handling,
exception handling and concurrency control.

Data base models are not usually employed for specifying systems software and,
indeed, many are poorly designed for this purpose. The main problem is that many
models only incorporate the *primitive* operations needed for data manipulation. They
assume that procedural and control structure capabilities are provided by some host
programming language. Unfortunately, the data structuring facilities of the model
are often badly mismatched with those of the language. This causes specifications
to acquire an unnecessary complexity. However, the semantic hierarchy model contains
its own control and procedural capabilities, and the fourth section demonstrates that
this model can give simple, intuitive specifications for four classical systems software data types -- binary tree, stack, queue and symbol table.

DATA BASE MODELS

To appreciate a data base approach to software specification, it is helpful to
briefly review the development of data base models. Since there is a large, and
growing, number of data base models it is impossible to consider each one individually.
Fortunately, they can be categorized into five quite distinct classes. In order of
sophistication (and roughly historical development) these classes are the *file*,
hierarchic [ACM 76], *network* [ACM 76], *relational* [ACM 76] and *semantic* classes

([Bachman 77], [Chen 76], [Copeland 78], [Hammer 78], [Kent 78], [Mylopolus 78], [Shipman 79], [Smith 77b]). Models from the first three classes are in active use in commercial data base systems. Relational data base systems are just beginning to enter the commercial field, while semantic models are still in the research stage.

The development of data base models has been driven largely by one problem -- to simulate, in an acceptably efficient manner, the activities of a business enterprise. The early models were developed in the days of sequential secondary storage devices. These models were predominantly concerned with representation details and supported only a limited simulation semantics. As hardware has improved, it has become possible to support a more sophisticated semantics. Since the emphasis of this paper is on specification, the representation aspects of the data base models will be largely ignored.

A data base model consists of five (semantic) components: a data space, a type definition language, manipulation primitives, a predicate language, and control structures. The *data space* contains a set of individuals and certain relationships between them. The *type definition language* is used to define constraints on the relationships in the data space. Individuals in the data space may be created and destroyed, and their relationships modified, via the *manipulation primitives*. The *predicate language* allows individuals to be identified by their semantic properties. Predicates and manipulation primitives may be embedded in *control structures* to form complete data base procedures.

DATA SPACE

Model Class	Individuals	Relationships		
	type/primitive partition	instance-of	attribute-of	orderings
file	Yes	prim x type	prim x prim	prim x prim
hierarchic	Yes	prim x type	prim x prim	prim x prim
network	Yes	prim x type	prim x prim	prim x prim
relational	Yes	prim x type	prim x prim	-
semantic	Yes	indiv x type	indiv x indiv	-

Figure 13: The data space for each class of model

Figure 13 describes the data space for each class of data base model. All models partition individuals into *types* and *primitives*. The set of types is assumed to remain relatively unchanged during the lifetime of a particular data base — however, the set of primitives may change quite rapidly. All models also capture the *instance-of* relationship between an individual and a type. For example, the individual Joe may be an instance of the type janitor.

In general, if an individual A is an instance of an individual B, then B is certainly a type. However, A may be *either* a primitive *or* a type. If A is indeed a type then B is a *higher-order* type relative to A. Higher-order types can occur quite frequently in data bases. For example, the type employee-type is of a higher order than the type janitor since janitor is an instance of employee-type. Only the semantic models support higher order types. All other models require that the instances of types be primitive individuals.

All models also support the *attribute-of* relationship between individuals. An individual A is an attribute of an individual B if B relates A to other individuals. As an example, consider the marriage in which Joe marries Mary. This marriage is an individual and the individuals Joe and Mary are its attributes. As another example, consider the university class in which Jack teaches Joe and Mary about mathematics. In this case, Jack, Joe, Mary and mathematics are attributes of this particular class. The attributes of an individual have a separate existence before they are related by the creation of the individual itself. For example, Joe and Mary exist before they are involved in their marriage.

The semantic models support the *attribute-of* relationship between *any* pair of individuals regardless of whether they are types or primitives. In particular, types can both be attributes of other individuals and also have other individuals as their attributes. This capability is frequently useful in data bases. For example, the type janitor may be an attribute of Joe, and the union Local-35 may be an attribute of janitor. All other models only support the *attribute-of* relationship between primitive individuals.

Some data base models support orderings over primitive individuals such as *next-to* or *next-with-common-attribute-to*. Such orderings are primarily exploited for efficiency reasons and do not necessarily reflect any semantic qualities. Furthermore, a semantic ordering of individuals can always be captured by giving each individual an appropriate attribute. Special ordering relationships are therefore superfluous from a semantic viewpoint. In the relational and semantic models, ordering relationships are not explicitly provided.

Figure 14 shows the properties of the type definition languages for each class of data base model. A type definition specifies two distinct kinds of constraints over the *instance-of* and *attribute-of* relationships in the data space. These are *subtype* constraints and *component type* constraints. If a type A is a subtype of a type B then every instance of A is also an instance of B. An instance of a type B is only allowed to have instances of a type A as its attributes if A is a component type of B.

TYPE DEFINITION LANGUAGE

Model Class	Subtypes		Component Types		
	support	meta-structure	single attributes	multiple attributes	meta-structure
file	No	---	Yes	No	Two-level Inverted Tree
hierarchic	No	---	Yes	No	Inverted Tree
network	No	---	Yes	No	Recursive Hierarchy
relational	No	---	Yes*	No	Recursive Hierarchy*
semantic	Yes	Hierarchy	Yes	Yes	Recursive Hierarchy

*The original formulation of Relational Model did not fully support component types; however, it was extended to do so in [Smith 77a].

Figure 14: The type definition languages for each class of model.

If a type definition specifies that A is a subtype of B, it means that every instance of A has at least *two* types. For example, if janitor is a subtype of employee then Joe is both a janitor and an employee. Multiple types cannot be handled satisfactorily by most data base models -- they require some additional mechanism for distinguishing when instances of different types are the *same* individual or *different* individuals. Only the semantic models adequately support subtypes. The declaration of subtypes via type definitions imposes a hierarchic metastructure over the set of types.

Assume that A is a component type of B. The type B has *single* A attributes if each B instance has at most one A attribute. Otherwise, the type B has *multiple* A attributes. For example, the type marriage may have component types groom and witness. In this case, marriage has a single groom attribute but multiple witness attributes. The declaration of component types via type definitions imposes a second hierarchic metastructure over the set of types. However, unlike the subtype meta-structure, the component type metastructure may be recursive.

All data base models support component types with single attributes, although the hierarchic metastructure is often severely restricted. For example, the hierarchic models limit the metastructure to an inverted tree[*] whereas the file models only allow a two-level inverted tree. These semantic limitations allow simple and effi-cient representation schemes to be used. Only the semantic models allow component types with multiple attributes. The other models require an additional mechanism for distinguishing when instances with different attributes (of the same component type) are the same individual or different individuals.

The development of type definition languages can be summarized in the following way. Before the semantic models, development was largely concerned with efficient representations for supporting single attribute component types. The semantic models ignore these representation issues and concentrate on fully supporting subtypes and component types. These two type disciplines impose two distinct hierarchic meta-structures over types.

Both of these metastructures correspond to forms of successive *abstraction* which make it easier to understand the complex relationships in the data space. A subtype hierarchy corresponds to successive *generalization* of types by taking their union. A component type hierarchy corresponds to successive *aggregation* of types by taking their cartesian product. Generalization and aggregation are important issues in data base design [Smith 78a]. It is important to keep in mind that the hierarchic metastructures are *semantic structures* and not just arbitrary *representational schemes*.

Figure 15 shows the manipulation primitives for each class of model. The *create* operation forms a new individual in the data base and states the type(s) to which it belongs and the attribute(s) that it involves. In general, the more sophisticated the type definition language, the more complex a create operation needs to be. The *destroy* operation removes an individual from the data base. The *modify* operation changes the types and/or the attributes of an *existing* individual.

The create and destroy operations can only be applied to primitive individuals, since the creation or destruction of types[**] affects the semantic constraints on the data space. However, modify operations can be applied to individuals of any order.

---

[*] A *tree* is a hierarchy in which each node has at most one *incoming* edge. An "inverted tree" is a hierarchy in which each node has at most one *outgoing* edge.

[**] Some data base models provide a *metaprimitive* for the creation of new types and definition of their subtypes and component types.

With the exception of the file model, all models allow manipulation on an individual-
by-individual basis. The file model, due to restrictions imposed by sequential
access storage media, does not allow modification and requires all individuals to be
created or destroyed in one entire operation.

MANIPULATION PRIMITIVES

Model Class	create	destroy	modify	basis
file	Yes	Yes	No	Entire
others	Yes	Yes	Yes	Individual

Figure 15: The manipulation primitives for each class of model.

Figure 16 shows the predicate languages for each class of data base model. A
predicate exploits the type metastructure of a data base to identify individuals by
their semantic properties. All languages provide binary relations (or functions)
over individuals which mean *attribute-of*, *instance-of* and *identity*. These primitives
allow individuals to be identified via their attributes and types. However, the file
model only allows "simple" predicates to be formed which test "key" attributes. The
hierarchic and network models allow boolean combinations of predicates, while the
semantic and relational models provide a full first-order logic capability.

Predicate languages for semantic models obtain additional expressive power by
letting variables range over *all* individuals (of any order), rather than just over
primitive individuals. This enables types to be quantified and also allows types to
be identified by their attributes, their instances and (if present) their own higher-
order types. Notice that, even with these capabilities, predicates are still
expressed in a first-order logic. This is possible since the notion of "type" is
captured by the non-logical primitive *instance-of* and not by the semantics of the
logic itself.

The predicate languages for the file, hierarchic and network models contain
sequencing relations, such as *next-to* or *next-with-common-attribute-to*, between
individuals. These primitives allow individuals to be identified relative to various
sequential orderings which are defined over them. As described earlier, these
sequential orderings are primarily exploited for efficiency reasons and are semantically

PREDICATE LANGUAGE

Model Class	Functions (F) and Relations (R)			Variable Range	Logical Power	Sequencing Relations
	instance-of	attribute-of	identity			
file	R	F	R	Primitive individuals	Simple	Yes
hierarchic	R	F	R	Primitive individuals	Boolean	Yes
network	R	F	R	Primitive individuals	Boolean	Yes
relational	R	F	R	Primitive individuals	First-order Logic	No
semantic	R	R	R	All individuals	First-order Logic	No

Figure 16: The predicate languages for each class of model.

superfluous. A major contribution of the relational model was to hide the housekeeping details associated with the use of sequencing primitives.

The operations invoked by data base users are constructed by embedding predicates and manipulation primitives in *control structures*. Most data base models do not explicitly provide control structures. Instead, they are assumed to be provided by a host programming language that is interfaced with the data base model. This approach introduces unnecessary complications since the data definition facilities of the host language and the data base model are usually mismatched. Indeed, the host language facilities are usually more *representation* oriented (e.g., *array* or *record* structures) than the model facilities. As a result, it is necessary to build facsimiles of data base individuals within host language types. It is very difficult to smoothly integrate a conventional programming language (e.g., Cobol or Pascal) and a data base model without compromising one or the other. Some interesting developments in this direction include Pascal-R [Schmidt 77] and Plain [Wasserman 78b].

To avoid interfacing difficulties, it is essential that a data base model provide its own control structures. This approach is taken in some semantic models, for example Taxis [Mylopolus 78] and the semantic hierarchy model discussed in the next section. Control structures are needed to define *functions* and *procedures*. Functions, when invoked with the necessary parameters, identify individuals or sets of individuals within the data space. Functions are defined in terms of predicates expressed in the predicate language. Procedures have side-effects which change the state of the data space via the manipulation primitives. Procedures may also be functional in that their invocations identify individuals. Procedures need control structures for *conditional* execution and for *sequencing*. Both functions and procedures need control structures for *recursion* or *iteration*.

THE SEMANTIC HIERARCHY MODEL

The purpose of this section is to describe the *semantic hierarchy* model. The most critical aspects of this model are its data space, type definition language and update primitives and so these will be specified quite formally. The predicate language and control structures are more familiar and will be described more cursorily.

> *Definition 1:*
> A *data space* D is a 7-tuple $<I_t, I_p, N, \psi, \varepsilon, \equiv, \pi>$
> where:
> - I_t is the set of *type* individuals,
> - I_p is the set of *primitive* individuals,
> - N is the set of individual *names*,
> - $\psi: N \xrightarrow[\text{into}]{1:1} I$ is the name/individual mapping where
> $I = I_t \cup I_p$,
> - $\varepsilon \subseteq I \times I_t$ is the *instance-of* relationship,
> - $\equiv \subseteq I \times I$ is the *identity* relationship, and
> - $\pi \subseteq \varepsilon \times I$ is the *attribute-of* relationship.

A data space contains a set I of individuals which is partitioned into types (I_t) and primitives (I_p). These individuals are intended to be analogs of *real-world* objects. Individuals may have names (N). A name forms the *external* representation of an individual for purposes of input and output. It is not required that an individual have a name, but if it does, the name must be unique and apply to no other individual. The mapping ψ from names to individuals is therefore *one-to-one* and *into*.

The relationship ε is the *instance-of* relationship between an individual and a type. The relationship $\equiv$ is the *identity* relationship on the set of individuals. The relationship π is the *attribute-of* relationship between an *instance of a type* and another individual. The previous section actually oversimplified the *attribute-of* relationship by suggesting that it occurred between one individual and another. In fact, it is the *instantiation of a type* (i.e., an individual together with one of its types) that is important rather than just the individual itself. The motivation for this treatment is easily understood with the aid of an example.

Figure 17 is a pictorial representation of a data space in which individuals are represented by dots, names by strings positioned near the named individual, and ε and π relationships by edges. The figure contains three types - marriage, parson, and groom. M1 and M2 are instances of marriage, while Joe is an instance of both groom and parson. The π relationship shows that Joe is the parson attribute of marriage M1 but the groom attribute of marriage M2. If π were treated simply as a relationship between individuals, this distinction would not be possible.

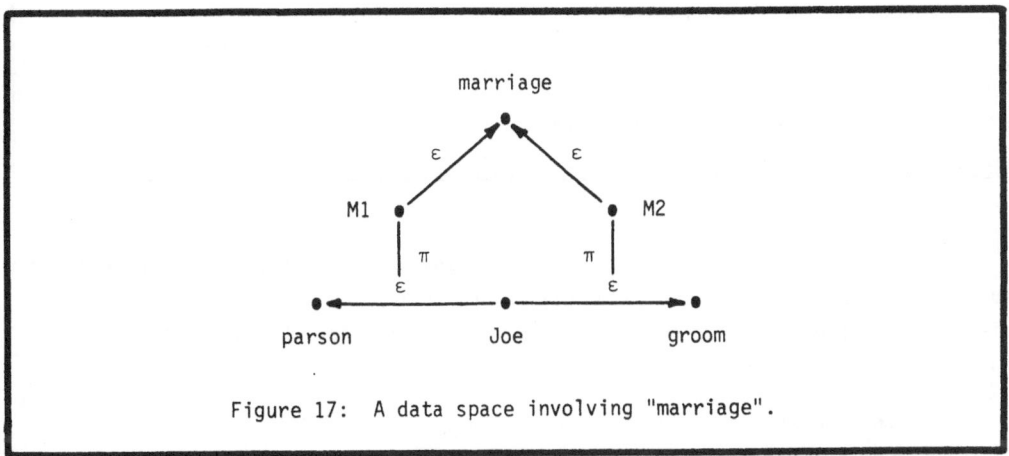

Figure 17: A data space involving "marriage".

A second example of a data space, this one involving higher order types and attributes of types, is shown in Figure 18. C3 is an instance of car and car is an instance of vehicle-type. Vehicle-type is therefore a higher order type. Car has the parking-lot attribute SE. This indicates that cars in general, rather than specific cars, have the SE lot. SE is therefore an attribute of a type. C3 has the maker attribute Ford, while Ford in turn has the location attribute Detroit.

186

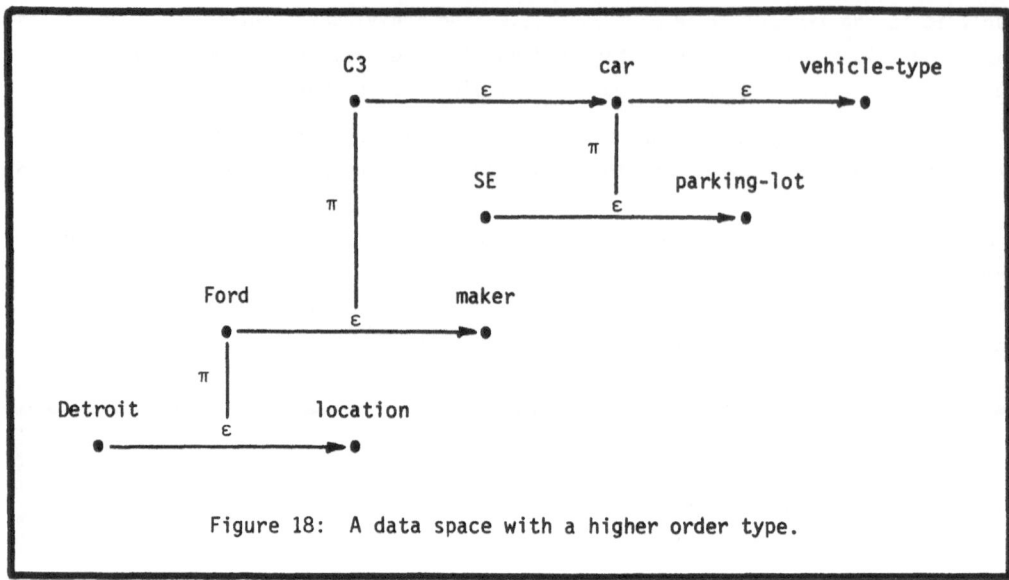

Figure 18: A data space with a higher order type.

It should be clear that a data space with many individuals will be very difficult to access and manipulate unless some discipline is imposed on relationships. Such a discipline is provided by a *type definition*, or *schema*, for the data space.

> *Definition 2*:
> A *type definition* S is a 3-tuple $\langle N_t, sub, com \rangle$ where:
> - $N_t \subseteq N$ is the set of type names,
> - $sub \subseteq N_t \times N_t$ is the *subtype-of* metarelationship, and
> - $com \subseteq N_t \times N_t$ is the *component-type-of* metarelationship.

A type definition for a data space includes the names (N_t) for the types of the data space. It will be assumed here that the set of types is fixed for the lifetime of the data base. The metarelationship *sub* between type names determines when one type is a subtype of another type. The metarelationship *com* between type names determines when one type is a component type of another type.

A special notation will be used for type definitions. Using this notation, types are listed separately together with their subtypes and component types. For example, the definition that the type vehicle has subtypes car, truck and plane and component types maker, weight and cost will be written:

   def vehicle: *sub*
       car, truck, plane
     com
      maker, weight, cost
     end

The metastructure of the other types in this definition would be expressed in a similar way. For example, the metastructure of the type plane may be expressed:

   def plane: *sub*
       cargo-plane, passenger-plane
     com
      maker, weight, cost, wingspan, ceiling
     end

Notice that the component types maker, weight and cost have been repeated from the supertype vehicle. It is not essential to do this but it is useful to collect all the relevant component types in one place. This notation for type definitions is similar to, but simpler than, McCarthy's *abstract syntax* [McCarthy 62].

  The effect of a type definition is to place constraints on the data space. A data space is consistent with a type definition if it satisfies all the constraints.

  Definition 3:
  A data space D is *consistent* with a type definition S *iff* for U, V in
  N_t, u, v in I and p in I_p:
  • $(\exists U)(p \in \psi(U))$
  • $U \; sub \; V \supset (\forall u)(u \in \psi(U) \supset u \in \psi(V))$
  • $u \; \underset{\pi}{\overset{\psi(U)}{}} \; v \supset (\exists V)(v \in \psi(V) \wedge U \; com \; V)$

The first constraint requires that every primitive individual be an instance of some type. Recall that $\psi(U)$ is the individual (in this case, a type) named U. The second constraint ensures that an instance u of a subtype U is also an instance of the type V. The notation $u \overset{U}{\underset{\pi}{}} v$ means that *u is a U-attribute of v* - formally, $u \in V$ and $<u,U> \pi v$. The third constraint ensures that an individual v is an instance of some type V having a component type U when u is a U-attribute of v.

  Figure 19 shows a data space that is consistent with the type definition of vehicle and therefore has attributes of all the types allowed for plane and vehicle. If V1 were made an instance of cargo-plane or passenger-plane then additional attributes would be allowed according to their type definition.

  When a data space is initially created, it contains as individuals only the types given in the type definition and the relationships ϵ and π are empty. It is easy to show that this initial data space is consistent. A manipulation operation on the data space is only defined if the resulting data space would be consistent. The primitive manipulation operations are *create*, *destroy* and *modify* and they apply to

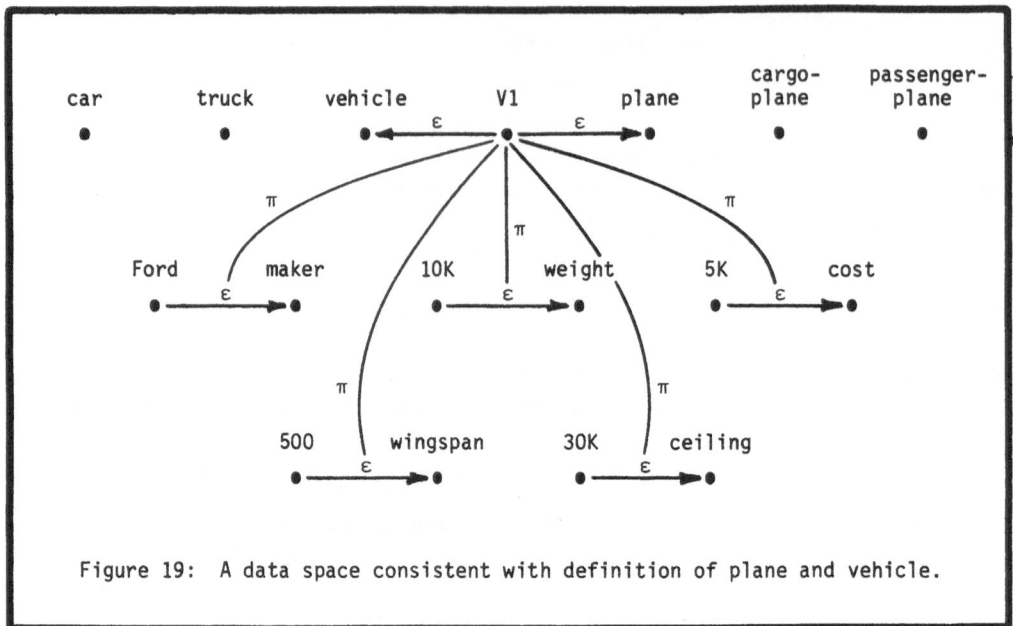

Figure 19: A data space consistent with definition of plane and vehicle.

single individuals. The syntax and semantics of these three primitives are defined in Figure 20.

When a (primitive) individual is created, it may be given a name, and its types and attributes must be specified. The name is optional since an unnamed individual can still be identified via a predicate. The semantics of the *create* operation are simply to include the name in N, to form a new individual in I_p and to extend ψ, ε and π in the obvious way. These extensions are computed from the existing data space and performed *simultaneously* to form the new data space.

When a (primitive) individual is destroyed, it is removed from I_p and its name is removed from N. This has the side effect of removing from ε and π (which are only defined over $I_p \cup I_t$) all tuples that involve the destroyed individual.

The modification of an individual may involve removals and additions to both its types and attributes. This requires appropriate changes to be made in ε and π. Notice that *modify*, unlike *create* and *destroy*, has no impact on N or I_p. Types may therefore be modified. In fact, types *must* be modified to enter their properties following the initial creation of a data space. In general, when the types of an individual are changed, there must be corresponding changes to its attributes to insure consistency with the type definition.

The predicate language of the semantic hierarchy model is a first-order language

CREATE

    Syntax: *create* n: *types*
                             A, B
                       attributes
                           c: C, d_1: D, d_2: D
                       end

    Semantics: Perform the following

            i) $N \cup \{n\}$ provided n is new
           ii) $I_p \cup \{x\}$ where x is a new individual
          iii) $\psi \cup \{<n, x>\}$
          iv) $\varepsilon \cup \{<x, \psi(A)>, <x, \psi(B)>\}$
           v) $\pi \cup \{<\psi(c), \psi(C), x>, <\psi(d_1), \psi(D), x>, <\psi(d_2), \psi(D), x>\}$
               provided $c \in C$, $d_1 \in D$ and $d_2 \in D$.

DESTROY

    Syntax: *destroy* n;

    Semantics: Perform the following

            i) $N - \{n\}$
           ii) $I_p - \{\psi(n)\}$

MODIFY

    Syntax: *modify* n: *types*
                          remove A
                          add B, C
                       attributes
                          remove d: D, e: E
                          add f: F
                       end

    Semantics: Perform the following

            i) $\varepsilon - \{<\psi(n), \psi(A)>\}$
                 $\cup \{<\psi(n), \psi(B)>, <\psi(n), \psi(C)>\}$
           ii) $\pi - \{<\psi(d), \psi(D), \psi(n)>, <\psi(e), \psi(E), \psi(n)>\}$
                 $\cup \{<\psi(f), \psi(F), \psi(n)>\}$

                 Figure 20: The manipulation primitives.

with a set N of individual symbols, binary relation symbols ε and $\equiv$, and a ternary relation symbol π. The set N is changeable in that individual symbols may be added or removed. The semantics of the predicate language is determined, at any point in time, by the state of the data space. The universe of discourse, over which all variables range, is I. Each individual symbol n in N is interpreted as the individual $\psi(n)$. The relation symbols are interpreted by their corresponding relations in the data space. Figure 21 gives a type definition for a data space and also illustrates several predicates over that data space.

Predicates may be used for the purpose of *function definition*. A function F, which takes as a parameter an instance x of a type X and which returns a *single* instance y, may be defined in terms of a predicate P(x, y) as follows[*]:

$$F(x: X) \equiv y \mid P(x, y)$$

On the other hand, if the function returned a *set* of instances, it would be defined as:

$$F(x: X) \equiv \{y\} \mid P(x, y)$$

Relative to the type definition in Figure 21, functions to return the manager of a managee and the salary of an employee could be defined as:

$$\text{MANAGER}(x: \text{managee}) \equiv y \mid y \overset{\text{manager}}{\underset{\pi}{}} x$$
$$\text{SALARY}(x: \text{employee}) \equiv y \mid y \overset{\text{salary}}{\underset{\pi}{}} x$$

Function applications may be used in place of individual symbols in a predicate. Such usage can often reduce the number of variables and quantifiers in a predicate. For example, the predicate P5(x) in Figure 21 could be written as:

$$\text{P5}(x): x \varepsilon \text{ manager} \wedge \text{SALARY}(\text{MANAGER}(x)) \equiv \text{SALARY}(x)$$

Function definitions may be recursive. For example, a function which returns the chain of managers above a particular managee may be defined as:

$$\text{MNGRCHN}(x: \text{managee}) \equiv$$
$$\{y\} \mid y \equiv \text{MANAGER}(x) \vee y \varepsilon \text{ MNGRCHN}(\text{MANAGER}(x))$$

In addition to predicates, the *create* operation may also be used for function definition. A function F with parameter x of type X may be defined as:

$$F(x: X) \equiv create : \textit{types}$$
$$Y, \ldots$$
$$\textit{attributes}$$
$$x: X, \ldots$$
$$\textit{end}$$

In this case an individual, whose types include Y and whose attributes include x: X,

---

[*]Before this notation is used, a theorem should be proved to the effect that the transformation operations on the data space guarantee that at most one individual will satisfy the predicate.

```
def employee type:  end

def employee:  sub
                  manager, managee, janitor, engineer
               com
                  salary
               end

def manager:  end                    def janitor:  com
                                                       broom-closet
def managee:  com                                   end
                 manager
              end                     def engineer:  com
                                                        office
                                                     end
```

P1(x): x is the office of the engineer Tom.

$$: \quad x \overset{\text{office}}{\underset{\pi}{}} \text{Tom}$$

P2(x): x is the employee type of Joe

$$: \quad x \; \varepsilon \; \text{employee type} \land \text{Joe} \; \varepsilon \; x$$

P3(x): x is an attribute of Jim.

$$: \quad (\exists y)(x \overset{y}{\underset{\pi}{}} \text{Jim})$$

P4(x): x is an employee type that contains no managers.

$$: \; x \; \varepsilon \; \text{employee type} \land (\forall y)(y \; \varepsilon \; x \supset (y \notin \text{manager}))$$

P5(x): x is a managee who earns the same as his manager.

$$: \; x \; \varepsilon \; \text{managee} \land (\exists s)(\exists y)(s \overset{\text{salary}}{\underset{\pi}{}} x \land s \overset{\text{salary}}{\underset{\pi}{}} y \land y \overset{\text{manager}}{\underset{\pi}{}} x)$$

Figure 21: A type definition and some predicates for a data space.

is created and returned as the value of the function application. This facility is extremely useful as it allows nameless individuals to be identified by a function application.

Predicates, manipulation operations and the *if-then-else* construct may be used to define *procedures*. As an example, consider a procedure which raises to $1000 the salary of a janitor if he currently receives $800 and otherwise fires him.

```
RAISE/FIRE(x:  janitor):
    if SALARY(x) ≡ 800
    then modify x:  attributes
                       remove 800: salary
                       add 1000: salary
                    end
        else destroy x;
```

It is often useful to apply procedures to all individuals in a given set. For this purpose a *for each* iterator is provided. For example, to process all janitors in a set S, it is only necessary to write:

```
PROCESS(S: set janitor): for each x ε S do RAISE/FIRE(x)
```

The *behavioral* semantics of a type is characterized by its operations in much the same way as its *structural* semantics is characterized by its subtypes and component types. Type definitions are therefore extended to allow the inclusion of operators for each type. A *function* is associated with a type if the function can be applied to, or can identify, *any* instance of that type. A *procedure* is associated with a type if the procedure can create, modify or destroy *any* instance of that type.

Some operations may be associated with several types. For example, if a type has subtypes then any operation associated with the type is also associated with each subtype. Further, if a function requires parameters of several types and identifies instances of yet another type, then the function is associated with all these types. To avoid pointless duplication of definitions, only operation *names* will be associated with types. Definitions of operations will remain global to all types.

As an example, the association of the previously defined operations MANAGER, SALARY, MNGRCHN, RAISE/FIRE, PROCESS with the types employee and janitor is shown below:

```
def employee : sub
                   manager, managee,
                   janitor, engineer
               com
                   salary
               functions
                   SALARY
               end
```

```
def janitor : com
                broom-closet
             functions
                SALARY
             procedures
                RAISE/FIRE, PROCESS
             end
```

Notice that SALARY is associated with both employee and janitor since it can be uniformly applied to any instance of these types. However, MANAGER is not associated with either employee or janitor since the function is only defined for instances of managee. The procedure RAISE/FIRE is associated with janitor but not with employee for similar reasons.

SYSTEM SOFTWARE SPECIFICATIONS

The semantic hierarchy model is a culmination of the long development of data base models described in the second section. This model should therefore be satisfactory for specifying a wide class of *commercial applications* software. However, it needs to be demonstrated that the model is sufficiently rich to specify the more abstruse concepts utilized in *systems* software. Accordingly, this section provides specifications for four common systems structures -- binary tree, stack, queue and symbol table.

Figure 22 gives a specification for a simple kind of binary tree in which all "data" appears at the terminal nodes and the descendants of a node are not ordered. This specification is entirely functional -- trees can be identified by the function applications which create them but not by any names. There are two subtypes of tree -- comp (composite tree) which has tree as its component type and prim (primitive tree) which has data as its component type. Note the recursive coupling of tree and comp.

Two create functions, PRIM and COMP, have been specified. PRIM can create any instance of prim and COMP can create any instance of comp. PRIM and COMP are therefore associated with prim and comp respectively, but neither one is associated with tree. Notice that the type definition for comp does not specify whether its component type is single attribute or multiple attribute. This information is supplied by the definition of COMP.

Even though the specification of a tree is quite simple, the data space produced by creating a tree can be quite complex. For example, Figure 23 shows the data space produced by the functional application:

COMP(PRIM(a), COMP(PRIM(a), PRIM(b)))

To simplify the figure, types are represented by lines rather than dots. Notice that, while data individuals have names, no tree individuals have names. Nevertheless,

```
    def tree:   sub
                   prim, comp
                end

    def prim:   com
                   data
                functions
                   PRIM
                end

    def comp:   com
                   tree
                functions
                   COMP
                end

    PRIM(d: data) ≡ create:   types
                                 prim, tree
                              attributes
                                 d: data
                              end

    COMP(e1, e2: tree) ≡ create:   types
                                      comp, tree
                                   attributes
                                     e1: tree, e2: tree
                                   end
```

Figure 22:   A specification for a tree.

tree individuals can be identified by their properties using the predicate language.

Figure 24 gives a specification for a stack. First, it is necessary to think of a stack from a data base viewpoint. Consider, for example, a stack of books. Each book has certain attributes that are independent of its being in a stack. However, when a book enters a stack (i.e., it becomes a stacked-book) it acquires one additional attribute -- the book below it on the stack.

To specify a stack of items, a type s-item (stacked-item) is defined. When an item becomes an instance of s-item, it may have attributes atts (which are independent of its being stacked) and also the attribute s-item (which is the item below it on the stack). The component types of s-item are therefore defined as atts and s-item. TOP is simply a function defined in terms of a predicate on the data space. PUSH, when given the atts of a new item, creates an individual of type s-item. Notice that this individual only acquires an s-item attribute if it is not the bottom of the stack. POP destroys the top item on the stack.

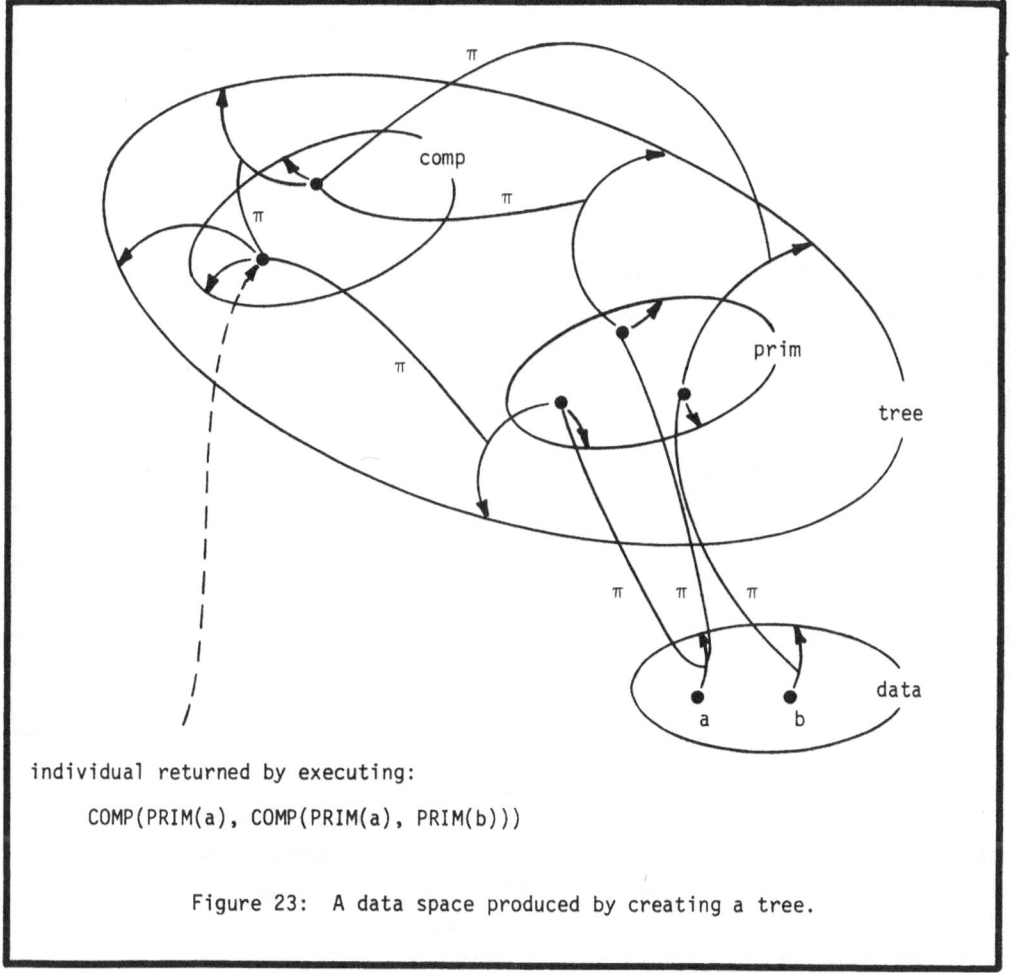

individual returned by executing:

    COMP(PRIM(a), COMP(PRIM(a), PRIM(b)))

Figure 23: A data space produced by creating a tree.

In Figure 24, items are assumed to exist only as long as they remain on the stack. By way of comparison, Figure 25 gives a specification for a queue in which items exist whether they are on the queue or off. Such independent existence is necessary for many applications. The queue specification assumes that the following definition occurs as part of the global type definition:

        def item : *sub*
                  q-item, ...
                com
                  att, ...
                end

This ensures that an item can have its independent attributes atts before becoming an instance of the subtype q-item.

```
    def s-item:  com
                    s-item, atts
                 functions
                    TOP
                 procedures
                    PUSH, POP
                 end

    TOP ≡ y | y ∈ s-item ∧ (∀x)¬(y  s-item  x)
                                       π

    PUSH(a: atts): if (∀x)(x ∉ s-item)
                   then create:  types
                                    s-item
                                 attributes
                                    a: atts
                                 end
                   else create:  types
                                    s-item
                                 attributes
                                    TOP: s-item, a: atts
                                 end

    POP:  if (∃x)(x ∈ s-item) then destroy TOP


                Figure 24:  A specification for a stack.
```

FRONT and REAR are functions defined by predicates on the data space. All that happens when an item enters a queue is that it acquires a new type q-item and a new attribute (the preceding item on the queue). When an item leaves the queue, it simply loses the type q-item. This has the effect of simultaneously removing the q-item attribute for the previous item on the queue. ENTER and LEAVE are therefore *modify* operations rather than *create* and *destroy* operations.

Figure 26 gives a specification for a symbol table. This example is drawn from [Guttag 77] where an algebraic specification for the same kind of symbol table is presented. The symbol table is designed for the compilation of block-structured languages. A new naming scope is created when a block is entered and then destroyed when the block is left. As each declaration in a block heading is encountered a symbol is formed from an identifier and other attributes. Each symbol is added to the symbol table. When an identifier is encountered in the body of a block, the symbol in the most local scope with this identifier must be retrieved. An identifier must not be declared twice in the same block.

```
    def q-item:   com
                    q-item
                  functions
                    FRONT, REAR
                  procedures
                    ENTER, LEAVE
                  end
```

FRONT $\equiv$ y | y $\in$ q-item $\wedge$ ($\forall$x)$\neg$(x $\overset{q\text{-item}}{\underset{\pi}{}}$ y)

REAR $\equiv$ y | y $\in$ q-item $\wedge$ ($\forall$x)$\neg$(y $\overset{q\text{-item}}{\underset{\pi}{}}$ x)

```
    ENTER(i: item):  if (∀x)(x ∉ q-item)
                       then modify i:  types
                                         add q-item
                                       end
                       else modify i:  types
                                         add q-item
                                       attributes
                                         add REAR: q-item
                                       end


    LEAVE:  if (∃x)(x ∈ q-item)
              then modify FRONT:  types
                                    remove q-item
                                  end
```

Figure 25: A specification for a queue.

-From a data base viewpoint, a symbol table is not a "table" at all but a data space containing two principal types — symbol and block. A symbol is an abstract individual whose attributes include its identifier (id), the block in which it was declared and other attributes (atts). A block is also an abstract individual and has one attribute of interest — the block which encloses it. Accordingly, Figure 26 lists the component types of symbol as id, atts and block, and those of block as block.

Consider first the operations associated with block. CURRENT is a function which identifies the current block via a predicate. ENCLOSING is a function which identifies the block enclosing a given block b. ENTERBLOCK creates a new block whose attribute is the current block. LEAVEBLOCK simply destroys the current block. Now consider the operations associated with symbol. ADD creates a new symbol in the current block with the declared id and atts — provided the id has not already been declared in this block. RETRIEVE, when given an id, checks to see if a symbol with this id exists within an accessible block. If it does, RETRIEVE invokes a recursive

def symbol: *com*   *def* block: *com*
         id, atts, block   block
        functions   *functions*
         FIND, RETRIEVE   CURRENT, ENCLOSING
        procedures   *procedures*
         ADD   ENTERBLOCK
        end   LEAVEBLOCK
                                       end

$\text{FIND(i: id, b: block)} \equiv \textit{if } (\exists s)(s \in \text{symbol} \wedge b \stackrel{\text{block}}{_\pi} s \wedge i \stackrel{\text{id}}{_\pi} s)$

$\qquad\qquad\qquad \textit{then } s \mid (s \in \text{symbol} \wedge b \stackrel{\text{block}}{_\pi} s \wedge i \stackrel{\text{id}}{_\pi} s)$
$\qquad\qquad\qquad \textit{else } \text{FIND(i, ENCLOSING (b))}$

$\text{RETRIEVE(i: id)} \equiv \textit{if } (\exists s)(\exists b)(s \in \text{symbol} \wedge b \stackrel{\text{block}}{_\pi} s \wedge i \stackrel{\text{id}}{_\pi} s)$
$\qquad\qquad\qquad \textit{then } \text{FIND(i, CURRENT)}$

$\text{ADD(i: id, a: atts)}: \textit{if } \neg(\exists s)(s \in \text{symbol} \wedge i \stackrel{\text{id}}{_\pi} s \wedge \text{CURRENT} \stackrel{\text{block}}{_\pi} s)$
$\qquad\qquad\qquad \textit{then create}:$ *types*
                                    symbol
                               attributes
                                i: id, a: atts, CURRENT: block
                               end

$\text{CURRENT} \equiv y \mid y \in \text{block} \wedge (\forall b)(b \in \text{block} \supset \neg(y \stackrel{\text{block}}{_\pi} b))$

$\text{ENCLOSING(b: block)} \equiv y \mid y \in \text{block} \wedge y \stackrel{\text{block}}{_\pi} b$

$\text{ENTERBLOCK}:$ $\textit{if } (\forall x)(x \notin \text{block})$
                $\textit{then create}:$ *types*
                                    block
                                 end
                $\textit{else create}:$ *types*
                                    block
                               attributes
                                CURRENT: block
                               end

$\text{LEAVEBLOCK}: \textit{if } (\exists x)(x \in \text{block}) \textit{ then destroy } \text{CURRENT}$

Figure 26: A specification for a symbol table.

function FIND which finds the symbol with attribute id in the most local block.

The four specifications above illustrate several important properties of the semantic hierarchy model that are not provided by all other specification languages. First, the predicate language allows individuals with certain properties to be identified in a *declarative* way. It is not always necessary to define a procedure which *searches* for those individuals. Second, the semantics of data sharing and side-effects are captured in a rich and natural fashion. Both the types and attributes of an individual may be changed dynamically. The semantic distinction, between a) modifying an existing individual, and b) destroying that individual and creating a new one, is retained. No notion of storage cell or pointer is used, and it is not necessary to "simulate" modification by recreating a new copy. Finally, the specifications provide a direct guideline to implementors as to how data types should be represented. It is essentially a question of deciding how the ε and π relationships are to be encoded.

CONCLUSIONS

The data base approach to system specification is to directly model the world (real or abstract) which underlies the system. Abstract entities in this world are represented by *individuals* in the model. The structure of the world is captured via the notions of *type* and *attribute*. These notions are sufficiently flexible to encompass higher-order types and type attributes. The metastructure of the world is expressed by the constructs *subtype* and *component type*. These constructs support the important abstractions of generalization (union) and aggregation (cartesian product).

It is sometimes stated [Hammer 76] or implied [Liskov 75] that such data base models, even though they are high-level, are nevertheless *arbitrary* computer representation schemes. The authors disagree with this assessment. It is important to distinguish *structure* (which is imposed by the world) from *representation* (which is arbitrarily imposed on top of structure for the purposes of computer implementation). The facts that "Joe is an instance of employee" and that "janitor is a subtype of employee" are incontrovertible properties of the world — they are not arbitrary representation decisions. On the other hand, the fact that "employee is a file which includes the record Joe" is an arbitrary representation decision.

As mentioned in the second section, many early data base models included both structural and representational aspects and the two were not carefully separated [Kent 78]. A reader of papers on these models (e.g., [ACM 76]) would be forgiven for assuming that data base models are representation oriented. However, the semantic models are deliberately designed to avoid representation and focus on structure. The only disagreement between these semantic models is which structure is important.

An important problem with *abstract data types* (as formulated by [Liskov 74]) is that not only do they suppress representation details but they also suppress structural information about subtypes and component types. It is not at all clear how *subtypes* can be handled in the context of abstract data types. For example, should a create operation on a type call create operations on each of its subtypes? If so, how are the attribute parameters passed to subtypes and how is it recognized that precisely the *same* individual is involved throughout? The parameter types declared for operations on an abstract data type give some clue to its *component types*. However, it is not possible to determine precisely the component types without analyzing the specification of the operations. Some work has been done on exploiting abstract data types for data bases [Weber 78] but there are still difficulties with the approach [Smith 78b].

Data base models explicitly support *sharing* and *side-effects*. Sharing is provided by a *naming* mechanism (based on predicates) which allows different operations to access and manipulate the *same* individual. There is no notion of operations making *copies* of an individual's structure for private usage. Side-effects are a natural consequence of sharing when the *create*, *destroy* and *modify* primitives are used. It is recognized that sharing and side-effects make software more difficult to verify with current techniques. However, if these two phenomena naturally occur in the underlying world, as they frequently do, they should be supported by the specification language. It may be necessary to develop more powerful verification techniques for data base models.

Data base technology has developed, over many years, a wealth of techniques for specifying and efficiently implementing commercial applications software. This paper has only dealt with the specification techniques. All evidence points to the fact that these techniques are equally pertinent for systems software specification. It remains to be seen whether data base implementation techniques are also effective for systems software.

A number of advantages of non-procedural descriptions of software systems were
mentioned by Alan Shaw and John and Diane Smith during the presentation of their
papers. Shaw claimed that regular-expression-based description techniques support
having multiple views of a system, permit analysis of a system during its development, and permit the hiding of mechanisms used to produce the system's behavior.
The benefits of a data base description paradigm claimed by the Smiths were the
availability of a variety of techniques for modelling, and design and implementation, and the ability to suppress representational detail.

Jack Wileden offered a different characterization of the virtues of non-
procedural description techniques. He delineated three characteristics of non-
procedural descriptions which he felt led to their value both as development notations and as a basis for other valuable tools. First, non-procedural descriptions
may be *non-prescriptive*, focusing on system behavior without unnecessarily defining
an implementation for achieving this behavior. Second, *redundant* descriptions may
be prepared, affording the opportunity to assess an eventual implementation by comparing the behavior it produces with an independently prepared description of
required/desired behavior. Finally, descriptions using a non-procedural technique
may be *orthogonal* to those reflecting the system's design and/or implementation, providing a different viewpoint by which a different set of system characteristics,
relating to the purposes rather than the operation of the system, may be exhibited.

In discussing the breadth of applicability of non-procedural description techniques, and in particular their usefulness for describing concurrent systems,
Wileden brought up the problem of resolution:

> The expression-based techniques provide explicit representations
> of concurrent activity while in the data base approach, concurrency is
> represented implicitly. In this regard, though, it should be noted
> that the issue of a satisfactory representation for actual concurrency
> in expression-based descriptions, alluded to by Shaw, remains unre-
> solved. While both interleaving and the "unordered with respect to a
> partial ordering" approach* are adequate for many applications, neither
> they nor any other current technique really captures the notion of
> actual concurrency. While they can be interpreted as meaning "these

---

*The two approaches are actually equivalent, since extending the partial ordering to
its associated set of consistent total orderings (completing the partial ordering)
[Grief 77] has the same effect as enumerating the strings represented by the interleave.

events may occur in any order, including perhaps simultaneously,"
these representations do not permit a distinction to be made between
"the order of these necessarily sequential events is immaterial"
(e.g., two independent write operations to a shared data base) and
"actual simultaneous activity is acceptable (or desirable)." Techniques supporting more accurate, higher-resolution representations of
concurrency must be found if the explicit concurrency description of
expression-based approaches is to prove genuinely useful to software
developers.

In the discussion generated by this observation, other aspects of the resolution
problem were brought out. Paul Zeiger felt that a major contributing factor was
defining events as indivisible and consuming non-zero time. Steve Zilles pointed
out that the lack of a notion of an abstraction relation among events and a concomitant event hierarchy was a serious defect. Bob Keller felt another problem was
the inability to describe illegal sequences as well as legal sequences. The conclusion from this part of the discussion was that there are a number of aspects to the
problem and a number of solution approaches, but more work, including exploratory
usage, on this aspect of regular-expression-based description techniques is required
before the problem can be understood, let alone solved.

Wileden then addressed the issue of the suitability of the techniques discussed
by Shaw and the Smiths for different types of systems and different types of development activities, although he pointed out it was a "slippery topic" lacking inarguable
characterizations:

The notion of "naturalness" with respect to a descriptive technique is intuitively appealing but difficult to define with much
precision. For our purposes, naturalness can be viewed as the ability to easily construct comprehensible descriptions which capture
the essential features of the object being described. On that basis
it seems that both the expression-based and data base techniques are
fairly natural for software system description, but that the degree
of naturalness varies for different types of systems or different
views of a given system.

In particular, expression-based techniques seem more natural for
activity-oriented system descriptions while the data base approach
appears more natural for *state-oriented* system descriptions. This
observation is not particularly startling, since the expression-
based techniques are couched in the terminology of 'event occurrences,' 'entity flow' and 'procedure activations' while data base
models were originally developed to describe the state of a collection of objects and their interrelationships. However, it does

perhaps shed some light on the limitations of the naturalness of each descriptive approach and suggest some guidelines for the usage of the respective approaches. For instance, expression-based descriptions of software systems primarily concerned with information modification (data base management systems being the obvious example) are most natural when they focus on the manipulations themselves (e.g., operation ordering in a shared data base) and quite unnatural for describing the results of those manipulations. On the other hand, data base models are rather unnatural for describing a software system (such as a process control application or an operating system) which is primarily concerned with a stream of activity, being much better suited to describing the state changes in information structures used to support the activity. This may explain why the examples of systems programming software descriptions offered in the Smith paper were essentially low-level data structure descriptions rather than high-level specifications for the operating system or compiler which might use those structures in performing its activity.

Certain software systems, such as the examples cited above, may be so strongly oriented toward either activity or information modification as to make one technique substantially more natural than the other for use in describing them. Many other systems, however, can be usefully viewed from either perspective, and hence may be described with nearly equal naturalness using either technique. A compiler, for instance, can be viewed both as a modifier of information (translating one representation into another) or as a performer of activities (scanning, parsing, generating code, etc.). In such a situation, either an expression-based technique or the data base approach could be used in describing the system. Depending upon the choice, either an activity-oriented viewpoint or a state-oriented viewpoint would be obtained. Which is the more natural would then depend upon the developer's own proclivities.

The thrust of the discussion generated by these comments was, as expressed by Chuck Bradley, that both activity-oriented and state-oriented system descriptions can be used (and useful) for any particular system during any pre-implementation phase, and it really depends on what needs to be expressed. Bob Snowdon proposed that there might be a good deal of benefit from looking at operating systems from a data base point of view since this would allow one to get away from details that obfuscate the system's overall function and behavior. Steve Zilles seconded this, expressing the feeling that when one wants to describe a system's purpose the data base view would be important, but when the description is more implementation-oriented, the event view would be more useful. Lee Osterweil supported Wileden's contention by pointing out that the more successful requirements definition systems employ a relational, and hence data base, viewpoint.

Pamela Zave argued the necessity of having a descriptive notation that could be uniformly employed during the entire pre-implementation lifetime of a system and from which other descriptions could be (hopefully, but not necessarily, automatically) derived:

> Data base models and event expressions seem to be perfectly ortho-
> gonal models of system properties, but either extreme of this space
> versus time dichotomy is relatively far from the procedural system
> description techniques in practical use. The less a description
> resembles one's everyday design notation the more likely it is to cast
> fresh light on the subject, but the less likely it is to be easily
> integrated, as a modelling and feedback tool, into design practice.
> This is really an intolerable situation, because as long as it exists,
> these theoretical tools will be, *by nature*, irrelevant to practical
> design. The reason is much the same as that for the unpopularity of
> preparing program documentation: in the deadline-pressured world of
> the working designer or programmer, preparing alternative descriptions
> that have no well-defined or enforceable relation to the product
> system may be regarded as "busy work."

> I think that the solution to this problem lies in finding design
> languages (preferably one, if that is possible) that are rich enough
> for practical use, formal, and which would support event and data
> base models (and hopefully others) as *projections* of the system at
> its current level of abstraction. The need for projections of system
> descriptions, analogous to an architect's two-dimensional views of a
> building, is being cited with increasing frequency. Such languages
> would make possible full integration of non-procedural descriptions
> into the development process, where they could function as ortho-
> gonal, hierarchical, and enforceable abstractions.

Zave then gave an overview of a purely functional notation [Zave 79] which she has been developing and which she feels is a candidate for a uniformly applicable nota-tion. She reported that, on the basis of using the notation in the development of an adaptive, distributed processing algorithm for the finite element method useful in many numerical analysis problems, the notation had proved to be easy-to-use and natural, had provided an elegant model with "clean" underlying algebraic semantics, had provided a medium which facilitated the collaborative design efforts by special-ists in different fields (namely, numerical analysis and software design), and had stabilized the development effort by introducing a record of the design that less-ened the effect of personnel attrition and the tendency to rush to code.

Chapter VII. Analysis Tools

The focus of this chapter is on application of software analysis tools and techniques to the pre-implementation phases of software development. The presentation by Ralph London, provided in written form by London and Larry Robinson, covers formal verification tools and techniques. Topics discussed include methodological concerns, application of verification ideas to language design, automated verification systems, new capabilities required, and future directions in verification tool technology.

The paper by Dick Fairley is concerned with software validation tools and techniques, automated validation tools, current issues in software validation, and the role of validation in the pre-implementation phases of the software lifecycle.

Discussant Lori Clarke presents thoughts on software validation. Her remarks concern establishing the absence of certain types of errors by testing, reasons why validation and verification techniques are not widely used during pre-implementation, and how validation and verification techniques fit into an encompassing software development environment.

The interplay between formal specification techniques and formal verification is addressed by discussant Larry Robinson. He discusses the role of specifications, summarizes the HDM (Hierarchical Development Methodology) system, and indicates several research areas in formal specification and verification.

THE ROLE
OF
VERIFICATION TOOLS AND TECHNIQUES

Ralph L. London*
Information Sciences Institute
University of Southern California

and

Lawrence Robinson
Ford Aerospace and Communications Corporation

INTRODUCTION

Before talking about verification, we must have a definition. For the purposes
of this discussion, verification is the mathematical proof of consistency between a
program and its specification. It should be distinguished from the "verification" in
"verification and validation," which refers to other methods such as testing. Note
that the term "consistency" was used, rather than "correctness," because verification
is not an absolute determination that the program is perfect. Thus, verification is
not a guarantee. A verification can fail for any (or all) of several reasons:

- The program needs to be changed.
- The specification needs to be changed or perhaps is incomplete.
- The theorem prover cannot arrive at a proof.

However, verification can increase one's confidence that a program meets its specification, because verification can evaluate many more cases than testing can.

Verification technology at the present time generally specifies and proves only
functional properties of a program, and not performance properties, although the
latter is sometimes possible.

Verifiability is a useful property for a system to have, even if the system is
not verified. Verifiability has already affected many areas of software engineering,
including programming language design and the construction, specification, and decomposition of systems. It is expected to have even more effect as it becomes more
widely known and applied.

The use of verification technology is not restricted to proving the consistency

---

*Due to other commitments, I was unable to produce a written version of my oral
presentation, so Larry Robinson prepared this synopsis and interpretation of my
remarks. I thank him for doing so.

of programs and specifications. Verification in its broadest sense can be said to encompass reasoning about programs, specifications, and even requirements and designs.

METHODOLOGICAL CONCERNS

Verification has important application in the methodology of developing software systems. In writing specifications one must think about the properties to be proved about them and the processes required to reason about them.

Specifications should be written in a modular fashion, with information hiding in mind. The decomposition of the system should be based on the (public) specifications alone. Verification provides one test for success of specifications. Other tests include

- Utility
- Comprehensibility
- Power
- Modifiability

Both the programs and proofs should be modifiable at low cost. This is absolutely essential for large systems, which are extremely costly to change (the costs to change proofs are often greater). Both methodology and tools should provide strong support for such modifications. Incremental systems and languages with abstract data types, which require a minimal amount of the proof to be redone if the system changes, are steps in this direction.

The reasoning process of verification should be used in task definition and design, as well as implementation and proof. An example of this is found in methodologies such as Alphard, which combine specification, implementation, and verification. A specific instance is the Alphard generator mechanism [Shaw,M 77] which is a control abstraction.

There is a great deal to be gained by determining certain properties of specifications and producing system-relevant data from the specifications themselves. Some properties of algebraic specifications can be determined, e.g., sufficient completeness, finite termination, and unique termination. There are online tools that can execute (in an inefficient way) a program based on its algebraic specification alone. Direct execution can be performed on abstract model specifications as well.

APPLICATIONS TO LANGUAGE DESIGN

Many of the new programming languages have been designed with verification considerations in mind. Some improvements in language design can be traced to the
influence of verification techniques.

Euclid [Lampson 77a] contains various kinds of assertion statements: pre- and
post- conditions, invariants, and in-line assertions, a special case of which is the
language-defined legality assertions. These can be checked at runtime or used in
verification. It is advisable for a programmer to put assertions in his or her program, whether or not it is to be verified. The Euclid procedure mechanism has rules
which prevent aliasing (see below). The original definition of a Euclid module
definition was flawed. This was recognized when proof rules were later written.

Alphard [Wulf 76] has a complete facility, with proof rules, for designing and
verifying abstract data types. Alphard has a specification mechanism built into the
language, and currently uses abstract model specifications (other specifications are
possible). The language contains parameterized types, so that for example, a stack
for any type (having certain properties motivated by verification concerns) can be
specified,verified, and implemented once, and then instantiated when a particular
stack (e.g., stack of integer) is declared. A prominent feature of Alphard is the
generator mechanism, by which a programming language statement iterating through a
collection of elements of an abstract data type can be written independently of the
actual algorithm for choosing each element. Thus, an iteration statement may look
like:

for x in S do <statements in x> od;

The algorithm for iterating through the collection (in a sense, the "for x in S"
part) is included in the specification of the abstract data type.

Ada [Ichbiah 79] has used many of the mechanisms of the newer languages. Although it is a large language, a large subset of it is verifiable. In fact a formal
semantics of Ada has been developed using denotational semantics (a formalism developed by Scott and others). It has pointed out some ambiguities in the original
language definition.

One of the issues in language design is aliasing, in which a single object may
be known by two different names. The aliasing problem occurs when it is possible to
pass variables by reference. Thus, two different (formal) variables in a procedure
might be referring to the same object, for a particular call. Since for simplicity
the proof rules for most languages make the assumption that variables are independent
and distinct, aliasing cannot be allowed, or else a proof is easily achieved for a
program that is actually inconsistent. On the other hand, proof rules have been
written which properly account for aliasing. One must decide whether the added

mechanism is appropriate in a practical sense (rather than theoretically) to permit aliasing. Many language designers have chosen to retain aliasing.

However, having a verifiable language does not solve all problems in verifying software. One must also look at the problem domain, and ask: "What will verifications look like for programs in language X or those for doing task Y?"

CURRENT VERIFICATION SYSTEMS

There are several running verifications systems in the research community. It should be emphasized that these are primarily research-oriented systems, and not necessarily suited to the verification of production software. They are all implemented in some dialect of Lisp. In all cases, additional information is available from the designers and in the literature.

The Affirm system ([Gerhart 79b], [Musser 79], [Thompson 79]), developed at the USC Information Sciences Institute, is for the algebraic specification and verification of abstract data types and Pascal-like programs which use these types in expressions and assertions. A natural deduction theorem prover uses powerful rewrite rule facilities and user-directed proof steps to prove program verification conditions and properties of data types. Additional features include tools for the analysis of algebraic specifications and a library of data types. Experiences include the specification and partial proof of a large file updating module and the proof of several high-level properties in the application areas of protocols and security kernels.

The Gypsy system ([Ambler 77], [Good 78]) is located at the University of Texas at Austin. Gypsy is a language for both specifying and implementing programs. Important applications to date have been for communications systems, for which Gypsy has special-purpose language constructs and proof rules. The verification system maintains the complete state of a system as it is being developed (both specifications and implementation). If any part of a system is changed, the system can identify the proofs that must be redone. This incremental approach reduces much of the effort in verifying programs.

The verification system at SRI International is based on the Boyer-Moore theorem prover and on HDM (Hierarchical Development Methodology) [Robinson 75]. The Boyer-Moore theorem prover proves theorems in a theory based on recursive functions and inductively defined objects. HDM is a methodology for formally specifying (using the specification language SPECIAL [Robinson 77]), implementing, and verifying programs. The computational model of HDM is a hierarchy of abstract machines. The verification system is intended to be used with many different implementation languages. It currently works for Modula and a subset of Jovial J73.

The Artificial Intelligence Laboratory at Stanford University has developed a verification system based on a version of Pascal with extensions [Luckham 79]. The theorem proving power of the system is divided into two parts. The very fast simplifier, including a decision procedure, contains built-in knowledge about common data structures such as numbers, arrays, records, and list structures as well as certain uninterpreted function and predicate symbols. The very general "rulehandler" uses user-supplied axioms and, if included, hints on their use to reason about structures not handled by the simplifier. The range of successful verification includes sorting, scheduling, parsing, compiling, concurrency, and the absence of certain runtime errors.

NEW CAPABILITIES

Several improvements over current verification systems are needed before verification can be made useful in production environments. Several desirable capabilities can be identified.

Context-oriented verification. Current verification systems do not provide enough information if the proof effort fails. Usually the theorem prover fails to prove a particular formula, but it is often difficult to tell why the proof failed, especially in terms that are relevant to the program being proved. Often the notation for proof makes it difficult to go back to the original program text. If the system stores this context information, it can be made available to the person performing the proofs so that he or she can correct the program or the specification (or supply the correct lemma). One problem in capturing the context of a verification is to provide the human engineering to allow users to take maximum advantage of the facility (most verification systems could provide more in the way of human engineering).

Incremental verification. Once a proof has been found for a program, minor changes to the program (or its specification) will frequently result in a new proof that is similar to the original proof, perhaps sharing many components. Current verification systems, except for the Gypsy system, do not take advantage of this phenomenon, so all proofs must often be redone if the smallest change takes place. Considering the cost in CPU time of verification, this is a great waste of resources. Even if a program is not greatly modified during its lifetime, incremental facilities can take advantage of the fact that the first attempt to prove a program often fails, because of errors in the program or specification (or because the theorem prover does not have enough information). However, part of the proof that failed can often be used after the errors are corrected. Note that the context capability and the incremental capability could share much mechanism.

Increased theorem-proving capability. Perhaps the greatest problem for verification researchers is that the theorem provers are not nearly as powerful as we would like them to be. No theorem provers operate without some form of user assistance. Because theorem proving is an undecidable problem, this difficulty cannot be completely eliminated. However, much use can be made of domain-specific knowledge, especially if the domain is decidable. This is an advantage of the Stanford Pascal Verifier and the Affirm system (when it has a well-behaved set of rewrite rules). The Boyer-Moore theorem prover is unique in that it can automatically perform proofs by induction, but it often requires the insertion of lemmas to "help" the theorem prover decide which inductions to choose.

New specification methods. Current specification techniques are often too low-level for the tasks required of them (e.g., requirements specification). In addition, they cannot be easily extended to new domains (e.g., ballistic missile defense). The specification techniques of the future must overcome these difficulties while maintaining their generality and ability to interface to state-of-the-art theorem provers.

FUTURE DIRECTIONS

Verification research and development should take on the following new directions, if it is to be of ultimate use.

Demonstration of utility. The utility of verification systems should be demonstrated by applying them to software problems in the field. It is only then that we will be able to see what verification systems can and cannot do. More experiments should be performed, especially those which produce statistics on the cost-effectiveness of verification techniques throughout the software life cycle. Verification is known to be extremely costly, but its cost may be justified by its benefits, especially in reduced costs for testing, integration, and maintenance. Only experiments can determine this.

- Expansion of user groups. Almost all use of verification systems has been by the builders of these systems or other researchers. Experimental use of verification systems should be expanded to include programmers with some familiarity with formal mathematics. It is acknowledged that the average programmer may not be able to make use of verification techniques. However, there are many programmers who can; if there are tools available, they should.

New task applications. So far, verification has been used in very limited domains, such as data structures and number theory. Other tasks -- such as network protocols, data base management systems, and compilers -- should also be attempted or expanded.

Decomposition techniques. More studies should be made of decomposition techniques, for both programs and data structures, to see how they affect verification. Those techniques that decompose (and hopefully reduce) the proof effort are favored.

Standard types. Many abstract data types are used extensively for many different applications. Libraries of specifications for abstract data types should be kept (perhaps in schematic form) so that maximum use can be made of existing specifications and implementations.

SOFTWARE VALIDATION
AND
PRE-IMPLEMENTATION ISSUES

Richard E. Fairley

Computer Science Department
Colorado State University

During the past few years, increasing attention has been focused on
the development of automated tools and systematic techniques for software validation. The benefits of automated tools and systematic techniques include better product quality, and increased productivity and
job satisfaction for the user. This paper surveys recent developments
in software validation, with a view toward the relationship between
validation tools and techniques and the pre-implementation phases of
software development.

INTRODUCTION

Software validation is the process of determining the level of conformance between an operational software system and its specifications. Validation involves
examining the software in various ways with the intention of finding errors (departures from the specifications). The two major categories of software errors are
design errors—errors in interpreting the requirements — and logic errors — errors
in implementing the design. A software system can be validated and still exhibit
unsatisfactory performance, due to unsatisfactory specifications.

Validation attempts to determine how well a software system conforms to its
specifications. Specifications typically include user requirements, implementation
constraints, functional structure of the system, detailed design specifications,
test plans, project milestones, and documentation standards. It is often convenient
to partition specifications into the categories of requirements specifications,
functional specifications, design specifications, and implicit specifications. Although the categories are somewhat arbitrary, the general trend is for requirements
specifications to describe the external view of the system, while functional specifications indicate system structure (modules, interfaces, data flow), and design
specifications describe the processing algorithms and data structures to be used in
an implementation. Implicit specifications are unstated assumptions concerning
standards of practice, quality, operating procedures, and general conduct of the
project. Unfortunately, the unstated assumptions are often in conflict between
customers and developers, and among development personnel. One goal of systematic
specification techniques is to make explicit as many implicit assumptions as
possible.

Systematic development of software involves the preparation of a series of specifications; each successive specification is (or should be) consistent with all previous specifications, and elaborates them in greater detail. Ideally, the specifications to which a software system is being validated will be explicit, complete, consistent, concise, unambiguous, and testable. In reality, specifications are almost always ambiguous, incomplete, inconsistent, incorrect, vague, untraceable, untestable, and changeable. Reducing these problems is a major role for automated tools and systematic techniques in the pre-implementation phases of software development.

In the following sections of this paper, systematic techniques and automated tools for software development are surveyed, current issues in software validation are discussed, and some observations on the relationship of software validation to the pre-implementation phases of software development are presented.

We conclude this section of the paper with the following proverbs for software validation:

> The purpose of validation is to demonstrate the presence of errors; not their absence.
>
> Conducting the validation process with the intention of finding no errors will usually succeed.
>
> Real software systems are never error-free.
>
> The best validation procedure is the one that has maximum likelihood of discovering the maximum number of errors.
>
> Debugging is the process of fixing known errors; validation is the process of discovering unknown errors.
>
> The number of remaining errors in a software system is proportional to the number of discovered errors.
>
> Programmers should never validate their own software; nor should development organizations.
>
> Automated tools and systematic techniques can help good people do a better job, but they can never replace hard work, creativity, or intuition.

SYSTEMATIC VALIDATION TECHNIQUES

Several techniques have been, and are being developed to facilitate systematic validation of software; they include structured walkthroughs, static analysis, dynamic testing, symbolic execution, reliable testing theory, error estimation techniques, test case assessment, systematic testing strategies, and independent validation. In this section of the paper, we review each of these briefly. Formal verification (proof of correctness) techniques and computing system performance measurement are not discussed in this paper.

Structured Walkthroughs

A structured walkthrough is a validation technique by which each programmer's work is reviewed by other project members. Prior to the walkthrough session, the reviewee provides each reviewer with a copy of the appropriate code and documentation. During the walkthrough session the reviewer "walks through" the code; explaining inputs, processing algorithms, data flow, and outputs. A recording secretary notes problems that arise during the session. Emphasis is placed on discovering problems and not on the resolution of problems. It is the reviewer's responsibility to follow up on all noted problem areas and to report solutions at a subsequent meeting. Each project member's work is reviewed during separate walkthrough sessions. It is important to note that managers should not attend walkthroughs, and that the walkthrough session should not be used as a direct evaluation of the project member's performance. Walkthroughs are often used as project milestones. Related techniques include code inspection, wherein a team reads code against a checklist of common errors, desk checking, and the tried and true technique of talking to a colleague.

Static Analysis

In static analysis, the program text is examined but the code is not executed. Thus, a structured walkthrough is a form of static analysis; however, the term "static analysis" is generally reserved to denote an automated examination of static program structure. Information that can be obtained by static analysis includes: 1) syntactic errors; 2) number of occurrences of source statements by type; 3) cross-reference maps of identifier usage; 4) analysis of how the identifiers are used in each statement (data source, data sink, calling parameter, dummy parameter, subscript, etc.); 5) subroutines and functions called by each routine; 6) unitialized variables; 7) variables set but not used; 8) isolated code segments that cannot be executed under any set of input data; 9) departures from coding standards (both language standards and local practice standards); and 10) misuses of global variables, common variables, and parameter lists (incorrect number of parameters, mismatched types, uninitialized input parameters, output parameters assigned to but never used, constants linked to output parameters, parameters never used for either input or output, etc.)

Some static information, such as error messages and cross-reference maps, is easily obtained by syntactic analysis; other information, such as variables set but never used on any subsequent control path (the live variable problem) requires sophisticated algorithms similar to those used in code optimizing compilers. It is not surprising that static analysis closely resembles certain aspects of compilation - both processes are concerned with analyzing the structure of programs.

Dynamic Testing

Dynamic testing involves derivation of a test plan, design of test cases, execution of the test cases, and evaluation of the results. The three major categories
of dynamic tests are functional tests, logical tests, and boundary value tests.
Functional test cases are derived from the requirements specifications and the functional specifications. The purpose of functional testing is to determine system performance under normal operating conditions. Computation of nominally correct output
values from nominal inputs, acceptance of inputs and delivery of outputs in the
desired formats, exhibition of satisfactory response time, and evaluation of memory
space and other resource utilization are typical candidates for evaluation by functional tests.

In contrast, logical tests are concerned with the manner in which the code performs its computations. Logical test cases are derived from the design specifications, from static analysis and structured walkthroughs, and from careful inspection
of the code by testing personnel. Items to be validated by logical testing include
arithmetic, error handling, initialization, interfaces, and timing. Arithmetic is
tested for two reasons: to check the precision of calculations and to determine
sensitivity to inaccuracies in the input data. Error handling is tested for processing of illegal data (e.g., attempting to find the square root of a negative number),
correctness of internal logic (e.g., pushing onto a full stack, popping an empty
stack), and response to environmental problems (e.g., input/output channel failure).
Initializations are tested to ensure that items are initialized to the correct
values for various execution and re-execution sequences.

Both data and control interfaces are candidates for logical testing. Data interfaces are manifest in the parameters passed between routines and in the protocol of
access to common data areas and data bases. Control interfaces exist in the invocations and the entry and exit points of modules. Design specifications often require
that certain routines be inaccessible from certain other routines and that certain
calling sequences be observed. All of these interface items are candidates for
validation.

There are several measures of timing: response time (best, worst, average), CPU
time, elapsed time, relative time spent in each routine, and relative time spent in
each statement. Timing information is essential for improving the efficiency of a
program. Programs often spend as much as 95% of execution time in 5% of the code,
and that 5% is often counterintuitive to what the programmer might guess.

Boundary value test cases are both functional and logical in nature. Boundary
values and singular points from the input domain, pathological characteristics of
processing algorithms, and quirks in the data structures are all candidates for
boundary value tests. Worst case analysis, sensitivity analysis of the specifications

and algorithms, and the programmer's intuition are all sources of boundary value test cases.

Note that initializations and interfaces can be validated by static analysis or by dynamic testing. In general, static analysis and dynamic testing are complementary approaches to software validation: Static analysis provides global information concerning program structure, while dynamic tests can be used to investigate detailed issues in depth. Static analysis often raises questions which are best answered by a well-designed dynamic test. For example, static analysis can be used to determine initialization of variables, but a dynamic test might demonstrate that a DATA statement was incorrectly used to initialize a Fortran variable at compile time when in fact the variable should have been reinitialized on each invocation of the routine. Static analyzers are often designed to issue warning messages that call attention to error prone and questionable programming practices which can then be investigated further by dynamic testing (e.g., variable X initialized in a DATA statement).

Symbolic Execution

In symbolic execution [Cheatham 79], a program is "executed" by assigning symbols to the input variables instead of assigning literal values, as is done in normal execution. Expressions are "evaluated" by assigning symbolic values to the operands and by then simplifying the resulting symbolic expressions. Evaluation of assignment statements results in a symbolic expression being associated with the left-hand-side variable. When that variable is referenced in subsequent statements, the current symbolic value of the variable is used. Boolean expressions are evaluated in a similar manner, and path expressions are derived to reflect the assumed "true" or "false" evaluation of booleans in branching statements. Loop transversal can be summarized by invariant expressions. In this manner, the values of output variables are determined as expressions involving the input variables and the execution paths traversed in computing the output expressions. The values of output expressions are thus boolean functions of the input variables. These symbolic output expressions are useful for a variety of purposes: Visual examination of the output expressions may reveal errors in the computation; for a given execution path through the program, it may be possible to find values for the input variables that cause the path expression to evaluate to "true". These input values then represent a set of test data that will force an actual execution of the program to follow that control path (in general, this problem is undecidable). Other applications of symbolic execution include detection of infeasible paths through the program, exposure of semantic errors in the code, informal verification of the code, and formal proofs of correctness. Symbolic execution is a natural bridge between dynamic testing and inductive proofs of correctness.

Reliable Testing Theory

Recently, investigations have been focused on the issue of reliable testing. A reliable test is one that is guaranteed to expose errors of a particular type, if they exist in the system. For example, static analysis can be guaranteed to find all uninitialized variables in a module under restrictions such as: the variable is local to the module under investigation, and the variable does not appear as a parameter in a subprogram call prior to its usage as a data source. Currently, investigators are focusing on the restrictions that must be placed on programs, specifications, and testing techniques in order to produce reliable tests. The goal is to develop a complementary set of testing techniques, each of which locates particular types of errors.

Error Estimation Techniques

Perhaps the most difficult issue in software validation is establishing an estimate of the number and severity of remaining errors in the system. Ideally, one should be able to establish a "tight" estimate of the remaining errors, and then allocate resources (based on a tight estimate of the resources required per error) to permit discovery and correction to some predetermined level (e.g., 95% or 99% error removal). In practice, there are no known methods for producing tight estimates, and no known methods for estimating the resources needed to find a given percentage of the errors in a system.

In the absence of solid, quantitative methods for error estimation, the following techniques are often utilized: historical data, error seeding, dual testing teams, rules of thumb, and predictive models. The use of historical data assumes prior experience with similar systems developed in a similar environment using personnel of similar competence, and that adequate records were maintained during previous projects to allow an analysis of errors. Violation of any one of these assumptions can invalidate historical models.

Error seeding involves intentional introduction of known, but undisclosed, errors into a system. At some later time the ratio of detected seeded errors to detected unseeded errors is used as an indication of the number of remaining unseeded errors. Alternately, one might assess the completeness of test coverage by introducing an error into the program and determining the ability of existing test cases to discover that type of error.

Some projects have utilized two independent validation teams [Ramamoorthy 78]. An analysis of errors detected by both teams and errors detected by only one team is used as a basis for estimating undetected errors.

Rules of thumb are based on local and/or industry wide averages. They often come from historical data. For example, it might be known that integration testing on a similar project found five errors per 1000 statements, and that 30% of the errors were implementation errors and 70% were design errors. Also, it might be known that two errors per 1000 statements were found during the first year of operation.

Predictive models are statistical in nature. Parameters are measured, such as elapsed time between error discoveries, complexity of program structure, or ratio of seeded errors to unseeded errors discovered. From the parameters, a statistical estimate of the number of remaining errors is calculated. Because the models are statistical in nature, one can never be certain that the assumptions of the model apply to the project, or that the model is accurate for the particular project.

Test Case Assessment

Ascertaining the "goodness" of a set of test cases is also a difficult issue. In general, a good set of test cases is understood to be a set that exercises the program functions and program logic in a manner that will expose a large number of design and implementation errors. Different considerations apply in assessing the goodness of test cases for individual modules and assessing test cases for systems (collections of modules).

In module testing, one would ideally assess both function and logic by exhaustively testing every possible set of input data from the input domain. In practice, this is not possible. As an alternative for testing program logic, one might attempt to supplement the functional and boundary value tests by partitioning the input domain into a set of equivalence classes such that every execution path through the program is exercised at least once by some test case. In practice, this is also impossible for most programs, due to the large number of equivalence classes created by looping constructs. A less satisfactory, but feasible, approach is to augment the functional tests and boundary values tests with logical test cases so that the entire set of test cases will exercise every branch in the module to every possible destination. This results in traversal of every arc in the program graph. An even less satisfactory, but more easily achieved, criterion is execution of every statement in the module at least once by the set of test cases.

Branch coverage and statement coverage testing are not entirely satisfactory because the sequence in which statements are executed often plays a critical role in exposing program errors. Determining the critical paths to be tested and deriving test cases to traverse those paths is one of the most difficult and subjective tasks in software validation. For example, it is often difficult to find test cases that will exercise the error handling code. (As a sidelight, it has been observed that a competent programmer will derive a set of test cases that typically achieve only 60%

to 70% statement coverage in a module [Miller 79].)

Design of system level test cases is even more subjective than the design of
module tests. System level testing is typically concerned with discovering subtle-
ties in the interfaces, decision logic, control flow, recovery routines, throughput,
capacity, and timing of the entire system. Careful planning is required to determine the extent and nature of system testing to be performed and to establish the
criteria by which the results will be evaluated. System test planning should be an
integral component of the functional specification and design phases of the project.

Systematic Validation Strategies

Validating a collection of routines is best accomplished using a systematic
strategy. Three basic strategies are the big-bang method, the bottom-up method, and
the top-down method. Variations on these basic strategies include the sandwich and
extended sandwich methods. Big-bang validation is the least desirable method.
First, the individual routines are validated in isolation. Then, the entire collection of routines is validated in one massive integration step. The disadvantage of
big-bang validation is the combinatorial complexity that results when a collection
of routines is integrated in one large step rather than by a series of incremental
steps.

Bottom-up validation is the classical strategy. It consists of module validation, followed by subsystem validation, followed by system validation. Advantages
of bottom-up validation are that test conditions are generally easy to create, and
that test results are readily observed. Disadvantages of bottom-up testing include
the requirement for a test harness for each module and subsystem, and the complexity
of system integration as subsystems are combined into successively larger units.

Top-down validation starts with the top level routine and one or two immediately
subordinate routines (this assumes a hierarchical system structure). After this top
level "skeleton" has been validated, it becomes the test harness for immediately
subordinate routines. Top-down validation requires the use of program stubs to
simulate the effect of routines below the level of those being validated. Top-down
testing offers several advantages:

- The top-level routines provide a natural test harness for the lower
  level routines.
- System integration testing is minimized.
- Errors are localized to the new modules and interfaces being added.
- Validation of a skeletal program allows demonstration of simulated
  system capabilities.

Top-down validation is particularly attractive when combined with top-down design and implementation; validation is then distributed throughout the system development cycle.

In many situations, it is not possible to adhere to a strict top-down validation strategy. For example, it may be difficult to find top-level input data that will result in appropriate input values to test a lower level module in a particular way. Also, it may be difficult to observe the results produced by the lower level modules. In addition, the top levels of the system may provide a very expensive test harness. In some cases, it may not be possible to use stubs to simulate modules below the current level of testing (e.g., input-output drivers, interrupt handlers). Thus, it may be necessary to test certain low-level modules first. The sandwich strategy is preferable in situations such as these. Sandwich validation is predominately top-down, but bottom-up techniques are used on certain modules and subsystems. This mix alleviates many of the problems of pure top-down validation and retains the advantages of the top-down strategy for subsystem and system integration. Extended sandwich validation subjects each module to extensive validation in isolation prior to inserting the routine into a top-down or bottom-up structure.

Independent Validation

It is generally acknowledged that software validation is best accomplished by personnel who are not involved in the development process. The Department of Defense has developed the concept of independent validation and verification of software (IV&V), whereby an independent organization, using independent tools and techniques, validates the system. It is argued that an independent organization will be more objective, and free from internal management pressures. Other advantages cited for IV&V include increased motivation, specialized skills, and healthy competition.

Projects utilizing IV&V usually achieve the desired levels of quality within schedule and budget; however, the cost of performing IV&V is typically 20% of the total software development cost ([Thayer 75], [Hartwick 77]). The cost of performing IV&V may render the technique unusable for all but the most critical projects. As an intermediate step, many organizations use an independent validation group within the parent organization. These validation groups range from one or two persons functioning as quality control personnel within a project to independent quality assurance departments within the company.

AUTOMATED VALIDATION TOOLS

The desire to improve quality, increase productivity, and increase job satisfaction has resulted in the development of numerous automated validation tools. These tools include automated module test drivers, test data generators, environment

simulators, static analyzers, dynamic testers, symbolic executers, automated proof
systems, and validation libraries. This section of the paper briefly surveys these
tools, excluding automated proof systems.

Module Drivers

Module drivers provide an environment (calling sequences, global data structures)
in which an individual routine can be tested. Drivers pass input data to the routine
and examine output values returned from the routine. Module drivers are often developed manually and often constitute a large portion of the total code written on a
project. Automated module drivers permit the specification of test cases (both inputs and expected outputs) in a descriptive language. The driver tool then executes
the routine on the test cases, compares the outputs to expected outputs, and reports
discrepancies. Some drivers can also be used as stubs for top-down testing. Test
cases are written for the stub and when the stub is invoked by the routine under
test, the driver tool examines the inputs to the stub and returns the corresponding
outputs to the routine. Automated test drivers include AUT [Heuermann 74], MTS
[MSPL 72], TESTMASTER [GE 77], and TPL [Panzl 78].

Test Data Generators

Test data generators are of two varieties: those that generate files of random
data values according to some predefined format, and those that generate test data
for particular execution sequences. As an example of the latter category, symbolic
executers, such as ATTEST, can sometimes be used to derive a set of test data that
will force execution of the program to follow a particular control path [Clarke 76].
Similarly, the generation of test cases from formal specifications is done in the
TESTER system [Peterson 76].

There are other tools that do not generate test data, but do aid in the planning
of test cases. For example, static analyzers can identify the minimum number of
paths that must be executed in order to achieve test coverage of all decision
branches in a module [Krause 73].

Environment Simulators

Environment simulators are sometimes used during integration testing to simulate
the operating environment in which the software will be expected to function. Simulators are used in situations where operation in the actual environment is impracti-
cal. These situations include: development of software for a non-existent machine,

simulation of real time inputs from a non-existent or costly system, and situations where live testing is impossible (e.g., anti-ballistic missile defense systems). Examples of environment simulators include PRIM [Gallenson 75], for emulating non-existent machines, and the Saturn Flight Program Simulator [Jacobs 70].

Static Analyzers

Static analyzers are software tools that examine programs and attempt to discover errors such as uninitialized variables, inconsistent interfaces between routines, variables initialized but never used (on a particular control path; on all control paths), unreachable code segments, and violations of programming standards (local and language standards). Typical static analyzers are AUDIT [Culpepper 75], DAVE [Fosdick 76], FACES ([Ramamoorthy 74], [Ramamoorthy 75]), and RXVP ([Miller 75], [GR 75]). AUDIT detects uninitialized variables and violations of ANSI Fortran standards. DAVE detects errors such as uninitialized variables, errors in subprogram interfaces, and errors in COMMON block alignment in Fortran programs. In addition, DAVE identifies questionable and error-prone constructs such as variables set but never used, and passing constants as arguments to output parameters in subroutines. FACES and RXVP have similar capabilities.

Dynamic Testers

Dynamic testing tools collect, format, and display information needed to ascertain the outcome of test cases. The biggest advantage of dynamic testing is that the behavior of the software can be observed in its actual operating environment, under actual operating conditions. The types of information obtained by dynamic testers includes structural information, execution summary statistics, control flow, data flow and data sensitivity information, environmental information, and dynamic assertion checking. Information concerning program structure (types, scopes, and usages of identifiers; statement types; input and output variables to statements and code blocks; static nesting levels; control flow graph; call graph, etc.) is usually provided by a static analysis of the program text prior to dynamic testing.

Execution summary statistics include ranges of variable values, statement execution counts, and timing estimates. Control flow and data flow information provides the sequences of values assigned to variables and the sequences of statement execution. Data sensitivity shows the effects of input data inaccuracies and finite word length by tracing the numerical significance of a computation. Environmental information includes identifier accessing, parameter passing, and procedure evaluation environments. Assertions are checked by comparing asserted behavior to actual behavior in the execution sequence. Assertions can be local to a particular time in the execution history, or global over some segment (perhaps all) of the program's execution history.

Techniques for implementing dynamic testing tools include hardware monitors, interpreters, and history collection. Hardware monitors are widely used for overall performance measurement of a computing system, but are of limited value for testing particular programs within a system. Interpreters function by maintaining and updating the program's computational state at each step in the execution sequence. They are thus suitable for providing snapshot information concerning the computation, but require augmentation in order to furnish global information or summary statistics.

Execution histories are collected by inserting extra subroutine calls into the source code, generally by using a preprocessor. An execution history contains the complete set of execution states (or some subset) in incremental form. Thus, summary information is readily available, changes in execution states can be traced either forward or backward in execution time, and arbitrarily complex assertions can be checked without forethought. On the other hand, the user cannot stop execution at an arbitrary point, change the execution state in various ways, and continue execution, as is possible when using an interpretive system, because the execution history is a post-mortem data base of program behavior.

ACES [Ramamoorthy 73], ISMS [Fairley 75], PET [Stucki 77], and RXVP ([Miller 75], [GR 75]) are typical dynamic testing tools. ACES allows the user to specify valid ranges for designated variables, and when the specified values are exceeded an error message is generated. PET provides various types of information concerning the execution of Fortran programs: it produces a listing of the number of times each statement in the program was executed, and the number of times each branch direction was taken. The first, last, minimum, and maximum values assigned to selected variables are reported, as are the minimum and maximum values of DO-loop variables. The relative percent of time spent in each subprogram is also reported. In addition, PET has a dynamic assertion processing capability. For example, assertions of the following form can be processed:

    ASSERT A(I) ≠ A(J) FOR ALL (I,J) (1:8)
       WHERE I ≠ J LIMIT 2 VIOLATIONS HALT

The sample assertion statement will cause program termination the second time the first eight elements of array A are not all different when the associated Fortran statement is executed.

RXVP has similar capabilities to PET. ISMS is a history collection and analysis system which is useful for both debugging and testing purposes. In particular, the entire execution history (or some subset) can be viewed as a motion picture of program behavior (at the source level) in the control flow, data flow, or combined domains; either forward or backward in execution time. ACES, PET, and RXVP operate on Fortran programs, while ISMS is a debugging and testing tool for Algol60 programs.

Symbolic Executers

Symbolic execution systems have been developed for several programming languages: ATTEST [Clarke 76] and DISSECT [Howden 78] symbolically execute Fortran programs, EFFIGY [Darringer 78] operates on programs written in a subset of PL/1, and SELECT [Boyer 75] symbolically executes LISP programs. Goals for these systems include automatic generation of output expressions as functions of the input variables and computation paths, detection of infeasible paths through the program, detection of semantic errors in the code, automated generation of test data, informal verification of programs, and formal program verification (proofs of correctness).

All of these systems are experimental in nature. There are no production versions of symbolic executers, although some validation systems have utilized symbolic execution techniques (e.g., FACES [Ramamoorthy 74] and [Ramamoorthy 75]). Problems to be overcome in symbolic execution of source code include handling of loops, symbolic evaluation of subscripts and pointer variables, and treatment of non-linear inequalities in path predicates.

Validation Libraries

An automated library is often the focal point for software development projects. The library typically consists of a data base containing all project documents, source code, object code, test cases, error reports, etc., in machine readable form. Utility programs such as text editors, compilers, report formatters, and management information tools allow easy access to, and manipulation of, materials. Automated library systems include the Software Factory [Bratman 75], PDS [Davis 77], and SCCS [Rochking 75]. Projects that do not incorporate full scale development libraries sometimes utilize validation libraries to maintain code, test cases, error reports, and status information.

CURRENT ISSUES IN SOFTWARE VALIDATION

Previous sections of this paper have mentioned some problem areas and some current research directions in software validation. This section summarizes the issues.

Test Case Design

Dynamic testing is by nature a sampling process. The goal of validation is to infer system quality from a limited number of test cases. The design problem is thus to devise a set of test cases that have maximum likelihood of detecting the maximum number of errors of maximum severity. Testable specifications, static analysis, structured walkthroughs, symbolic execution, a systematic validation strategy, functional, boundary value, and logical tests, and systematic measures of test coverage all contribute to the successful design of test cases. However, it must be recognized that test case design is currently an art form that is practiced with varying degrees of success. Given that a limited number of test cases cannot in general exercise all paths through a module, which paths are the critical ones? How can they be identified and how can test data be derived to force execution of these paths? What are the goals of system level testing, and how can achievement of those goals be measured?

Automated Generation of Tests Cases

Ideally, one would hope that test cases (as opposed to test data), could be derived in an algorithmic manner from functional and design specifications (expressed in a formal notation), and from an analysis of the source program text. One goal of research in symbolic execution is to automatically generate test data for selected execution paths. However, little work has been done to provide guidance in the selection of paths. A goal of research in program mutation [Sayward 78] is to evaluate the ability of test cases to discover particular kinds of errors; however, the method provides no guidance in selecting the test data to be evaluated.

Documentation

Documenting the validation aspects of a software development project encompasses the following areas: documentation that software requirements satisfy user requirements and system requirements; documentation that functional specifications and design specifications satisfy the requirements specifications (a report on walkthroughs, simulations, etc.); documentation of the validation plan (techniques, objectives, schedules, resources); documentation of the validation procedure (techniques, conditions, environment, expected results); documentation of test case design (criteria, techniques, inputs, expected outputs); and a test report (results, explanation of deficiencies, modifications made, assessment of completeness, assessment with respect to requirements specifications). At the present time, there is no standard format for these documents, nor is there uniform agreement on what the documents should contain.

Size and Complexity of Validation Tools

Software validation is a deceptively complex task, and the tools for automated validation are correspondingly complex. Most validation tools are very large complex programs that require extensive computer resources for their operation. For example, a symbolic executer typically contains a parser, a symbolic interpreter, an expression simplifier, an inequality solver, and an interactive dialog package. The expense of implementing and operating automated validation tools has resulted in limited usage of all but the most elementary tools on a routine production basis. Validation tools must be made more compact, more reliable, more efficient, more general in their capabilities, and easier to use before they will achieve widespread usage.

Evaluation of Voluminous Output

Another problem shared by all validation tools is the human engineering issue of what information to display to the user, and how to format the information in a meaningful way. For example, static analyzers often print warning messages that describe error-prone and questionable constructs in the subject program. In fact, one or two true errors may be buried in the reams of warning messages produced, but, overwhelmed by the mass of information, the user may overlook the errors. Similarly, execution histories collected by dynamic testing tools can contain all execution events from a particular test run, or from a set of test runs, thus producing large amounts of data. Errors may be buried in the execution history, but the user may not observe them unless the proper questions are posed at the proper points in the execution history, and are answered in the proper ways. Symbolic executers manipulate computational expressions, which can become very long and complex, even when an expression simplifier is used. In particular, the output expressions derived by symbolic execution may be so complex that the user may overlook errors in the expressions, or errors implied by the expressions.

Integrated Tools

It is obvious that no single validation tool or technique is suitable for validating complex software systems. An integrated set of tools would permit application of different tools to the investigation of different issues, and the tools would be compatible so that the output of one would provide input information for the next. For example, static analyzers often raise questions to be investigated by dynamic testing. An example of an integrated tool is the SADAT system, which consists of a static analyzer, a dynamic analyzer, a test data generator, and a path

predicate calculator [Amschler 78]. The facility is not as general as might be
hoped for, but it does indicate a trend toward integrated systems. Issues to be
addressed in integrated systems include finding the best combination of tools for
particular projects and particular error types, and how to implement compact, efficient collections of tools.

Problems of Special Purpose Systems

   Validation techniques have tended to evolve around validation of small to medium
size programs written in procedural programming languages for execution on sequential machines. Investigators have correctly realized that problems at this level
must be solved before systematic validation of more complex systems can be undertaken. Thus, little is known about systematic validation of real time systems and
transaction driven systems, where the unpredictable pattern of interrupts makes repro-
duction of test cases difficult; or about validating data base systems, where test
cases must exercise access protocols and critical regions in an observable manner;
or about validation of parallel and distributed systems, where scheduling, timing,
and synchronization constraints, must be validated; or about validation of mathematical software, where finite word length and intricate decision logic often make the
design of test cases and interpretation of test results difficult; or about validation of the software component in command and control systems, where simulation of
the external environment may be difficult; or about the problems of validating
extremely large software systems.

Validation of Large Scale Systems

   There are no well-defined techniques or validation tools for testing large scale
systems. Because the development of large scale systems involves many people over
long periods of time, effective validation requires careful coordination, scheduling,
and configuration control. All of the previously mentioned techniques, tools, and
issues are magnified in importance. It is essential that detailed test plans be
derived from the functional requirements and design specifications, that walkthroughs and simulations be performed during detailed design and implementation,
that the system be developed as a collection of functionally independent modules,
and that a systematic validation strategy (top-down, bottom-up, sandwich) be
utilized. Beyond this, there is a lack of knowledge concerning the influence of
various design and development methodologies, the types of problems peculiar to
large scale systems, or the scaling effects encountered in adapting known tools and
techniques to the validation of large scale systems.

Empirical Studies

As in most areas of software engineering, there is a severe lack of empirical
knowledge concerning the utility of various validation tools and techniques. Those
few studies that have been performed tend to raise more questions than they answer.

The three basic techniques of empirical study in software engineering are case
studies, controlled experiments, and evaluation studies [Howden 79]. Case studies
determine the effects of using a particular method on a particular project. While
case studies can produce useful data, it is difficult to compare different methods
used on different projects. Controlled experiments involve the use of different
teams and different methods on the same project. The difficulty with controlled
experiments is that software development projects are so complex that establishing
identical control over the many independent variables in the experiment is virtually
impossible.

An evaluation study determines the properties of a particular method on a carefully selected set of test cases. The major problem with evaluation studies is
determining that the selected set of test cases are representative of the class of
interest.

It is evident that there are problems with all three empirical methods of
evaluating validation tools and techniques. However, the absence of a coherent
theory of validation will force us to rely on these methods in the foreseeable
future.

Testing Theory

Ideally, every validation tool and technique would be based on a particular
theory of error detection in software. An integrated set of tools and techniques
could then be developed with known detection characteristics. In practice, there is
very little theory to guide the development of validation tools and techniques.

The seminal paper in testing theory is by Gerhart and Goodenough [Goodenough 75].
According to Gerhart [Gerhart 79a] development of testing theory has lagged behind
pragmatic developments for several reasons. First, researchers have failed until
recently to realize the necessity of a theoretical framework. Second, many researchers have found program proving to be more attractive, with its connections to
mathematical logic and the programming process, than testing with its statistical,
experimental, *a posteriori* flavor. Third, testing is an extremely difficult theoretical problem; combinatorial complexity and undecidability issues abound. This
has made development of a uniform framework of basic definitions and accepted
terminology difficult.

A comprehensive theory of testing must encompass logical and statistical issues, experimental methodology, management issues, psychology, and the relation of testing to methods used in the pre-implementation and implementation phases of software development. Advances in testing theory will require better terminology (definitions and axioms), development of theorems concerning the feasibility and effectiveness of various techniques, integration of software development methods into the validation process, and experimentation to determine the empirical validity of the theory.

RELATIONSHIP OF VALIDATION TO PRE-IMPLEMENTATION CONSIDERATIONS

This section of the paper examines the relationships between software validation and the pre-implementation phases of software development. Emphasis is placed on applying the previously discussed material to pre-implementation needs and objectives. There are many analogies, many unexplored avenues, and a few irrelevancies.

Techniques

Structured walkthroughs are presently utilized in all phases of software development. In the pre-implementation phases the major goal of a structured walkthrough is to demonstrate that the current specification is internally consistent, and consistent with all previous specifications. Structured walkthroughs are often used as project milestones and management control points.

Static analysis can be used at the specification level to establish completeness, consistency, and lack of ambiguity. For example, the SREM system performs a consistency check on the dimensional units of parameters that appear in interfaces between modules [Alford 77].

Dynamic testing is specific to implemented code, but many of the concepts are applicable to pre-implementation. For example, the categories of functional tests, boundary value tests, and logical tests can be used to validate detailed design specifications against requirements specifications and functional specifications.

Symbolic execution of functional specifications has been explored by Darringer [Darringer 79]. Symbolic execution is attractive at the functional level because looping constructs, inequalities, subscripts, and pointers are absent.

Reliable testing theory has not, to our knowledge, been applied at the pre-implementation level. However, reliable testing theory provides an interesting framework for evaluating formal notations for specification. Are there notations that facilitate discovery of certain classes of errors in certain types of specifications?

Error estimation techniques such as historical data, error seeding, dual teams, and rules of thumb appear to be equally appropriate to the pre-implementation and implementation phases of software development. To our knowledge, predictive models have not been applied at the pre-implementation level.

Systematic validation strategies such as top-down, bottom-up, and sandwich validation have direct counterparts at the design level. In fact, system design strategies are more numerous than systematic validation strategies. Examination of design strategies might indicate new directions for validation.

Independent validation is currently applied to all phases of software development. At the pre-implementation levels, validation of specifications is generally referred to as verification, but we avoid that terminology to prevent confusion with formal verification techniques that are used to establish a formal correspondence between specifications and code.

Automated Tools

Automated tools for software validation are not directly applicable to pre-implementation because they function specifically at the code level. However, there are many cross connections between validation tools and pre-implementation specifications. For example, formal specifications should facilitate automatic generation of test data for the code. Static analyzers should be able to accept specifications and code as inputs, and produce yes/no answers to certain questions of conformity (in general, this is the automated proof of correctness problem, but there are many interesting sub-problems). Is it possible to build environment simulators (perhaps in conjunction with symbolic executors) to provide the environment in which to exercise functional specifications?

Issues

The issues in software validation have direct counterparts at the pre-implementation levels of software development:

> How can one best devise a limited number of test cases that have maximum likelihood of detecting the maximum number of errors in the pre-implementation specifications?
>
> How can test cases be derived from a given level of specification to demonstrate consistency with previous specifications, and to demonstrate conformity of the code?
>
> What types of documentation are appropriate at each state of development? What should be the form and content of documentation?
>
> How can automated tools for all phases of software development be

made more efficient, more compact, more reliable, easier to use, and more general in their capabilities?

How can software development tools be engineered to provide the proper information at the proper time, and to encourage the user to explore the proper issues at the proper time?

Can an integrated set of software tools be developed to facilitate all phases of the software lifecycle?

What types of pre-implementation tools and techniques are appropriate for the development of special purpose systems (real time, data base, distributed, mathematical, command and control, and large scale systems)?

Empirical studies and theoretical models are sorely needed at every level in software engineering. Case studies, controlled experiments, and evaluation studies have the same strengths and weaknesses at the pre-implementation levels as at the validation level. Ideally, every software development tool and technique would be based on a particular theory of software development.

A comprehensive theory of software development must eventually encompass system analysis and design, programming methodology, project management, communication skills, the psychology of goal-oriented groups, and the technological lifecycle. Perhaps a truly comprehensive theory of software development will remain an unattainable goal by which our efforts will be judged.

SUMMARY

This paper has surveyed the field of software validation. The importance of specifications, and problems with specifications in the validation process were stressed. A set of proverbs for software validation was presented. Validation techniques surveyed included structured walkthroughs, static analysis, dynamic testing, symbolic execution, reliable testing theory, error estimation techniques, test case assessment, systematic testing strategies, and independent validation.

Automated tools for software validation were surveyed. They include automated test drivers, test data generators, environment simulators, static analyzers, dynamic testers, symbolic executers, and validation libraries.

Current issues in software validation were discussed. The issues include test case design, automated generation of test cases, documentation, size and complexity of validation tools, integrated sets of tools, problems of special purpose systems, validation of large scale systems, empirical studies, and testing theory.

The relationship of validation concerns to pre-implementation considerations was discussed. It is apparent that validation and pre-implementation issues are closely related. In many cases identical concerns apply at both levels, and in some cases progress in one area provides insight into problems in the other area.

In the past, research at the pre-implementation level and research at the validation level have tended to be isolated areas. It is hoped that this paper, and companion papers in the conference proceedings, will encourage closer cooperation between researchers in the pre-implementation and validation areas.

Although many of the software life cycle charts display validation, verification, and/or testing as a separate phase in the cycle, it was generally agreed that validation and verification activities should be carried out continuously throughout the entire life cycle. In fact, these activities often act as feedback loops to further refine the outputs of previous phases of the life cycle; for example, validation or verification may cause refinement in the requirements. The goal of verification and validation methods is to increase confidence that a given software system is consistent with the specifications of that system. Unfortunately, neither method can contribute much to analyzing whether the specified system actually solves the problem as intended. This latter problem can, to some extent, be addressed "recursively," but ultimately one has to accept the specifications without further logical reasoning or proofs. "But is that what was intended?" is not a mathematical question.

The analysis methods discussed for verification and validation were limited in scope to work primarily with the code of a system. This situation is quite natural since most work has been directed towards techniques for analyzing code. The code is the most easily analyzed description because both the methodology for developing the description and the notation used are well-defined for coding activities. Work needs to be done to attempt to extend code analysis techniques to the other phases of the life cycle, and to enhance the integration of analysis tools throughout.

Much of the discussion was devoted to the presentation of prepared remarks by the discussants for this session, Lori Clarke and Larry Robinson. In these remarks, Clarke commented on Dick Fairley's first proverb: "the purpose of validation is to demonstrate the presence of errors, not their absence." She felt that this:

> ... reflects the current status of most validation tools, but not what I
> consider to be the desired status. A major weakness of many validation
> tools is that when no errors are found, it is unclear what has actually
> been achieved. Usually after validating a program, one has more confi
> dence in the reliability of the program. This confidence, however, may
> be unfounded. Certainly, if a validation tool can assure the absence
> of some class of errors, then that justifiably increases confidence in
> the program. Subsequently, if an error is found, only non-proven as
> pects of the program need be examined for the source of the error.
>
> Static analysis tools, particularly those for data flow analysis,
> guarantee the absence of certain errors. Dynamic analysis and sym
> bolic execution systems address a wider class of errors than static

analysis systems, but only for a subset of the program. Thus, these tools only guarantee the absence of a class of errors for the analyzed subset of the program. If this subset is well chosen, then perhaps stronger inferences can be made about the program's reliability. More work, supported by empirical results, needs to be done in this area.

Lori Clarke also provided a number of comments on why verification and validation techniques have not received more use during the pre-implementation phases:

Both Fairley and London point out that the vast majority of existing validation and verification tools are aimed at analysis during the implementation phase. This is not surprising since coding is the best understood phase in the software life cycle. Only recently have the pre-implementation phases of requirements, specifications, and design become recognized and their need established. (There is still disagreement, as is evident in the literature, on the number, names, and functionality of these phases.) To provide analysis during the pre-implementation phases, notations to express the resulting product and methods to support systematic development during each of these phases are needed.

Notational descriptions for the pre-implementation phases are only beginning to be investigated. English is usually too ambiguous, even for the requirements phase. Some of the more formal notations, such as algebraic specifications, seem more appropriate as secondary forms of description rather than as primary forms. A secondary description provides redundancy that can be useful during analysis, but is too concise to be the primary medium for communication. The development of satisfactory and well-accepted notations for the pre-implementation phases will evolve as our experience with such notations expands. Programming languages, the notational medium for the coding phase, still pose many controversial issues and are forever undergoing change. Pre-implementation languages will probably undergo this same type of metamorphosis as they mature.

Methods to support program development during each life cycle phase are also desired. Analysis techniques can then be developed to monitor adherence to a development method. In general, program development methods facilitate analysis since they generally impose some rigor on the development process. For example, loop analysis during symbolic evaluation is easier on structured code than on unstructured code to such an extent that it is usually not undertaken on the latter.

With respect to how verification and validation techniques fit within a more encompassing development environment, Clarke offered these observations:

Software analysis is just one component of a support system to facilitate software development. Such a support system should provide at least the following set of capabilities during all phases of the life cycle:

- Creation and editing capabilities that are knowledgeable about the notations, development methods, and existing environment. Support for a large number of users working on a shared project should be provided.

- Report generation capabilities that provide both graphical and tabular representations of the current state of a developing software project. A wide spectrum of management and programming reports should be available.

- Testing capabilities that facilitate the execution or simulation of the proposed system during all phases of development and that support regression testing.

- Analysis tools to detect errors and incomplete structures. This encompasses a wide range of tools including static analysis, data flow analysis, symbolic evaluation, dynamic analysis, and verification.

Fortunately, much of the information needed to accomplish these tasks is related. A data base of program information should be created and maintained during software development. A shared program data base would eliminate the inefficiency of each analysis method gathering similar information. Moreover, it would facilitate the integration of analysis methods within and between software development phases. Information gathered by one analysis method could be utilized by another method. Such a data base could be used to monitor the incremental growth of a software project and to facilitate comparisons between phases.

Clarke's overall conclusions were that:

Analysis tools for the pre-implementation phase of the software life cycle are few. This is not surprising based on the current state of research in these areas. Analysis methods as well as other support capabilities must follow the development of better notations and methods to facilitate program development during these phases. Many of the analysis techniques developed for the coding phase should be applicable to the pre-implementation phases. However, analysis methods for the coding phase, though more developed than analysis tools for the other phases, are still, for the most part, experimental prototype systems. There is still more work to be done in this area. Empirical studies are needed to understand the strengths and weaknesses of the existing analysis methods. These studies should lead to the development of more integrated tools that combine the strengths of various analysis methods. Such an integration of analysis techniques should be considered within each phase of the software development life cycle as well as between different phases.

The discussion then turned to the technique of program mutation. The method of creating program mutations by exchanging variables, operators, or labels, omitting statements, etc., and then executing the mutated program with its test data can detect errors on the executed program paths but may not detect all errors. Program mutation may, however, address one class of bugs which are difficult to find with other analysis methods: misspelled variable names that collide with other variables. Carl Hewitt noted that in other scientific disciplines theories are tested by independent validation, and not by mutation. Others expressed skepticism concerning the combinatorial explosion of the mutation method.

A major deficiency of the mutation method, and of most other validation techniques is that they fail to detect missing path errors. Test data that will not reveal missing code in a program will not reveal the error in a mutated program. In general, no validation method that relies solely on the code can detect a failure to satisfy the specification.

Lori Clarke also noted an interesting aspect of verification. Students were assigned small programs to write and verify. All of the programs were "proved" correct, but not all of them were (the act of writing "QED" does not, by itself, vouch for an acceptable proof). This points to the need for some form of consistency checking in verification; e.g., proof checkers and automated verification systems. It also emphasizes that proofs have various standards, levels of formality, and varied criteria of acceptability (i.e., proofs are accepted by sociological agreement).

Larry Robinson, in his remarks, turned attention to formal specification and verification and their interplay. His comments are covered by the following writeup which he kindly prepared:

> We are concerned here primarily with tools for testing and formal verification (hereafter called simply "verification"). There are several distinctions to be made. Testing is a mature and usable technology for software engineering. Verification, on the other hand, exists primarily in the research community, and needs some development before it is ready for production use. This commentary will address verification and its use in software tools and environments.
>
> Verification is not ready to be used in production software environments for the following reasons:
>
> - More research must be done to solve some theoretical problems, particularly in improving the power of theorem provers and in developing proof rules for useful application domains.
> - Verification techniques must be better integrated into the software life cycle. Verification is extremely sensitive to the specification technique, the programming language, and even the structure of the system being verified. Thus, a complete methodology

that includes verification will probably place constraints on all of the above factors.

- Once the first two goals have been met, a set of tools must be developed that provides a complete and continuous software development environment. A "bag of tricks" will not suffice.

If these three cannot be solved, then verification will not become useful as a software development technique.

In spite of the research nature of formal verification techniques, some aspects of verification can be used today. Ralph London has already pointed out some of them in his comments. I will try to point out others. It is particularly important to visualize the impact of verification in the pre-implementation phases of software development, since at present verification is usually performed after the programs have been written.

The Role of Specifications

Verification is concerned mainly with how to achieve a proof once all the ingredients -- programs and formal specifications -- are present. How the programs and specifications are developed is another matter. Sometimes the specifications are developed after the program, sometimes before. In many cases the specifications are considered "annotations" to the program.

Before discussing these issues, it is necessary to define what a specification is. At the conference on Specifications of Reliable Software (Boston, 1979), the term "specification" was being used with the following meanings, sometimes simultaneously in the same discussion:

- A statement of system requirements.
- An informal statement of what the system actually does.
- A formal statement of what the system actually does (i.e., the assertions used in program verification).

In this discussion, "requirements statement" refers to the first item, "informal specification" to the second, and "specification" or "formal specification" to the third.

In an ideal environment, formal specifications can be important for reasons other than verification. Formal specifications can be extremely important in the software life cycle, perhaps more important than the actual code. Specifications are read by the users of the system and by the other system developers, while code may not be read by anyone except the person writing (or maintaining) it. A specification can be a contract between the user and the developer of a piece of software. Specifications should be written before the implementation takes place.

The following set of steps for system development is proposed:

1) Statement and analysis of the system requirements.
2) Formal specification of the interface of the system to its external environment.
3) Decomposition of the system into component parts.
4) Formal specification of the interface of each of the components and of the interconnection of the components to make the system.
5) Implementation of each of the components.
6) Verification of the correctness of the system. Testing should also be performed at this point.

Formal specifications can also be of use even if the system is not verified. The specifications help in getting all of the system interfaces precisely defined, thus making integration easier. Because most of the errors in systems occur in interfaces, formal specifications should have a favorable impact on system reliability, although this has not been verified experimentally as yet.

There are two kinds of verification possible:

• Verifying that the implementation of a system meets its specifications. This is the standard kind of verification to which Ralph London refers.

• Verifying that the specifications are consistent with some formal statement of a system's requirements. This kind of verification is becoming particularly useful to verify security properties of a system, and has been used in some secure operating system projects.

To verify that the system's implementation meets some formally stated requirements, both types of verification are required.

HDM: Example of Existing Work

Ralph London has already described some of the current verification efforts. This section describes some of the work being done at SRI International and at Ford Aerospace on HDM (Hierarchical Development Methodology) [Robinson 75], which has made some steps in addressing pre-implementation issues using verification techniques.

HDM is a set of techniques, supported by languages and tools, for designing, formally specifying, implementing, and verifying systems. It is based on a computational model that describes how computations in a system takes place.

The HDM computational model is based on an abstract machine, which provides a set of operations, and an abstract program, which executes

sequences of instructions on the abstract machine. An abstract machine
can be implemented in hardware or software. To the users of the abstract
machine it does not matter which: they see only the formal specifications
of the abstract machine's interface. In a software implementation, an abstract program is written for each operation of the abstract machine to
be implemented. A system is described as a hierarchy, or sequence, of
abstract machines, in which each abstract machine is implemented on the
abstract machine at the next lower level of the hierarchy.

Formal specifications for each abstract machine are written in a
nonprocedural specification language called SPECIAL (SPECIFication and
Assertion Language). The specifications for each operation are assertions about how the values of the abstract machine's state variables
change as a result of invoking the operation. Techniques have been developed to prove that an abstract program meets a set of specifications,
that an abstract machine is correctly implemented by a set of programs
running on another abstract machine, and that invariants on the state
variables of the abstract machine are logically valid. A particular
application of these techniques allows a proof that a SPECIAL specification obeys the rules of military multilevel security.

There are several online tools to support HDM that have been developed at SRI International:

- A parser and type-checker for SPECIAL
- A checker for interconnections among the specifications of the
  system.
- A verification-condition generator (a tool that, given a program
  and a specification, generates formulae that imply the program's
  correctness) for correctness of implementation. The implementation language is a simple low-level language into which programs
  in high-level languages (such as Modula and Jovial J73) can be
  translated.
- A theorem generator for the multilevel security proofs mentioned
  above.

The formulae generated by the last two tools must then be proved by the
Boyer-Moore theorem prover, also developed at SRI International but not
specific to HDM. These tools are a first step toward a full set of formal specification and verification tools. However, they require too much
effort from the user and they are not well-integrated. An environment
which does not suffer these problems is described in the next section
of this discussion.

HDM has been used to design the following large systems, for which
implementation (and possible verification) is either planned or in progress:

- KSOS-11 (Kernelized Secure Operating System) is a multilevel, secure version of UNIX to run on a Digital Equipment PDP-11/70. Ford Aerospace and Communications Corporation is developing the system under contract to the Department of Defense (DoD). The system has been designed and formally specified, and its implementation and verification are now in progress.

- KSOS-6 is a multilevel, secure version of UNIX to run on a Honeywell Level 6, with some modifications to improve its security. Honeywell Corporation is developing the system under contract to DoD. The system has been designed and formally specified, and its implementation and verification are now in progress.

- PSOS (Provably Secure Operating System) is a new operating system, based on domains and capabilities, for which hardware was specially designed. SRI International conceived the system originally for DoD (in fact, HDM was originally developed to write the first formal specifications for PSOS). A procurement for its detailed design, implementation, and verification is now in progress.

- SIFT (Software Implemented Fault Tolerance) is an ultra-reliable system to be used in aircraft control. SRI International is developing the system under contract to NASA Langley Research Center. The system was designed and formally specified, and its implementation and verification are now in progress. A model of the system's intended response to hardware faults was developed (the system is supposed to tolerate any single fault and reconfigure around it), and the specifications are to be proved consistent with the model.

From designing these systems, much has been learned that will allow improvements to HDM and succeeding methodologies; much more will be learned when these systems have been implemented. The major lessons are:

- The languages and tools can be improved to be better-integrated and easier to use.

- More power -- to specify certain phenomena such as concurrency -- is required.

- Formally specifying a system can result in benefits even if verification is not attempted. The rigor of formal specifications has uncovered potential design errors in the KSOS-11 system before they might otherwise have been discovered. In the KSOS-11 project the formal specifications were used as a basis for the system's informal prose specifications.

HDM is but one example of a broad-based methodology. Gypsy [Ambler 77], developed at the University of Texas at Austin, is another.

Needs for Specification and Verification Tools

To have a good environment for specifying and verifying systems, a set of integrated tools is needed. Clearly all of the tools mentioned above as a part of HDM are required. The following would also be desirable.

Development data base. This keeps track of the current state of the system, including specifications, programs, and records of proofs. All

changes to the system are done through this tool, which can keep track
of possible inconsistencies as a result of a given change. To resolve
the inconsistencies, the tool could either make necessary changes to
other parts of the system or could indicate to the user the places where
changes should be made. This tool would keep track of versions and releases of a given system, and could recover a past version of a system.

Incremental capability. Whenever changes are made to a system, much
rechecking has to be done. If the system is to be verified, the proofs
have to be redone as well, often at considerable cost. The incremental
capability tries to minimize the amount of rechecking to be done after a
change -- including proofs -- to determine whether the changes have left
the system in a consistent state. This tool would make use of information
provided by the development data base, as well as its own knowledge of the
dependencies among different parts of the system. These dependencies are
closely related to the computational model being used. In the HDM computational model, for example, there is a great emphasis on allowing
units a maximum amount of independence (e.g., a change in an implementation of an abstract machine that satisfies the specifications does not
affect any software at levels above the original abstract machine).

Specification execution. This is a tool that is particularly well-
suited to pre-implementation considerations. This tool would, given
only the formal specification of a piece of software, simulate its behavior. Thus, it would be possible to test a program that uses a piece
of software that has been specified but not implemented. This is a good
basis for top-down implementation, providing a test frame mechanism without having to build one separately or use the limited concept of stubs.
Such a tool would also be useful for potential users to see how an entire
system is to operate based on the formal specification; users who do not
know how to read formal specifications can see if the system will behave
as intended. Such a tool has already been developed for algebraic specifications as part of the Affirm system [Thompson 79].

Research Areas

As formal specification and verification *per se* is a research area,
all of its aspects are going to be the subject of basic research, for
the present time. However, I am going to point out areas that are in
particular need of research.

Properties of Systems. Most specification and verification environments are satisfactory for specifying and proving properties of individual
programs. However, for production software it is necessary to be able to

prove the properties of entire systems of programs. Such systems may
share information in unusual ways, and many (often subtle) assumptions
between parts of the system exist. Thus, verifying properties of systems
is more than just a matter of verifying several programs. More emphasis
should be placed on the "systems" aspects of software verification. Abstract data types and modules are a starting point, but more must be done.

Computational Model Research. Every programming language is based on
a computational model as described above. Often, in specification and
verification techniques, the model is lost, having been replaced by a few
"axioms" that attempt to formalize the computations taking place. When
there is a need to extend the computational model (e.g., to encompass
concurrency), a few more axioms are added. Some problems with the adding of axioms are:

- The axioms may be inconsistent.
- Because of the discrepancy between the computational environment and the axioms, it is difficult to check whether the axioms
  correspond to the actual computational environment, especially
  for more complex ones.
- There is a tendency to choose axioms that are close to what one
  wishes to prove.

These tendencies raise questions about the soundness of proofs based on
such axioms. More attention should be given to a careful definition of
the computational model, perhaps using operational or functional definitions. Then what used to be axioms could be formally demonstrated on the
basis of these more complete definitions.

New Kinds of Specification Techniques. Almost all verification
techniques are based on the inductive assertion method, originally developed by Floyd and Hoare. These techniques imply a specification
method based on assertions. However, other specification methods have
been shown to be useful of late. Of particular interest are applicative
techniques, in which the action of software systems is modeled by a mathematical function (and sequencing, concurrency, and data flow are modeled
by manipulating the functions, their arguments, and results), and grammatical techniques, in which the structure of the input and output data
can be specified as a grammar and the processing of data can be specified
by attaching actions to the rules of the grammar. It seems that applicative techniques are useful for determining the overall logical structure of the problem and the system to solve it (so applicative techniques
may also be useful for requirements statements). Grammatical techniques
seem to be useful in cases where the data has a complex structure. These
specification techniques can be explored further, and -- if possible --

verification techniques for them should be developed.

Short-term Payoffs. The ultimate benefits of verification are still a long way off. However, there is much verification technology that can be used in the short term. Specification without verification, as mentioned above, has already been demonstrated to be beneficial. Furthermore, it now seems possible to construct a "production-oriented" verification system, which would not be as powerful as some of the existing systems but could prove limited properties of programs with minimum user intervention (or sophistication). Some possible properties could be the "clean termination" properties: termination of loops, subscripts in range, pointer behavior. These properties could be proved without requiring users to write assertions.

Conclusion.

It seems that specification and verification technology has enormous potential for improving the quality of software. The problem remains for researchers to determine a subset of this technology to be used immediately. Since that has not been done yet, we can talk mostly of potential rather than results.

Chapter VIII. Summary

On the evening before the final session, the participants divided into three subgroups to consider the following issues:

> Where to next with respect to Support Systems?
> Where to next with respect to Specification Languages?
> Where to next with respect to Analysis Techniques?

Recommendations from the three "subcommittees" follow.

WHERE TO NEXT WITH RESPECT TO SOFTWARE DEVELOPMENT SUPPORT SYSTEMS?

This report was compiled and delivered by Nico Habermann. It is divided into four topics:

- Why are software development support systems not widely used at the present time?
- What are the major issues?
- What should we be doing now?
- What should we be doing in the future?

Reasons for Lack of Acceptance

1. The physical environment is often inadequate to support a software development system. Development support systems require hardware support, interactive computing capability, and fast-response terminals.

2. In the past, programmers were considered to be inexpensive, and support systems thought to be expensive. This attitude is slowly changing, but the cost effectiveness of development support systems, in terms of increased programmer productivity and product reliability, has not been widely demonstrated.

3. There is no accepted technique for demonstrating the benefits of a software development support system.

4. There is never adequate time or resources to develop a support system within the framework of a particular project, and there is a lack of incentive to develop support systems using company resources.

5. Investment of capital resources and manpower in the development of a support system is viewed as a high risk venture.

6. With isolated exceptions, such as UNIX and InterLisp, there has been a lack of imagination in designing and developing support systems.

7. Failures of the past, and oversell of inadequate systems, have made managers and programmers cautious in their approach to software development support systems.

Major Issues in Software Development Support Systems

1. There are several ways to categorize a software development project:

   • number of levels of management
   • size of project team and duration of project
   • size, type, and complexity of product

The predominant viewpoint will determine the type and level of support system needed.

2. Toolboxes provide a coherent collection of relatively small, individual tools with uniform interfaces between tools. They can be used in various combinations to achieve various results. Support systems maintain the state of the project and have knowledge of the objects being manipulated. This provides more context, but perhaps less flexibility, than a toolbox. Some projects benefit from toolboxes, while support systems are more appropriate for other projects.

3. File systems and data bases can be used to maintain project information. It is not clear which data organization is appropriate in which situations.

4. Support systems can be designed to provide one uniform notation for all phases of a software development project, or to provide different notations in different phases. Considerable controversy surrounds the issue of whether a single language or multiple languages should be used.

Recommended Current Research Direction

1. Investigate the following specific issues:

   • Determine end user's project information needs.
   • Understand the organization of projects and people and determine the types and levels of support needed.
   • Determine what information to record.
   • Provide support for particular development methods and derive new development metaphors and viewpoints.
   • Integrate useful packages of tools into support systems.
   • Investigate extensibility issues for software development support systems.

2. Investigate the software development process to determine how the following specific facilities can be provided by support systems:

- Product visibility information
- Management information
- System construction and evaluation tools
- Program construction and evaluation tools
- Log history
- Version control and maintenance information.
- Project and product documentation

3. Determine the influence of the following hardware capabilities on the software development process:

- High resolution displays
- Terminal speed and screen size
- Intelligent terminals
- Computer networks

Recommended Future Research Directions

1. Continue to investigate all of the specific issues listed under item 1. of the previous section. Also, investigate the contributions to be made by the application of artificial intelligence techniques to the software development process.

2. Continue to investigate all of the specific facilities issues listed under item 2. of the previous section. In addition, investigate the incorporation of formal verification tools into all phases of the software development process.

3. Investigate future developments in hardware capabilities, including:

- Color graphics
- Voice recognition
- VLSI impact on intelligent terminals

4. Determine the mutual impact of software development support systems and the educational process on each other.

5. Find the correct approach to software development support systems by:

- making support systems widely available;
- generating much more data on how programmers spend their time, types of errors made, when bugs are found, etc.; and
- letting natural evolution and selection occur.

WHERE TO NEXT WITH RESPECT TO DESIGN LANGUAGES

This report was compiled and presented by Alan Shaw. In his prefatory remarks, Shaw noted that: 1) the original mission was to consider specification languages in general but the discussion centered mainly upon design languages, and 2) the sub-group was composed almost entirely of people from academia and industrial research institutions.

Scope of Applicability of Design Languages

Design languages are of use from the latter part of the requirements definition phase through the early part of the implementation phase.

Purposes of a Design Language

1. The language should allow the specification of a system's gross structural aspects when that structure is not completely worked out and has the status of being one of a number of hypothetical, candidate structures.

2. The language should support the derivation of information needed to answer questions about the candidate structures and their similarities and differences. This derivation could be accomplished in a variety of ways including simulation, analysis and inspection.

3. The language should facilitate the communication of the design to other people. This includes communication to requirements definers and system implementors.

Some Desirable Features of Design Languages

1. The languages should, following the trend established by several newly defined programming languages, permit abstraction and iterative refinement.

2. The languages should allow, collectively but not necessarily individually, the description of several different views of a system. Some views of possible utility are: data flow, data structure, process, event, communication, queue-based, and abstract machine. If a language or collection of languages focuses upon one view, then others should be easily derivable.

3. The languages should support the process of demonstrating the feasibility of a hypothetical system structure, for example, by the implementation of a proto-type.

4. The languages should be machine-executable so that some of a system's

dynamic properties can be obtained from the description.

Some Observations on the Current State of Affairs

1. There is a distinction, not always realized, between languages for use while designing and languages for expressing a design.

2. Common current-day languages for designing (as opposed to expressing a design) are generally informal and are of four major classes:

- pseudo-programming languages (e.g., pseudo-code, etc.)
- pictorial languages (e.g., block diagrams, data structure graphs, instance diagrams, etc.)
- state-oriented languages (e.g., finite-state models, etc.)
- activity languages (e.g., example traces, event sequences, flows, scripts, etc.)

3. There is a lack of data upon which to compare different design methods (such as Jackson, Yourdon, HDM, etc.) and different description techniques. Data are needed on, among other things: failures, successes, descriptive power, flexibility, and views which can be represented.

Main Conclusions

1. Work is needed on the experimental comparison and evaluation of existing design languages.

2. Much more needs to be done before truly effective design languages exist.

WHERE TO NEXT WITH RESPECT TO ANALYSIS SYSTEMS?

This report was compiled and presented by Dick Fairley. It is divided into two sections: short-term research directions, and long-term research directions.

Short-term Research Directions

1. Catalog, organize, and publicize existing tools. One reason analysis tools are not widely used is simple lack of awareness. The Institute for Computer Sciences and Technology of the National Bureau of Standards is inviting developers and users of software tools to participate in an exchange of information on testing and development tools.

2. Publish guidelines to analysis tools and techniques. Too often, only

researchers in the area of analysis tools are familiar with the benefits, short-comings, and tradeoffs between various analysis tools and techniques. This informa-tion must be disseminated on a much wider basis, through textbooks, and conference and journal papers.

3. Develop basic tools and programming environments. There are many simple, inexpensive analysis tools that could be, and should be, part of every programming environment, in the same manner as compilers and text editors. Some of these tools should be available for stand alone usage, and others as options in compilers.

4. Standardize low level modules. One way to reduce the analysis (and synthe-sis) problem is to make extensive use of standard routines for low level functions in a software system. In this manner, a high-level abstract machine foundation can be provided for software development.

5. Conduct controlled experiments. As in all areas of software engineering, analysis suffers from a lack of quantitative data on which to base decisions and pursue new directions. In the analysis area, two types of experiments are needed: those that collect and analyze error data, and those that determine the cost effec-tiveness and benefits of automated analysis tools.

6. Do systematic prototype development. There are many interesting ideas for analysis tools. Most of these proposals can only be evaluated by constructing a prototype system and experimentally determining its capabilities. A systematic approach to implementing and evaluating alternatives is needed.

7. Apply verification, validation, and formal verification tools and techniques to the pre-implementation phases of software development. All analysis tools and techniques are concerned with demonstrating the correspondence between actual (or simulated) and desired structure and behavior of a software system. Given appropri-ate notations, all of the techniques available at the source code level can be applied at the pre-implementation levels. In fact, some techniques, such as symbolic execution, appear to be less complex at the pre-implementation levels.

8. Study the influence of the application area. Although many analysis con-siderations are independent of the particular application area, many special purpose techniques can be applied to particular classes of systems. Conversely, many analy-sis techniques do not work for real-time and concurrent systems.

9. Learn from other disciplines. Every problem solving activity involves prob-lem definition, requirements analysis, design, implementation, and verification of the solution. Scientists, engineers, and architects have both general and speci-fic methods of analyzing their artifacts. Surely there is much to be learned from studying their methods.

Long-term Research Directions

1. Develop analysis tools and techniques for distributed systems. In the past, the majority of analysis efforts have been developed for applications programs and traditional systems software. Analysis techniques must be developed to account for the additional problems introduced by distributed computing systems.

2. Develop analysis tools and techniques for performance modelling. The major emphasis of current analysis efforts concerns the functional characteristics of software. To date, little has been done on analyzing the dynamic performance character-istics of a software system at the specification and design levels.

3. Develop analysis tools and techniques for systems requirements. System analysis (interactions of people, hardware, and software subsystems) is the least understood, and potentially most significant, phase of software development. Tools and techniques are sorely needed to analyze system requirements and determine the degree to which they satisfy the problem statement.

4. Incorporate knowledge bases and context into analysis tools. As in the case of design tools, the effectiveness of analysis tools could be greatly enhanced by developing tools that function in certain contextual environments, and make use of a knowledge base of the product being analyzed.

5. Apply verification and validation techniques and formal verification tech-niques to the pre-implementation phases of software development. This is both a short-term and long-term research direction.

6. Develop integrated analysis systems. There are many complementary approaches to the analysis of software systems (static analysis, dynamic testing, symbolic test-ing, formal verification) that might be integrated into an analysis system.

7. Develop quality metrics. If concrete quality metrics can be developed, they can be translated into software properties that result in desirable characteristics of the software product. Analysis tools can then be developed to identify weak areas, and to measure the quality of a software product.

8. Study the nature of errors. As new synthesis and analysis techniques are developed, certain classes of problems will be solved and new problems will be created. Continuing study of error patterns will be necessary to identify the strengths and weaknesses of new tools and techniques.

9. Increase fault tolerance. In other disciplines, fault tolerance is in-creased by increasing the redundancy of the system. Analysis tools should be developed to determine the degree of redundancy in a software system, and the in-fluence of redundancy on reliability.

10. Axiomatize the remaining trouble spots. Formal verification of source

programs is dependent on the existence of axioms that describe the semantics of the implementation language. Numerous trouble spots remain, such as the axiomatization of floating point numbers, and the aliasing of variables.

11. Influence curriculum developments. Software design and analysis tools will become widely used when programmers become familiar with their capabilities. This can best be accomplished as part of the educational process. Witness the spread in popularity of Pascal, which is partly due to the widespread use of Pascal in universities.

The discussion following the subcommittee reports began with a short presentation by Bob Snowdon and Dave Pearson in which they indicated their concern over the philosophy toward support systems and tools evidenced by the remarks throughout the workshop. Their worry was that if care is not taken, we will end up with a hodge podge of tools on the market which do not *really* help, in general, to produce good systems in every sense of that term. Further, they indicated that they felt some of the development systems now on the market could be seen as the beginning of this trend. They felt the major problem is that support system and tool developers may be distracted by specifics rather than paying attention to the general issues; they characterized this as a "great leap backwards." They concluded their remarks by indicating that their prognoses were intended to be both hopeful in the sense that they believed that there are "one or two" support system and tool developers in the world who are demonstrating concern for total systems development and also disparing in the sense that events, and an apparent lack of awareness of them, may well overtake us before we realize it.

The rest of the discussion covered a number of topics and is presented below in topical rather than chronological order.

SYSTEM LIFECYCLE

There was much additional discussion of the various phases of software projects. The standard waterfall chart with Requirements, Specifications, Design, Implementation, Coding and Maintenance was found to be inadequate to describe the actual life cycle of a software product. Bob Snowdon suggested that "systems morphology," a new framework which addresses the life cycle, could soon replace the standard "waterfall" view. Dick Fairley pointed out that development is a non-linear process; many procedures are performed recursively. This implies that CADES-like systems may be inadequate as they are state-change oriented and do not capture the complexities of nesting or loops.

The strongest complaint about the waterfall chart is that it shunts off 80% of the life cycle into the amorphous category, "maintenance." Tricia Santoni pointed out that the Navy is "drowning" in maintenance. Dick Fairley quoted figures citing maintenance as being 20% bug repair, 20% adaptation to new environments and 60% product enhancement. Given this view, maintenance should be renamed evolution and

the waterfall chart should be a loop instead of a linear sequence, in which Requirements, Specifications, Design, Implementation and Coding are considered as steps in
each iteration. Others identified the current view as being responsible for inadequate marketing strategies by software vendors: products should be priced to include maintenance over the long term.

DESIGNS, DESIGNING, AND DESIGN REVIEW

The proposed development support systems seem to address the design phase most
directly (or perhaps this is an area in which we are better versed than in requirements or specification phases). The discussion concerned two topics: how are designs done now, and what should the properties of designs be in the future.

Designs are communicated to implementors by large, English language documents.
These documents may not necessarily be produced at all; if they are not available
at the time of implementation, they will not be produced either due to lack of need
or lack of time. This may be less of a hindrance than first supposed, since the
design team is quite frequently the implementation team, so the design can be communicated informally. It was observed that even if the documents are produced, as they
are required to be in the military environment, and conform to a standard, all that
is standard within the document is the paragraph numbers. There is no commonality
among the components of design documents. After a document is produced, there is
no guarantee that it will be kept up to date with the evolving implementation which
inevitably requires design modifications. Steve Zilles observed that the non-
linearity of the development process inhibits the generation of linear model results
such as design documents. It is not clear in practice how the design document
differs from the requirements definition. Chuck Bradley pointed out that for many
applications, a strictly external view (I/O and performance) has been sufficient.

Paul Zeiger asked if design reviews are successful. Tom Love pointed out that
methodologies to deal with groups of people are needed here. Communication, group
organization, and group dynamics play a large role in the probability of success of
reviews. Steve Zilles identified structured walkthroughs as a well-known and successful technique that has been applied to Code, Pseudo-Code and Decomposition phases.
It was found that walkthroughs succeeded in finding coding errors, but were not that
successful at finding design errors. He remarked that the major objection to
current design documents is that they do not isolate the "important points" from
the non-relevant ones, and suggested that more structuring of the English within
the document should occur. Dick Fairley observed that a design review serves mostly
to get the reviewee to study his work prior to the meeting, which is probably the
major advantage of the process. Bill Riddle identified this function as the major

one behind all pre-implementation software tools and suggested that the major advantage of all tools is an enhanced ability to examine one's work.

The second phase of the discussion focused on the notion of executability of designs. Alan Shaw elaborated that this could range anywhere from some sort of simulation, analysis or measurement, all the way to mechanical program production. Objections were raised that this had the tendency to further blur the design-implementation distinction (as Ada does). Shaw replied that the generation of code was an extreme view, but should not be eliminated. Roy Campbell observed that the purpose of design is to determine feasibility, and that feedback is a good way of getting this information. Others pointed out some design techniques, such as the graphical ones (e.g., HIPO) do not lend themselves to execution and that orthogonal representations provide valuable insights without executability.

Terry Straeter had argued in an earlier session for increased software breadboarding to demonstrate feasibility, and this theme was carried on by Carl Hewitt. It was pointed out that executable designs offer this capacity early in the development process. Hewitt suggested that prototypes should be small and easy to generate so that they can be experimented with not only by the designers but by customers. George Cannon observed that there is a danger in letting the customer see a prototype because he may not then understand or appreciate the lag time between its production and the product's final emergence from the implementation phase. Others claimed that early prototyping freezes representation decisions too early. Bob Rosin responded that modules incorporated into the prototype provide the same functionality as the final product but they need not use the same representation.

NON-TECHNICAL CONSIDERATIONS

Many people argued that industry is not the place where a new wave of good tools will arise since industry cannot afford the failures (these are the purvue of academia). Contrarily, it was observed that universities cannot produce commercial software products because of the problems involved with distribution and maintenance. Taylor Booth claimed that there is not the same financial incentive to produce software products because of the ease of unauthorized use without remuneration. Others countered that even bootlegged systems like UNIX have been successfully and widely licensed to corporations that require product support.

Product maintenance was further identified as a problem unto itself. As soon as a product becomes successful, effort which could have gone to future products must now be expended on maintenance, making it less likely that a second success could come from the same group. Tom Love identified this as an example of the "pregnancy effect": by the time the situation becomes evident, its too late to do anything about it. Carl Hewitt noted that further compounding this is the Second System Syndrome, e.g., CTSS was followed by MULTICS. In retaliation, he said, emerges what could be called the "Third System Syndrome": rising from the ashes of a second system failure, a small group of people get together (perhaps at a Chinese restaurant in Cambridge at 3 a.m.) and revolutionarily design a new system. Bob Rosin pointed out that this was the genesis of UNIX. Gary Nutt argued that the impetus to get good, new tools will come from former students that have seen such tools in the university environment and agitate for them within their companies. Bob Rosin further argued that as soon as good tools become narrowly available, they cannot help but become widely so. Others felt that new tools would derive from industries which are their own best customers: for example, Tektronix makes good oscilloscopes because it uses oscilloscopes in its manufacturing process. This can work analogously for software.

SOFTWARE CATCHING UP TO HARDWARE

Nico Habermann observed that a changing hardware base means that software must be developed faster to keep up. Others suggested that we should design our systems independently of hardware because of this fluctuating foundation. Haberman was dubious that performance characteristics could be successfully maintained with such an approach. Vic Lesser suggested that our software development systems should be transportable to new hardware as the hardware below and the software above changes.

Productivity was conjectured to be declining as the software tasks increases in complexity. Bob Rosin rejected that view, citing an ability to solve quite rapidly tasks which might have taken weeks in the 1950's. Rather, Rosin cited Dijkstra's argument in the "Humble Programmer" paper that the reason for the mistaken observation is that we are tackling problems of different orders of magnitude than we were in the 1950's. In fact, it was suggested that our productivity has increased polynomially, but our problems have increased exponentially. Roy Campbell suggested that this should tend to induce smaller, self-contained tools, more easily understood and more successfully produced.

WHAT SYSTEMS TO USE

UNIX was largely agreed to be the outstanding system currently available, although Carl Hewitt pointed out that INTERLISP, MACLISP and EMACS have a similar functionality. Smalltalk, Mesa and Cedar were rejected due to unavailability of the hardware on which they run. Paul Zeiger asked what system he ought to use as a kernel for tools research on a new VAX. One opinion was that he should use UNIX but to be quite careful not to become satisfied with it or use it as a framework for the incorporation of new tools because this could lead to a unalterable dependence on a soon to be outdated tool.

George Cannon asked how we can induce programmers to accept others' products instead of writing their own. Bob Rosin answered that if the standard tools are easy to use and easy to access, the programmer would prefer the standard tool.

CONCLUSION

Some thought was given as to whether or not a follow-on workshop was warranted and when it should be. The consensus was that a follow-on workshop in about two or three years would be a good idea and should focus on what has been accomplished with respect to the short-term and long-term topics identified during this workshop.

A workshop such as this has no real conclusions; rather the "results" are a series of realizations which have all the more impact because one sees that there is extensive agreement concerning them and their importance. In the text, we have tried to highlight these realizations and faithfully reproduce the commentary on them given by the workshop participants; and in the introductory chapter we related many of the more central themes which emerged. As Gary Nutt observed with respect to tools, "not everything is perfect," but we hope that this workshop record is accurate and reflective of the participants' opinions.

Bibliography and References

(The items cited in Alan Shaw's paper are tagged EE, FE and/or PE, depending on whether they are concerned with event expressions, flow expressions and/or path expressions, respectively.)

ACM 76
Computing Surveys, 8, 1 (March 1976).

Alberts 76
D.S. Alberts. The economics of software quality assurance. *Proc. AFIPS National Computer Conf.,* (1976), pp. 433-442.

Alford 77
M.W. Alford. A requirements engineering methodology for real-time processing requirements. *IEEE Trans. on Software Engineering, SE-3,* 1 (January 1977), 60-69.

Ambler 77
A.L. Ambler, D.I. Good, J.C. Browne, W.F. Burger, R.M. Cohen, C.G. Hoch, and R.E. Wells. Gypsy: A language for specification and implementation of verifiable programs. *Software Engineering Notes, 2,* 2 (March 1977), 1-10.

Amschler 78
A. Amschler, L. Gmeiner and V. Voger. SADAT: Static and dynamic analysis and testing. *Digest of Workshop on Software Testing and Test Documentation,* Fort Lauderdale, Florida, (December 1978).

Andler 77
S. Andler and P.G. Hibbard. Types in Algol 68. *Proc. Fifth Annual III Conf. on the Implementation and Design of Algorithmic Languages,* IRIA, Le Chesnay, France, (May 1977), pp. 124-144. PE.

Andler 78
S. Andler. Synchronization primitives and the verification of concurrent programs. *Proc. Second International Symp. on Operating Systems,* IRIA, Le Chesnay, France, (October 1978). PE.

Andler 79
S. Andler. Predicate path expressions. *Proc. Sixth Annual ACM Symp. on Principles of Programming Languages,* San Antonio, Texas, (January 1979), pp. 226-236. PE.

Andrews 79
G. Andrews. Synchronizing resources. Tech. Report, Dept. of Computer Sci., Cornell Univ., (February 1979).

ANSI 75
ANSI/X3/SPARC Study Group on Data Base Management Systems: Interim Report 75-02-08. *SIGMOD FDT, 7,* 2 (1975).

Araki 78a
    T. Araki and N. Tokura. Flow languages are recursively enumerable. Programming
    Group Memo No. 78-01, Dept. of Info. and Computer Sci., Osaka Univ., Osaka, Japan,
    (November 1978). FE.

Araki 78b
    T. Araki and N. Tokura. Undecidability of the equivalence problem for flow
    expressions. To appear (in Japanese): *Trans. IECE Japan.* FE.

Araki 79
    T. Araki, T. Kagimosa and N. Tokura. Relations of flow languages to Petri net
    languages. Programming Languages Group Memo No. 79-01, Dept. of Info. and
    Computer Sci., Osaka Univ., Osaka, Japan, (February 1979). FE.

Bachman 77
    C. Bachman and M. Daya. The role concept in data models. *Proc. Very Large Data
    Base Conf. III,* (1977).

Baker,F 72
    F.T. Baker. Chief programmer team management of production programming. *IBM
    Systems J., 11,* 1 (1972), 56-73.

Baker,J 78
    J.W. Baker, D. Chester and R.T. Yeh. Software development by step-wise evaluation
    and refinement. SDBEG-2, Software and Data Base Engineering Group, Dept. of
    Computer Sci., Univ. of Texas, Austin, Texas, (January 1978).

Bell 77
    T.E. Bell, et al. An extended approach to computer-aided software requirements
    engineering. *IEEE Trans. on Software Engineering, SE-3,* 1 (January 1977), 49-60.

Bernstein 78
    P. Bernstein, J.B. Rothnie, N. Goodman and C.A. Papadimitriou. The concurrency
    control mechanism of SDD-1: A system for distributed data bases (the fully
    redundant case). *IEEE Trans. on Software Engineering, SE-4,* 3 (May 1978), 154-168.

Berzins 77
    V. Berzins. Denotational and axiomatic definitions for path expressions.
    Computation Structures Group Memo 153-1, Lab. for Computer Sci., Massachusetts
    Inst. of Tech., Cambridge, Massachusetts, (November 1977). PE.

Black 77
    R.K.E. Black. Effects of modern programming practices on software development
    costs. *Proc. Compcon 77,* Chicago, Illinois, (September 1977), pp. 250-253.

Boehm 73
    B.W. Boehm. Software and its impact: A quantitative assessment. *Datamation,*
    (May 1973), 48-59.

Boehm 75
    B.W. Boehm. The high cost of software. In Horowitz (ed.), *Pratical Strategies
    for Developing Large Software Systems,* Addison-Wesley, Reading, Massachusetts,
    (1975).

Boyer 75
    R.S. Boyer, B. Elspas and K.N. Levitt. SELECT: A formal system for testing and
    debugging programs by symbolic execution. *SIGPLAN Notices, 10,* 6 (June 1975),
    221-227.

Bratman 75
    H. Bratman. The software factory. *Computer, 8,* 5 (1975), 28-37.

Brinch Hansen 78
P. Brinch Hansen. Distributed processes: A concurrent programming concept. *Comm. ACM, 21,* 11 (November 1978), 934-941.

Brodie 78
M.L. Brodie. Specification and verification of data base semantic integrity. CSRG-91, Computer Systems Research Group, Univ. of Toronto, Toronto, Canada, (April 1978).

Brown 72
J.R. Brown and R.H. Hoffman. A survey of techniques and automated tools. TRW-SS-72-03, TRW Inc., Redondo Beach, California, (May 1972).

Brown 73
J.R. Brown, A.J. DeSalvio, D.E. Heine and J.G. Purdy. Automated software quality assurance. In Hetzel (ed.), *Program Test Methods,* Prentice-Hall, Englewood Cliffs, New Jersey, (1973).

Brown 74
J.R. Brown. Improving quality and reducing cost of aeronautical systems software through the use of tools. *Proc. Air Force Aeronautical Systems Software Workshop,* (April 1974).

Brown 75a
J.R. Brown. Why tools? *Proc. Computer Sci. and Statistics: Eighth Annual Symp. on the Interface,* (February 1975), pp. 310-312.

Brown 75b
J.R. Brown. Getting better software cheaper and quicker. In Horowitz (ed.), *Practical Strategies for Developing Large Software Systems,* Addison-Wesley, Reading, Massachusetts, (1975).

Brown 77
J.R. Brown. Functional programming final technical report. 29580-6001-RU-00, TRW Inc., Redondo Beach, California, (July 1977).

Brown 78
J.R. Brown. Programming practices for increased software quality. In *Software Quality Management,* Petrocelli Books, (1978).

BSTJ 78
Bell System Tech. J., 57, 6 (July-August 1978), part 2.

Burge 75
W.H. Burge. *Recursive Programming Techniques.* Addison-Wesley, Reading, Massachusetts, (1975).

Burke 78
J. Burke. *Connections.* Little-Brown, Boston, Massachusetts, (1978).

Caine 75
S.H. Caine and E.K. Gordon. PDL: A tool for software design. *Proc. AFIPS National Computer Conf.,* (June 1975), pp. 271-276.

Campbell 74
R.A. Campbell and A.N. Habermann. The specification of process synchronization by path expressions. In *Lecture Notes in Computer Science, 16,* Springer Verlag, Heidelberg, (1974), pp. 89-102. PE.

Campbell 76
R.H. Campbell. Path expressions: A technique for specifying process synchronization. Thesis, Computing Lab., The Univ. of Newcastle upon Tyne, England, (August 1976). (Also: UIUCDCS-R-77-863, Dept. of Computer Sci., Univ. of Illinois, Urbana, Illinois.) PE.

Campbell 79a
R.H. Campbell and R.B. Kolstad. Path expressions in Pascal. *Proc. Fourth International Conf. on Software Engineering,* Munich, Germany, (September 1979), pp. 212-219. PE.

Campbell 79b
R.H. Campbell, I.B. Greenberg and T.J. Müller. Path Pascal user manual. UIUCDCS-R-79-960, Dept. of Computer Sci., Univ. of Illinois, Urbana, Illinois, (February 1979). PE.

Campos 78
I. Campos and G. Estrin. SARA-aided design of software for concurrent systems. *Proc. AFIPS National Computer Conf.,* Anaheim, Calif., (June 1978), pp. 325-336.

Carlson 76
W.E. Carlson. Software research in the Department of Defense. *Proc. Second International Conf. on Software Engineering,* San Francisco, California, (October 1976), pp. 379-383.

Cheatham 79
T.E. Cheatham, G.H. Holloway and J.A. Townley. Symbolic evaluation and the analysis of programs. *IEEE Trans. on Software Engineering, SE-5,* 4 (July 1979), 402-417.

Chen 76
P.S. Chen. The entity-relationship model: Toward a unified view of data. *Trans. on Data Base Systems,* (March 1976), 9-36.

Clarke 76
L.A. Clarke. A system to generate test data and symbolically execute programs. *IEEE Trans. on Software Engineering, SE-2,* 3 (September 1976), 215-222.

Compte 78
D. Compte, G. Durrieu, O. Gelly, A. Plas and J.C. Syre. Parallelism, control and synchronization expression in a single assignment language. *SIGPLAN Notices, 13,* 1 (January 1978), 25-33. PE.

Conway 63
M.E. Conway. Design of a separable transition-diagram compiler. *Comm. ACM, 6,* 7 (July 1963), 396-408.

Cooprider 79
L.W. Cooprider. The representation of families of software systems. Ph.D. Thesis, Dept. of Computer Sci., Carnegie-Mellon Univ., Pittsburgh, Pennsylvania, (1979).

Copeland 78
G.P. Copeland. String storage and searching for data base applications: Requirements and strategy for implementation. Tech. Report, Tektronix Inc., Beaverton, Oregon, (1978).

Culpepper 75
L.M. Culpepper. A system for reliable engineering software. *IEEE Trans. on Software Engineering, SE-1,* 2 (June 1975), 174-178.

Dahl 72
O.J. Dahl. Hierarchical program structures. In Dahl, Dijkstra and Hoare, *Structured Programming*, Academic Press, London, (1972).

Darringer 78
J.A. Darringer and J.C. King. Applications of symbolic execution to program testing. *Computer*, *11*, 4 (April 1978), 51-60.

Darringer 79
J.A. Darringer. The use of symbolic execution in program testing. In *Software Testing*, Infotech International Ltd., Maidenhead, England, (1979), pp. 65-84.

Davis 77
C.G. Davis and C.R. Vick. The software development system. *IEEE Trans. on Software Engineering*, *SE-3*, 1 (January 1977), 69-84.

DeRemer 76
F. DeRemer and H. Kron. Programming-in-the-large versus programming-in-the-small. *IEEE Trans. on Software Engineering*, *SE-2*, 2 (June 1976), 80-86.

Dijkstra 72
E.W. Dijkstra. Notes on structured programming. In Dahl, Dijkstra and Hoare, *Structured Programming*, Academic Press, New York, (1972).

DoD 79
PEBBLEMAN: Department of Defense Requirements for the Programming Environment for the Common High Order Language. (January 1979).

Dolotta 76
T.A. Dolotta and J.R. Mashey. An introduction to the programmer's workbench. *Proc. Second International Conf. on Software Engineering*, San Francisco, Calif., (October 1976), pp. 164-168.

Elspas 72
B. Elspas, K.N. Levitt, R.J. Waldinger and A. Waksman. An assessment of techniques for proving program correctness. *Computing Surveys*, *4*, 2 (June 1972), 97-147.

Enslow 78
P.H. Enslow. What is a 'distributed' data processing system? *Computer*, *11*, 1 (January 1978), 13-21.

Erman 79
L.D. Erman and V.R. Lesser. The Hearsay-II system: A tutorial. In Lea (ed.), *Trends in Speech Recognition*, Prentice-Hall, Englewood Cliffs, New Jersey, (1979).

Estrin 78
G. Estrin and I. Campos. Concurrent software system design, supported by SARA at the age of one. *Proc. Third International Conf. on Software Engineering*, Atlanta, Georgia, (May 1978), pp. 230-242.

Fairley 75
R.E. Fairley. An experimental program-testing facility. *IEEE Trans. on Software Engineering*, *SE-1*, 4 (December 1975), 350-357.

Farber 75
D.J. Farber. A ring network. *Datamation*, (February 1975), 44-46.

Feldman 79
J. Feldman. High-level programming for distributed computing. *Comm. ACM*, *22*, 6 (June 1979), 353-368.

Flon 76
  L. Flon and A.N. Habermann. Towards the construction of verifiable software
  systems. *SIGPLAN Notices, 8,* 3 (March 1976), 141-148. PE.

Fosdick 76
  L.D. Fosdick and L.J. Osterweil. Data flow analysis in software reliablity.
  Computing Surveys, 8, 3 (September 1976), 305-330.

Freeman 80
  P. Freeman and A.I. Wasserman (eds.). *Tutorial: Software Design Techniques.*
  (Third Edition) IEEE, New York, (1980).

Gallenson 75
  L. Gallenson et al. PRIM User's Manual. ISI/TM-75-1, Information Sci. Inst.,
  Univ. of Southern California, Marina del Rey, California, (1975).

Gausler 77
  J.S. Gausler. The DOD defense systems software management program: Current status.
  Proc. Software Management Conf., (1977), pp. 5-11.

GE 77
  Fortran Test Procedure Language: Programmer Reference Manual. General Electric
  Corp., Schenectady, New York, (1977).

Gerhart 76
  S.L. Gerhart and L. Yelowitz. Observations of fallibility in applications of
  modern programming methodologies. *IEEE Trans. on Software Engineering, SE-2,*
  3 (September 1976), 195-207.

Gerhart 79a
  S.L. Gerhart. Workshop report: *Computer, 21,* 3 (March 1979), 99-100.

Gerhart 79b
  S.L. Gerhart and D.S. Wile. Preliminary report on the Delta Experiment:
  Specification and verification of a multiple-user file updating module. *Proc.
  Specification of Reliable Software Conf.,* Boston, Massachusetts, (April 1979),
  pp. 198-211.

Geschke 77
  C.M. Geschke, J.H. Morris Jr., and E.H. Satterwaite. Early experience with
  Mesa. *Comm. ACM, 20,* 8 (August 1977), 540-553.

Gimson 78
  R. Gimson. The application of a data model to the support of Fortran programs.
  PMM/79, Computing Lab., The Univ. of Newcastle upon Tyne, England, (1978).

Ginsburg 65
  S. Ginsburg and E.H. Spanier. Mappings of languages by two-tape devices.
  J. ACM, 12, (1965), 423-434.

Ginsburg 66
  S. Ginsburg. *The Mathematical Theory of Context-free Languages.* McGraw-Hill,
  New York, (1966).

Good 75
  D.I. Good, R.L. London and W.W. Blesdoe. An interactive program verification
  system. *SIGPLAN Notices, 10,* 6 (June 1975), 482-492.

Good 78
  D.I. Good et al. Report on the language Gypsy: Version 2.0 ICSMA-CMP-10,
  Certifiable Minicomputer Project, Univ. of Texas at Austin, Austin, Texas, (1978).

Goodenough 75
J.B. Goodenough and S.L. Gerhart. Towards a theory of test data selection. *IEEE Trans. on Software Engineering, SE-1,* 2 (June 1975), 156-173.

GR 75
RXVP User's Guide. RM-1942, General Research Corp., Santa Barbara, California, (1975).

Greif 77
I. Greif. A language for formal problem specification. *Comm. ACM, 20,* 12 (December 1977), 931-935.

Guttag 77
J.V. Guttag. Abstract data types and the development of data structures. *Comm. ACM, 20,* 6 (June 1977), 396-404.

Habermann 73
A.N. Habermann. Operations on shared data controlled by function modules in type definitions. Tech. Report, Computer Sci. Dept., Carnegie-Mellon Univ. Pittsburgh, Pennsylvania, (September 1973). PE.

Habermann 75a
A.N. Habermann. Path expressions. Computer Sci. Dept., Carnegie-Mellon Univ., Pittsburgh, Pennsylvania, (June 1975). PE.

Habermann 75b
A.N. Habermann. On the timing restrictions of concurrent processes. *Proc. Fourth Texas Conf. on Computing Systems,* Austin, Texas, (November 1975), pp. 1A/3.1-1A/3.6. PE.

Habermann 76
A.N. Habermann. *Introduction to Operating System Design.* SRA Inc., Chicago

Habermann 79a
A.N. Habermann. Implementation of regular path expressions. Tech. Report, Computer Sci. Dept., Carnegie-Mellon Univ., Pittsburgh, Pennsylvania, (1979). PE.

Habermann 79b
A.N. Habermann. A software development control system. Tech. Report, Computer Sci. Dept., Carnegie-Mellon Univ., Pittsburgh, Pennsylvania, (1979).

Hammer 76
M. Hammer. Data abstractions and data bases. *SIGMOD FDT, 8,* 2 (1976), 58-59.

Hammer 78
M. Hammer and D. McLeod. The semantic data model: A modelling mechanism for data base applications. *SIGMOD FDT,* (1978), 26-35.

Hanson 78
A.R. Hanson and E.M. Riseman. Visions: A computer system for interpreting scenes. In Hanson and Riseman (eds.), *Computer Vision Systems,* Academic Press, New York, (1978).

Hartwick 77
R.D. Hartwick. Test planning. *Proc. AFIPS National Computer Conf.,* 46, AFIPS Press, Montvale, New Jersey, (1977), pp. 285-294.

HB 76
The System Implementation Language LIS. Doc. 4549 EL/EN, CII-Honeywell-Bull, Louveciennes, France, (January 1976).

Hebalkar 79
P.G. Hebalkar and S.N. Zilles. TELL: A system for graphically representing software designs. *Proc. Compcon Conf.*, San Francisco, (1979).

Henderson 72
P. Henderson and R.A. Snowdon. An experiment in structured programming. *BIT*, *12*, (1972), 38-53.

Henderson 74
P. Henderson and R.A. Snowdon. A tool for structured program development. *Proc. IFIP Congress '74*, Stockholm, Sweden, (August 1974), pp. 204-207.

Henderson 75a
P. Henderson. Finite state modelling in program development. *SIGPLAN Notices*, *10*, 6 (June 1975), 221-227.

Henderson 75b
P. Henderson, R.A. Snowdon, J.D. Gorrie and I.I. King. The TOPD System. Tech. Report 77, Computing Laboratory, Univ. of Newcastle upon Tyne, England, (September 1975).

Henderson 79
P. Henderson, R. Gimson, G.D. Pratten and R.A. Snowdon. The maintenance of software with multiple versions. In *Structured System Design*, Infotech International Ltd., Maidenhead, England, (1979).

Henermann 74
C.A. Henermann, G.J. Myers and J.H. Winterton. Automated test and verification. *IBM Tech. Disclosure Bulletin*, *17*, 7 (1974), 2030-2035.

Hewitt 75
C. Hewitt and B. Smith. Towards a programming apprentice. *IEEE Trans. on Software Engineering*, *SE-1*, 1 (March 1975), 26-45.

Hoare 78
C.A.R. Hoare. Communicating sequential processes. *Comm. ACM*, *21*, 8 (August 1978), 666-677.

Hoare 79
C.A.R. Hoare. Remark made at IFIP WG 8.1 Conf. on Formal Models and Practical Tools for Info. System Design, Oxford, England, (April 1979).

Howden 75
W.E. Howden and L.G. Stucki. Final report: Methodology for effective test case selection, Phase II. MDC G5800, McDonnell Douglas Corp., (April 1975).

Howden 76
W.E. Howden. Experiments with a symbolic execution system. *Proc. AFIPS National Computer Conf.*, *45*, (1976), pp. 899-908.

Howden 78
W.E. Howden. DISSECT: A symbolic evluation and program testing system. *IEEE Trans. on Software Engineering*, *SE-4*, 1 (January 1978), 70-73.

Howden 79
W.E. Howden. Workshop report. *Computer*, *21*, 3 (March 1979), 100.

Huet 77
G. Huet, G. Kahn and P. Maurice. Environnement de programmation Pascal. Tech. Report, IRIA, Rocquencourt, France, (November 1977).

IBM 78
Extended PL/I Reference Manual. Software Technology Group, IBM T.J. Watson Research Center, Yorktown Heights, New York, (November 1978).

Ichbiah 79
J. Ichbiah et al. Preliminary Ada reference manual. *SIGPLAN Notices, 14*, 6 (June 1979).

IEEE 75a
Proceedings 1975 International Conference on Reliable Software, Los Angeles, California, (April 1975). (Also: *SIGPLAN Notices, 10*, 6 (June 1975).)

IEEE 75b
Proceedings First National Conference on Software Engineering, Washington, D.C., (1975).

IEEE 76
Proceedings Second International Conference on Software Engineering, San Francisco, California, (October 1976).

IEEE 78
Proceedings Third International Conference on Software Engineering, Atlanta, Georgia, (May 1978).

IEEE 79
Proceedings Fourth International Conference on Software Engineering, Munich, Germany, (September 1979).

IEEE TSE
IEEE Transaction on Software Engineering. IEEE, New York.

Ingalls 78
D. Ingalls. The Smalltalk-76 programming system. *Proc. Fifth Annual ACM Symp. on Principles of Programming Languages*, Tucson, Arizona, (January 1978), pp. 9-16.

Ivie 77
E.L. Ivie. The programmer's workbench: A machine for software development. *Comm. ACM, 20*, 10 (October 1977), 746-753.

Jackson 75
M.A. Jackson. *Principles of Program Design*. Academic Press, New York, (1975).

Jacobs 70
J.H. Jacobs and T.J. Dillon. Interactive saturn flight program simulator. *IBM Systems J., 9*, 2 (1970), 145-158.

Kagimasa 79
T. Kagimasa, T. Araki and N. Tokura. The descriptive power of flow expressions. (In Japanese) Tech. Group on Automata and Languages Memo AL-78-77, IECE, Japan, (January 1979). FE.

Kahn 71
R.E. Kahn and R.W. Crowther. Flow control in a resource-sharing computer network. *Proc. ACM/IEEE Second Symp. on Problems in Optimization of Data Comm. Systems*, (1971), pp. 108-116.

Katzen 76
H. Katzen. *Systems Design and Documentation: An Introduction to the HIPO Method*. Van Nostrand Reinhold, New York, (1976).

268

Kent 78
W. Kent. *Data and Reality*. North-Holland Publishing Co., Amsterdam, The Netherlands, (1978).

Kersten 79
M.L. Kersten and A.I. Wasserman. The architecture of the PLAIN data base handler. To appear: *Software Practice and Experience*.

Kersten 80
M.L. Kersten, A.I. Wasserman and R.P. van de Reit. Troll: A data base interface and testing tool. Submitted for publication, (1980).

Kieburtz 78
R.B. Kieburtz and A. Silberschantz. Access-right expressions. Report 44, U.T.D. Programs in Math. Sci., Univ. of Texas, Dallas, Texas, (1978).

Kimura 79
T. Kimura. Behavioral abstraction of communicating sequential processes. Tech. Report, Dept. Computer Sci., Washington Univ., St. Louis, Missouri, (January 1979). EE, PE.

King 76
J.C. King. Symbolic execution and program testing. *Comm. ACM*, *19*, 7 (July 1976), 385-394.

Krause 73
K.W. Krause, R.W. Smith and M.A. Goodwin. Optimal software test planning through automated network analysis. *Record 1973 IEEE Symp. on Computer Software Reliability*, IEEE, New York, (1973), pp. 18-22.

Lamport 78
L. Lamport. Time, clocks and the ordering of events in a distributed system. *Comm. ACM*, *21*, 7 (July 1978), 558-564.

Lampson 77a
B.W. Lampson, et al. Report on the programming language Euclid. *SIGPLAN Notices*, *12*, 2 (February 1977), 1-79.

Lampson 77b
B. Lampson and H. Sturgis. Crash recovery in a distributed data storage system. *Proc. Second Annual Brown Univ. Workshop on Distributed Computation*, Providence, Rhode Island, (1977).

Lauer 75a
P.E. Lauer and R.H. Campbell. A description of path expressions by Petri Nets. *Proc. Second ACM Symp. on Principles of Programming Languages*, Palo Alto, California, (January 1975), pp. 95-105. PE.

Lauer 75b
P.E. Lauer and R.H. Campbell. Formal semantics of a class of high level primitives for coordinating concurrent processes. *Acta Informatica*, *5*, (1975), 297-332. PE.

Lauer 77
P.E. Lauer, E. Best and M.W. Shields. On the problem of achieving adequacy of concurrent programs. *Proc. IFIP Working Conf. on Formal Description of Programming Concepts*, North-Holland, Amsterdam, The Netherlands, (August 1977). PE.

Lauer 78a
P.E. Lauer, M.W. Shields and E. Best. On the design and certification of asynchronous systems of processes. Part 1: COSY: A system specification language based on paths and processes; Part 2: Formal theory of the basic COSY notation. ASM/45 and ASM/49, Computing Lab., The Univ. of Newcastle upon Tyne, England, (March and June 1978). PE.

Lauer 78b
P.E. Lauer and M.W. Shields. Abstract specification of resource sharing disciplines: Adequacy, starvation, privacy and interrupts. *SIGPLAN`Notices*, *13*, 12 (December 1978), 41-59. PE.

Ledgard 73
H.F. Ledgard. The case for structured programming. *BIT*, *13*, (1973), 45-57.

LeLann 77
G. LeLann. Distributed systems: Towards a formal approach. In Gilchrist (ed.), *Information Processing 77*, North-Holland, Amsterdam, The Netherlands, (1977).

Lesser 79a
V.R. Lesser and D.D. Corkill. Functionally-accurate cooperative distributive systems. *Proc. International Conf. on Cybernetics and Society*, Denver, Colorado, (1979), pp. 346-353.

Lesser 79b
V.R. Lesser and L.D. Erman. An experiment in distributed interpretation. *Proc. First International Conf. on Distributed Computing Systems*, Huntsville, Alabama, (1979), pp. 553-571.

Lesser 79c
V.R. Lesser, D. Serram and J. Bonar. PCL: A process-oriented job control language. *Proc. First International Conf. on Distributed Computing Systems*, Huntsville, Alabama, (1979).

Liskov 74
B.H. Liskov and S.N. Zilles. Programming with abstract data types. *SIGPLAN Notices*, *9*, 4 (April 1974), 50-60.

Liskov 75
B.H. Liskov and S.N. Zilles. Specification techniques for data abstractions. *IEEE Trans. on Software Engineering*, *SE-1*, 1 (March 1975), 7-19.

Liskov 77
B. Liskov, A. Snyder, R. Atkinson and C. Schaffert. Abstraction mechanisms in CLU. *Comm. ACM*, *20*, 8 (August 1977), 564-576.

London 75
R.L. London. A view of program verification. *SIGPLAN Notices*, *10*, 6 (June 1975), 534-545.

Luckham 79
D.C. Luckham, S.M. German, F.W. Henke, R.A. Karp and P.W. Milne. The Stanford Pascal Verifier User Manual. Stan-CS-79-731, SVG-11, Computer Sci. Dept., Stanford Univ., Stanford, California, (March 1979).

Lycklama 78
H. Lycklama. UNIX on a microprocessor. *Bell Systems Tech. J.*, *57*, 6 (July-August 1978), part 2, 2087-2101.

McCarthy 62
 J. McCarthy. Towards a mathematical science of computation. *Proc. IFIP Congress
 '62*, North-Holland Publishing Co., Amsterdam, The Netherlands, (1962), pp. 21-28.

McNurlin 79
 A. McNurlin. Program design techniques. *EDP Analyzer*, *17*, 3 (March 1979).

Miller 75
 E.F. Miller. Methodology for comprehensive software testing. RADC-TR-75-161,
 General Research Corp., Santa Barbara, California, (1975).

Miller 79
 E.F. Miller. Program testing: An overview for managers. In *Software Testing*,
 Infotech International Ltd., Maidenhead, England, (1979), pp. 187-200.

Minsky 67
 M.L. Minsky. *Computation: Finite and Infinite Machines*. Prentice-Hall, Englewood-
 Cliffs, New Jersey, (1967).

MSPL 72
 Module Testing System (MTS) Fact Book. Management Systems and Programming Ltd.,
 London, England, (1972).

Musser 79
 D.R. Musser. Abstract data type specification in the Affirm system. *Proc. Specification of Reliable Software Conf.*, Boston, Massachusetts, (April 1979), pp. 47-57.

Mylopoulos 78
 J. Mylopoulos, P. Bernstein and H. Wong. A language facility for designing interactive data base: Intensive application. *SIGMOD*, (1978).

Ogden 78
 W.F. Ogden, W.E. Riddle and W.C. Rounds. Complexity of expressions allowing con-
 currency. *Proc. Fifth ACM Symp. on Prin. of Programming Languages*, Tucson, Arizona,
 (January 1978), pp. 185-194. EE, PE.

O'Neill 77
 J.T. O'Neill (ed.). *MUMPS Language Standard*. ANSI Standard X11.1-1977, Am.
 National Standards Inst., (1977).

Osterweil 76a
 L.J. Osterweil. A proposal for an integrated testing system for computer programs.
 CU-CS-93-76, Dept. of Computer Sci., Univ. of Colorado at Boulder, Colorado,
 (August 1976).

Osterweil 76b
 L.J. Osterweil and L.D. Fosdick. DAVE: A validation, error detection and documen-
 tation system for Fortran programs. *Software: Practice and Experience*, *6*,
 (September 1976), 473-486.

Osterweil 76c
 L.J. Osterweil and L.D. Fosdick. Some experience with DAVE, a Fortran program
 analyzer. *Proc. AFIPS National Computer Conf.*, *45*, (1976), pp. 909-916.

Osterweil 77
 L.J. Osterweil. A methodology for testing computer programs. *Proc. AIAA Conf. on
 Computers in Aerospace*, Los Angeles, California, (November 1977), pp. 52-62.

Panzl 78
 D.J. Panzl. Automatic software test drivers. *Computer*, *11*, 4 (1978), 44-50.

Parnas 71
D.L. Parnas. Information distribution aspects of design methodology. *Proc. IFIP Congress 71*, Ljubljana, Yugoslavia, (August 1971), pp. TA3/26-TA3/30.

Parnas 72
D.L. Parnas. On the criteria to be used in decomposing systems into modules. *Comm. ACM*, *15*, 12 (December 1972), 1053-1058.

Pearson 73
D.J. Pearson. CADES: Computer aided design and evaluation system. *Computer Weekly*, (July/August 1973).

Pearson 78
D.J. Pearson. A study in the pragmatics of operating system development. *Proc. 1978 International Symp. on Operating System Techniques*, Paris, France, (1978).

Pebbles 78
R. Pebbles and E. Manning. System architecture for distributed data management. *Computer*, *11*, 1 (January 1978), 40-47.

Peterson 76
R.J. Peterson. TESTER/1: An abstract model for the automatic synthesis of program test case specifications. *Proc. Symp. on Computer Software Engineering*, Polytechnic Press, New York, (1976), pp. 465-484.

Plasmeijer 78
R. Plasmeijer, J. van den Bos and J. Stroet. An implementation of high-level graphics tools. Informatica/Computer Graphics Memo, Univ. of Nijmegen, Nijmegen, The Netherlands, (December 1978). PE.

Pratten 78
G.D. Pratten and R.A. Snowdon. CADES: Computer-aided development and evaluation system. Tech. Report, International Computers Ltd., Stoke on Trent, England, (1978).

Ramamoorthy 73
C.V. Ramamoorthy, R.E. Meeker and J. Turner. Design and construction of an auto-mated software evaluation system. *Record of the 1973 IEEE Symp. on Computer Software Reliability*, IEEE, New York, (1973), pp. 28-37.

Ramamoorthy 74
C.V. Ramamoorthy and S.F. Ho. Fortran automatic code evaluation system (FACES). ERL-M466, Dept. of Electrical and Computer Engineering, Univ. of California, Berkeley, California, (1974).

Ramamoorthy 75
C.V. Ramamoorthy and S.F. Ho. Testing large software with automated software evaluation system. *IEEE Trans. on Software Engineering*, *SE-1*, 1 (March 1975), 46-58.

Ramamoorthy 78
C.V. Ramamoorthy, S.F. Ho and H.H. So. The role of software tools in a methodology for the development and validation of critical software for nuclear power plants. In Ramamoorthy and Yeh (eds.), *Tutorial: Software Methodology*, IEEE, New York, (1978).

Reed 79
D.P. Reed and R.K. Kanodia. Synchronization with event counts and sequences. *Comm. ACM*, *22*, 2 (February 1979), 115-123.

Reifer 75
 D.J. Reifer. Automated aids for reliable software. *SIGPLAN Notices*, *10*, 6 (June 1975), 131-142.

Riddle 72a
 W.E. Riddle. Modelling and analysis of supervisory systems. Ph.D. Thesis, Computer Sci. Dept., Stanford Univ., Stanford, California, (March 1972). EE.

Riddle 72b
 W.E. Riddle. The hierarchical modelling of operating system structure and behavior. *Proc. ACM 72 National Conf.*, Boston, Massachusetts, (August 1972), pp. 1105-1127. EE.

Riddle 73a
 W.E. Riddle. A method for the description and analysis of complex software systems. *SIGPLAN Notices*, *8*, 9 (September 1973), 133-136. EE.

Riddle 73b
 W.E. Riddle. A design methodology for complex software systems. *Proc. Second Texas Conf. on Computing Systems*, Austin, Texas, (November 1973), pp. 22.1-22.8.

Riddle 74a
 W.E. Riddle. The equivalence of Petri nets and message transmission models. SRM/97, Computing Lab., Univ. of Newcastle upon Tyne, England (August 1974). EE.

Riddle 74b
 W.E. Riddle. Message transfer expressions and their use in specifying synchronization constraints. RSSM/1, Dept. of Computer and Comm. Sci., University of Michigan, Ann Arbor, Michigan, (September 1974). EE.

Riddle 74c
 W.E. Riddle. The translation of path expressions into message transfer expressions. RSSM/2, Dept. of Computer and Comm. Sci., Univ. of Michigan, Ann Arbor, Michigan, (September 1974). EE, PE.

Riddle 75
 W.E. Riddle. Computer augmented design of complex software systems. *Proc. Fourth Texas Conf. on Computing Systems*, Austin, Texas, (November 1975) pp. 3A/2.1-3A/2.12. EE.

Riddle 77
 W.E. Riddle, J.H. Sayler, A.R. Segal and J.C. Wileden. An introduction to the DREAM software design system. *Software Engineering Notes*, *2*, 4 (July 1977), 11-23. EE.

Riddle 78a
 W.E. Riddle, J.C. Wileden, J.H. Sayler, A.R. Segal and A.M. Stavely. Behavior modelling during software design. *IEEE Trans. on Software Engineering*, *SE-4*, 4 (July 1978), 283-292. EE.

Riddle 78b
 W.E. Riddle, J.H. Sayler, A.R. Segal, A.M. Stavely and J.C. Wileden. A description scheme to aid the design of collections of concurrent processes. *Proc. 1978 National Computer Conf.*, Anaheim, California, (June 1978), pp. 549-554. EE.

Riddle 79a
 W.E. Riddle, J.H. Sayler, A.R. Segal, A.M. Stavely and J.C. Wileden. Abstract monitor types. *Proc. Specification of Reliable Software Conf.*, Boston, Massachusetts, (April 1979), pp. 37-43. EE.

Riddle 79b
W.E. Riddle. An approach to software system behavior description. *Computer Languages, 4,* (1979), 29-47. EE.

Riddle 79c
W.E. Riddle. An approach to software system modelling and analysis. *Computer Languages, 4,* (1979), 49-66. EE.

Ritchie 74
D.M. Ritchie and K. Thompson. The UNIX time-sharing system. *Comm. ACM, 17,* 7 (July 1974), 377-387.

Robinson 75
L. Robinson, K. Levitt, P. Neumann, and A. Saxena. A formal methodology for the design of operating systems software. In Yeh (ed.), *Current Trends in Programming Methodology, Vol. I,* Prentice-Hall Inc., Englewood Cliffs, New Jersey, (1977).

Robinson 77
L. Robinson and O. Roubine. SPECIAL: A specification and assertion language. Tech. Report CSL-36, SRI International, Menlo Park, California, (January 1977).

Rocking 75
M.J. Rochking. The source code control system. *IEEE Trans. on Software Engineering, SE-1,* 4 (December 1975), 364-370.

Ross 77
D.T. Ross and K.E. Schoman. Structured analysis for requirements definition. *IEEE Trans. on Software Engineering, SE-3,* 1 (January 1977), 6-15.

Sanguinetti 77
J.W. Sanguinetti. Performance prediction in an operating system design methodology. RSSM/32 (Ph.D. Thesis), Dept. of Computer and Comm. Sci., Univ. of Michigan, Ann Arbor, Michigan, (May 1977). EE.

Sanguinetti 78
J.W. Sanguinetti. A formal technique for analyzing the performance of complex systems. *Proc. CPEUG Conf.,* Boston, Massachusetts, (October 1978). EE.

Sanguinetti 79
J.W. Sanguinetti. A technique for integrating simulation and system design. *Proc. Conf. on Simulation, Measurement and Modeling of Computer Systems,* Boulder, Colorado, (August 1979), pp. 163-172. EE.

Sayward 78
F. Sayward, R. Demillo and R. Lipton. Program mutations: A new approach to program testing. *Proc. Software Specification and Testing Technology Conf.,* Office of Naval Research, (April 1978).

Schmidt 77
J.W. Schmidt. Some high level constructs for data of type relation. *Trans. on Data Base Systems, 2,* 3 (September 1977), 247-261.

Shaw,A 75
A.C. Shaw. Systems design and documentation using path descriptions. *Proc. 1975 Sagamore Computer Conf. on Parallel Processing,* Sagamore, Michigan, (1975), pp. 180-181. FE.

Shaw,A 78
A.C. Shaw. Software descriptions with flow expressions. *IEEE Trans. on Software Engineering, SE-4,* 3 (May 1978), 242-254. FE.

Shaw,A 79
A.C. Shaw. On the specification of graphics command languages and their processors. *Proc. IFIP Working Group 5.2 Workshop on Methodology of Interaction,* Selliac, France, (May 1979). FE.

Shaw,A 80
A. Shaw. Expression-based approaches to software description. In Riddle and Fairley (ed.), *Software Development Tools,* Springer-Verlag, Heidelberg, Germany, (1980).

Shaw,M 77
M. Shaw, W.A. Wulf and R.L. London. Abstraction and verification in Alphard: Defining and specifying iteration and generators. *Comm. ACM, 20,* 8 (August 1977), 553-564.

Shields 78
M.W. Shields and P.E. Lauer. On the abstract specification and formal analysis of synchronization properties of concurrent systems. *Proc. International Conf. on Math. Studies of Info. Processing,* Springer Verlag, Heidelberg, Germany, (1978). PE.

Shields 79
M.W. Shields and P.E. Lauer. A formal semantics for concurrent systems. *Proc. Sixth International Colloq. Automata, Languages and Programming,* Graz, Austria, (July 1979). PE.

Shipman 79
D.W. Shipman. The functional data model and the data language DAPLEX. *Trans. on Data Base Systems,* (1979).

Simon 62
H.A. Simon. The architecture of complexity. *Proc. Am. Phil. Soc., 106,* (December 1962), 467-492. Also in Simon, *Sciences of the Artificial,* MIT Press, Cambridge, Massachusetts, (1969).

Smith 77a
J.M. Smith and D.C.P. Smith. Data base abstractions: Aggregation. *Commm. ACM, 20,* 6 (June 1977), 405-413.

Smith 77b
J.M. Smith and D.C.P. Smith. Data base abstractions: Aggregation and generalization. *Trans. on Data Base Systems,* (June 1977), 105-133.

Smith 78a
J.M. Smith and D.C.P. Smith. Principles of data base design. New York Univ. Symp., (1978).

Smith 78b
J.M. Smith. Comments on the papers 'A software engineering view of data base management' by A.I. Wasserman and 'A software engineering view of data base systems' by H. Weber. *Proc. Very Large Data Base Conf. IV,* Berlin, Germany, (September 1978).

Smoliar 79
S. Smoliar. Using applicative techniques to design distributed systems. *Proc. Specification of Reliable Software Conf.,* Boston, Massachusetts, (April 1979), pp. 150-161.

Snowdon 73
R.A. Snowdon. PEARL: A system for the preparation and validation of structured programs. In Hetzel (ed.), *Program Test Methods*, Prentice Hall, Englewood Cliffs, New Jersey, (1973).

Snowdon 74
R. Snowdon. Interactive use of a computer in the preparation of structured programs. Thesis, Univ. of Newcastle upon Tyne, England, (1974).

Snowdon 78
R.A. Snowdon and P. Henderson. The TOPD system for computer-aided system development. In *Structured Analysis and Design*, Infotech International Ltd., Maidenhead, England, (1978).

Stavely 77
A.M. Stavely. Record of a TOPD design session. RSSM/54, Dept. of Computer and Comm. Sci., Univ. of Michigan, Ann Arbor, Michigan, (July 1977).

Stephens 78
S.A. Stephens and L.L. Tripp. Requirements expression and validation aid. *Proc. Third International Conf. on Software Engineering*, Atlanta, Georgia, (May 1978), pp. 101-108.

Stonebraker 76
M. Stonebraker, E. Wong, P Kreps, and G.D. Held. The design and implementation of INGRES. *Trans. on Data Base Systems, 1*, 3 (September 1976), 189-222.

Stucki 75
L.G. Stucki and G.L Foshee. New assertion concepts for self-metric software validation. *SIGPLAN Notices, 10*, 6 (June 1975), 59-71.

Stucki 76
L.G. Stucki. The use of dynamic assertions to improve software quality. Ph.D. Thesis, School of Engineering, Univ. of California at Los Angeles, California, (June 1976).

Stucki 77
L.G. Stucki. New directions in automated tools for improving software quality. In Yeh (ed.), *Current Trends in Programming Methodology, Volume II, Program Validation*, Prentice-Hall, Englewood Cliffs, New Jersey, (1977), pp. 80-111.

Swan 77
R.J. Swan, et al. CM*: A modular multi-microprocessor. *Proc. AFIPS National Computer Conf., 46*, (1977), pp. 627-634.

Tanenbaum 78
A.S. Tanenbaum. Implications of structured programming for machine architecture. *Comm. ACM, 21*, 3 (March 1978), 237-246.

Tanenbaum 80
A.S. Tanenbaum, J.W. Stevenson and H. van Staveren. Description of an experimental machine architecture for use with block-structured languages. Informatica Rapport, Subfaculteit Wiskunde, Vrije Universiteit, Amsterdam, The Netherlands, in press.

Teichroew 77
D. Teichroew and E.A. Hershey. PSL/PSA: A computer-aided technique for structured documentation and analysis of information processing systems. *IEEE Trans. on Software Engineering, SE-3*, 1 (January 1977), 41-48.

Teitelbaum 79
R.T. Teitelbaum. The Cornell program synthesizer: A microcomputer implementation of PL/CS. Tech. Report, Dept. of Computer Sci., Cornell Univ., Ithaca, New York, (1979).

Thayer 75
R.H. Thayer and E.S. Hinton. Software reliability: A method that works. *Proc. AFIPS National Computer Conf., 44,* AFIPS Press, Montvale, New Jersey, (1975), pp. 877-883.

Thomas 76
R.H. Thomas. A solution to the update problem for multiple copy data bases which use distributed control. Report 3340, Bolt, Beranek and Newman Inc., Cambridge, Massachusetts, (1976).

Thompson 79
D.H. Thompson and S.L. Gerhart. Affirm Reference Library: I, Reference Manual; II, Users Guide; III, Type Library; IV, Annotated Transcripts; V, Collected Papers. Info. Sci. Inst., Univ. of Southern California, Marina del Rey, California, (November 1979).

Tichy 79
W. Tichy. Software development control based on module interconnection. *Proc. Fourth International Conf. on Software Engineering,* Munich, Germany, (September 1979), pp. 29-41.

Torrigiani 77
P.R. Torrigiani and P.E. Lauer. An object oriented notation for path expressions. *Proc. AICA 1977, 3: Software Methodologies,* (October 1977), pp. 349-371. PE.

Torrigiani 78
P.R. Torrigiani. Synchronic aspects of data types: Construction of non-algorithmic solution of the banker's problem. In *Lecture Notes in Computer Science, 65,* Springer-Verlag, Heidelberg, Germany, (1978), pp. 560-583. PE.

van den Bos 78
J. van den Bos. Definition and use of higher level graphics input tools. *Computer Graphics, 12,* 3 (August 1978), 38-42. PE.

van den Bos 78a
J. van den Bos. Input tools: A new language construct for input-driven programs. *Proc. Europ. IFIP Conf.,* London, England, (October 1979). PE.

van den Bos 79b
J. van den Bos. High-level graphics input tools and their semantics. *Proc. IFIP Working Group 5.2 Workshop on Methodology of Interaction,* Selliac, France, (May 1979). PE.

Wasserman 74
A.I. Wasserman. Online programming systems and languages: A history and appraisal. Tech. Report #6, Lab. of Medical Info. Sci., Univ. of California, San Francisco, California, (1974).

Wasserman 78a
A.I. Wasserman et al. Software engineering: The turning point. *Computer, 11,* 9 (September 1978), 30-41.

Wasserman 78b
A.I. Wasserman, D.D. Sherniz and E.F. Handa. Report on the programming language PLAIN. Lab. of Medical Info. Sci., Univ. of California, San Francisco, California (1978).

Wasserman 79a
A.I. Wasserman. The data management facilities of PLAIN. *Proc. 1979 SIGMOD Conf.*, Boston, Massachusetts, (1979), pp. 60-70.

Wasserman 79b
A.I. Wasserman. USE: A methodology for the design and development of interactive information systems. In Schneider (ed.), *Formal Models and Practical Tools for Information Systems Design*, North-Holland Publishing Co., Amsterdam, The Netherlands, (1979), pp. 31-50.

Wasserman 80a
A.I. Wasserman. Information system development methodology. *J. Am Soc. for Info. Sci.*, (January 1980).

Wasserman 80b
A.I. Wasserman. The design of PLAIN: Support for systematic programming. *Proc. AFIPS National Computer Conf.*, *49*, (1980), pp. 113-122.

Wasserman 80c
A.I. Wasserman. Design and evaluation of a procedure-oriented exception-handling. Ih preparation, (1980).

Weber 78
H. Weber. A software engineering view of data base systems, *Proc. Very Large Data Base Conf. IV*, Berlin, Germany, (1978).

Welter 76
M. Welter. Counter expressions. RSSM/24, Dept. of Computer and Comm. Sci., Univ. of Michigan, Ann Arbor, Michigan (October 1976). EE.

Wileden 78
J.C. Wileden. Modelling parallel systems with dynamic structure. RSSM/71 (Ph.D. Thesis), Dept. of Computer and Comm. Sci., Univ. of Michigan, Ann Arbor, Michigan, (January 1978). EE.

Williams 75
R.D. Williams. Managing the development of reliable software. *SIGPLAN Notices*, *10*, 6 (June 1975), 3-8.

Wulf 76
W.A. Wulf, R.L. London and M. Shaw. An introduction to the construction and verification of Alphard programs. *IEEE Trans. on Software Engineering, SE-2*, 4 (December 1976), 253-265.

Yonezawa 77
A. Yonezawa. Specification and verification techniques for parallel programs based on message passing semantics. MIT/LCS/TR-91, Lab. for Computer Sci., Massachusetts Inst. of Tech., Cambridge, Massachusetts, (December 1977).

Yourdon 79
E. Yourdon and L.L. Constantine. *Structured Design*. Prentice-Hall, Englewood Cliffs, New Jersey, (1979).

Zave 79
P. Zave. Functional specification of asynchronous processes and its application to the early phases of system development. Dept. of Comp. Sci., Univ. of Maryland, College Park, Maryland, (March 1979).

Zelkowitz 79
M.V. Zelkowitz, A.C. Shaw and J.D. Gannon. *Principles of Software Engineering and Design*. Prentice-Hall, Englewood Cliffs, New Jersey, (1979). FE.

List of Attendees

Taylor L. Booth
University of Connecticut
  Department of Electrical Engineering
  and Computer Science

Charles Bradley
Digital Equipment Corporation

John Buxton
University of Warwick
  Department of Computer Science

Roy H. Campbell
University of Illinois at Urbana-Champaign
  Department of Computer Science

George R. Cannon, Jr.
Logicon, Inc.

Rick Cattell
Xerox Palo Alto Research Center

Lori Clarke
University of Massachusetts
  Computer and Information Science
  Department

Richard M. Cohen
The University of Texas at Austin
  Certifiable Minicomputer Project

Carl G. Davis
Department of the Army
  Ballistic Missile Defense Advanced
  Technology Center

Bryan Edwards
University of Colorado at Boulder
  Department of Computer Science

Richard Fairley
Colorado State University
  Computer Science Department

A. N. Habermann
Carnegie-Mellon University
  Department of Computer Science

Carl Hewitt
Massachusetts Institute of Technology
  Laboratory for Computer Science

Ray Houghton
National Bureau of Standards
  Institute for Computer Science

Robert M. Keller
The University of Utah
  Department of Computer Science

Norman L. Kerth
Tektronix Laboratories
  Computer Research Group

Sacha Krakowiak
Laboratoire d'Informatique et de
  Mathematiques Appliquees de Grenoble

Burt Leavenworth
IBM T. J. Watson Research Laboratories

Victor Lesser
University of Massachusetts
  Computer and Information Science Dept.

Ralph London
University of Southern California
  Information Sciences Institute

Tom Love
General Electric Information Services
  Company

Isao Miyamoto
Nippon Electric Company, Limited

Isaac Nassi
Digital Equipment Corporation

Gary Nutt
Xerox Palo Alto Research Center

Rod Oldehoeft
Colorado State University
  Computer Science Department

Leon Osterweil
University of Colorado at Boulder
  Computer Science Department

David J. Pearson
Bell-Northern Research Ltd.
  Advanced Development Systems

Lawrence J. Peters
Boeing Computer Services

Marvin Polan
Teledyne Brown Engineering

William Ralph
Colorado State University
  Computer Science Department

Jean-Claude Rault
Institut de Recherche D'Informatique et
  D'Automatique

William Riddle
University of Colorado at Boulder
  Computer Science Department

Lawrence Robinson
Ford Aerospace and Communications
  Corporation

Robert F. Rosin
Bell Telephone Laboratories

Sabina H. Saib
General Research Corporation

Patricia Santoni
Naval Ocean Systems Center

John Sayler
University of Michigan
  Department of Computer and
  Communication Sciences

Richard E. Schantz
Bolt Beranek and Newman Inc.

Al Segal
University of Michigan
  Department of Computer and
  Communication Sciences

Edmond H. Senn
National Aeronautics and Space
  Administration

Alan Shaw
University of Washington
  Department of Computer Science

Diane D. P. Smith
Computer Corporation of America

John Miles Smith
Computer Corporation of America

Robert Snowdon
International Computers Ltd.

Terry Straeter
General Dynamics Corporation

Tony Wasserman
University of California at
  San Francisco
Medical Information Science

Jack Wileden
University of Massachusetts
  Computer and Information Science
  Department

Pamela Zave
University of Maryland
  Computer Science Department

H. Paul Zeiger
University of Colorado at Boulder
  Department of Computer Science

Saydean Zeldin
Higher Order Software, Inc.

Stephen N. Zilles
IBM San Jose Research Division

S. Alagić, M. A. Arbib

The Design of Well-Structured and Correct Programs

1978. 68 figures. X, 292 pages
(Texts and Monographs in Computer Science)
ISBN 3-540-90299-6

Contents: Introducing Top-Down Design. – Basic Compositions of Actions and Their Proof Rules. – Data Types. – Developing Programs With Proofs of Correctness. – Procedures and Functions. – Recursion. – Programming With and Without Gotos.

Operating Systems

An Advanced Course

Editors: R. Bayer, R. M. Graham, G. Seegmüller
With contributions by numerous experts
Springer Study Edition
Reprint. 1979. 100 figures, 14 tables. X, 593 pages
ISBN 3-540-09812-7

Contents: Introduction. – Models: The Object Model: A Conceptual Tool for Structuring Software. Computer Organization and Architecture. – Issues and Results in the Design of Operating Systems: Naming and Binding of Objects. Issues in Kernel Design. Protection Mechanisms and the Enforcement of Security Policies. Synchronization in a Layered System. Reliable Computing Systems. Notes on Data Base Operating Systems. Common Carrier Provided Network Interfaces. Design Issues for Secure Computer Networks. – Future Outlook and Research Problems: On System Specification. Research Problems of Decentralized Systems with Largely Autonomous Nodes.

Springer-Verlag
Berlin
Heidelberg
New York

Software Engineering

An Advanced Course

Editor: F. L. Bauer
Springer Study Edition
Reprint. 1977. 93 figures, 8 tables. XII, 545 pages
ISBN 3-540-08364-2

Contents: Introduction: What the software engineer can do for the computer user. The design and construction of software systems. – Descriptional tools: Hierarchies. Language characteristics. Low level languages. Summary of a discussion session. Relationship between definition and implementation of a language. Concurrency in software systems. – Techniques: Modularity. Portability and adaptability. Debugging and Testing. Reliability. – Practical aspects: Project management. Documentation. Performance prediction. Performance measurement. Pricing mechanisms. Evaluation in the computing center environment. – Appendix: Software engineering.

Software Engineering Education

Needs and Objectives

Proceedings of an Interface Workshop
Editors: A. I. Wasserman, P. Freeman
1976. 18 figures. VIII, 159 pages
ISBN 3-540-90216-3

Contents: Industry needs for software engineering education. – University plants and programs in software engineering education. – Discussion topics. – Conclusion.

Springer-Verlag
Berlin
Heidelberg
New York